WILLIAM EWART GLADSTONE

SPIRITUAL LIVES

General Editor

Timothy Larsen

The *Spiritual Lives* series features biographies of prominent men and women whose eminence is not primarily based on a specifically religious contribution. Each volume provides a general account of the figure's life and thought, while giving special attention to his or her religious contexts, convictions, doubts, objections, ideas, and actions. Many leading politicians, writers, musicians, philosophers, and scientists have engaged deeply with religion in significant and resonant ways that have often been overlooked or underexplored. Some of the volumes will even focus on men and women who were lifelong unbelievers, attending to how they navigated and resisted religious questions, assumptions, and settings. The books in this series will therefore recast important figures in fresh and thought-provoking ways.

William Ewart Gladstone

The Heart and Soul of a Statesman

MICHAEL WHEELER

OXFORD
UNIVERSITY PRESS

Great Clarendon Street, Oxford, OX2 6DP,
United Kingdom

Oxford University Press is a department of the University of Oxford.
It furthers the University's objective of excellence in research, scholarship,
and education by publishing worldwide. Oxford is a registered trade mark of
Oxford University Press in the UK and in certain other countries

© Michael Wheeler 2025

The moral rights of the author have been asserted

All rights reserved. No part of this publication may be reproduced, stored in a retrieval
system, transmitted, used for text and data mining, or used for training artificial intelligence,
in any form or by any means, without the prior permission in writing of Oxford University
Press, or as expressly permitted by law, y licence or under terms agreed with the appropriate
reprographics rights organization. Enquiries concerning reproduction outside the scope
of the above should be sent to the Rights Department, Oxford University Press, at the
address above.

You must not circulate this work in any other form
and you must impose this same condition on any acquirer

Published in the United States of America by Oxford University Press
198 Madison Avenue, New York, NY 10016, United States of America

British Library Cataloguing in Publication Data

Data available

Library of Congress Control Number: 2024945900

ISBN 9780198881513

DOI: 10.1093/9780191990892.001.0001

Printed and bound by
CPI Group (UK) Ltd, Croydon, CR0 4YY

The manufacturer's authorised representative in the EU for product
safety is Oxford University Press España S.A. of el Parque
Empresarial San Fernando de Henares, Avenida de Castilla, 2 –
28830 Madrid (www.oup.es/en).

For the Warden and staff of
Gladstone's Library

Contents

Acknowledgements	ix
List of References and Abbreviations, and Textual Note	xi
Introduction	xiii
1. Walking in the light	1
2. True allegiance	27
3. Many mansions	51
4. Work while it is day	71
5. Manifest in the flesh	97
6. Fight the good fight	123
7. Athirst for God	149
8. Lead, Kindly Light	173
Selected Bibliography	195
Index	203
List of Series Titles	217

Acknowledgements

My warm thanks to Tim Larsen for inviting me to write this book and to Tom Perridge and Jamie Mortimer at Oxford University Press for all their support. Also Dr Rachel Cooper and Kavitha Yuvaraj.

I would like to thank Sir Charles Gladstone for permission to quote from the Gladstone Papers at the British Library. Also the staff at the British Library, Gladstone's Library, Lambeth Palace Library, the Athenæum, and the London Library, for their help in providing material from their collections, and to Sonja Schäfer, Historisches Archiv mit Rheinischem Bildarchiv, Köln, for responding to an archival request.

Special thanks are due to my trusty readers of draft chapters: Professor Chris Walsh and Greg Gardner. Their advice has been invaluable. Other friends have also been supportive: the Revd Terry Hemming, David Harte, Bruce Hunter, Mike Shaw, and Dr Ruth Windscheffel, wise Gladstone scholar. Supremely, my heartful thanks are due to Susan Woodhead, my darling wife, who has listened, read, and advised.

The book is dedicated to my friends and colleagues at Gladstone's Library, and especially to Revd Dr Andrea Russell, Warden, and her predecessor Revd Peter Francis.

Andover, Hampshire
March 2024

References and Abbreviations, and Textual Note

In the endnotes, the short notation of *The Gladstone Diaries*, ed. M. R. D. Foot and H. C. G. Matthew, 14 vols. (Oxford: Clarendon, 1968–94) is *Diaries*. Passages cited have been checked against the originals at Lambeth Palace Library, LPL, MSS 1416–55, unless otherwise stated, as in the travel diary of 1832 (BL, 44,818A), for example. Where minor errors occur in the printed diaries, the original is quoted here. Where several diary entries on consecutive days are quoted, a reference to the first entry only is given. Letters to Laura Thistlethwayte reprinted in *Diaries* have also been checked against the originals, LPL, MSS 2761–70.

For items from the British Library's Gladstone Papers, the short notation is BL followed by the volume number and, where relevant, folio number(s), 'f. 00', with 'r' for recto, 'v' for verso. Items from Lambeth Palace Library are indicated as LPL. GL refers to Gladstone's Library and GladCat to the transcription of his marginalia in his own books, available on the library's website.

Abbreviations

Hansard   *Hansard's Parliamentary Debates* (online)
ODNB   *Oxford Dictionary of National Biography* (online)
OED   *Oxford English Dictionary* (online)

Textual Note

In quotations from manuscripts, words underlined in the original are italicized. Insertions are indicated thus: ^ ^.

Introduction

The Rt Hon. William Ewart Gladstone, MP, FRS, DCL (1809–98), declined public honours and was known as 'Mr Gladstone' by his contemporaries, including Thomas Wemyss Reid, in the multi-authored biography that he edited in 1899, and John Morley, in the official tombstone biography (3 vols., 1903).[1] The leading statesman of nineteenth-century Britain, a figure who bestrode the political world like a Colossus, is 'Gladstone' to modern biographers. This brilliant but troubled man brought in twelve budgets as chancellor of the exchequer, served as prime minister four times, chaired 556 cabinet meeting, was the greatest orator among a generation of superb preachers and political speakers, and was the minister whose grasp of the public finances was second to none.

As a reader of biographies I have tended to look askance at those which use the given names of their subjects: the practice can seem either cosy or presumptuous. Nevertheless, in order to signal the difference between my approach and those of earlier biographers, the subject of my book is known as William, his baptismal name. (He was also known as 'Willy' to his closest friends and family members, and more widely as 'the people's William', whose reforms improved the lives of millions, later in life.) William's autobiographical fragments of 1892 included this disclaimer: 'I do not indeed intend in these notes to give a history of the inner life, which I think has with me been extraordinarily dubious, vacillating, and (above all) complex'.[2] This book is about the spiritual dimension of his complex inner life. In tracing the movements of his heart and soul, I work from the inner to the outer aspects of a rich and varied life, from his daily disciplines of prayer and reflection to his earnest attempts to follow the precepts of Christianity through action in the public realm and in private philanthropy, and in the writing of numerous reviews, articles, and books. Today, British politicians try to establish clear boundaries between their public profiles and their religious beliefs. Such a division would baffle William, who always sought to integrate and harmonize private and public worlds, even if he often failed.

As Angus Hawkins reminded us, Victorian politics was regarded as a practical moral activity, rather than the product of ideology or doctrine.[3] It was primarily religious rather than political concerns that engaged and motivated this most energetic of Victorian titans. Having been dissuaded from becoming a clergyman by his domineering father, he dedicated himself to church-building and to preaching at home. His priority as a young member of parliament was the defence of the Church of England, the 'many peculiarities' of which, he believed, 'as contradistinguished from dissenting bodies . . . afford greater advantages for the formation of a spiritual life'.[4] In this book, I consider his high regard for institutions, including marriage, the church, the state, the crown, charities, and Christian educational bodies. Much of his omnivorous reading and diligent private research focused upon religion. I emphasize his reliance upon devotional literature for support on his long spiritual journey: texts ranging from Augustine's *Confessions* and Thomas à Kempis's *The Imitation of Christ*, for William a 'golden book',[5] to obscure Victorian devotional works that spoke to him personally, have been largely overlooked by earlier biographers. His extraordinary diary, edited in fourteen volumes, reveals a lifelong commitment to the Christian faith, a firm belief in divine providence, and an acute awareness of his own sinfulness, registered through the workings of a hypersensitive conscience. By the time he formed his first ministry as prime minister, in 1868, he had undergone significant changes of heart and mind as he moved from Tory to Peelite to Liberal-Conservative positions, and from the evangelicalism of his upbringing to a high Anglican ecclesiology. Always a devout Christian and Anglican, he was sometimes enigmatic in his religious and political pronouncements, baffling his supporters and latterly infuriating his monarch. Operating at a time when parties played an increasingly significant role in both state and church, William remained an independent intellectual, eschewing party labels within the Church of England and working out his own stance in relation to specific Liberal party policies in politics. He was as much a man of letters as he was a politician. Later in his political career, the people's William appealed to public opinion through a series of national moral campaigns. His fiercest battles, however, were spiritual, as he castigated himself for falling short of the ideals set out in Jesus' sermon on the mount, particularly with regard to sexual desire. His longest crusade was against the enemy within.

My methodology is reconstructive historicist, with the aim of relating the spiritual life of an avowedly exceptional male figure to the religious culture of his age. Such a study is made possible by the unrivalled richness of the available source material, including around 25,200 daily entries in the diaries, the originals of which are at Lambeth Palace Library, 5,000 annotated books and 70,000 Glynne-Gladstone family letters at Gladstone's Library, Hawarden, and the 750 volumes of manuscript material—letters, sermons, essays, political and personal memoranda—held at the British Library.

The subjects chosen for Oxford's Spiritual Lives series are all 'highly influential, prominent figures (typically household names) whose eminence is not primarily based on a specifically religious contribution'. In the case of William Ewart Gladstone, the biographies published in the twentieth century tended to underplay the religious contribution to his life and reputation, as their focus was largely upon his public life, particularly in the field of politics. In the introduction to *Gladstone, God and Politics* (2007), a single-volume recasting of material from his two-volume biography *Gladstone* (1982, 1999), Richard Shannon pointed out that 'the religious dimension for any practical interpretational effect simply does not exist' in Roy Jenkins's prize-winning biography.[6] (Jenkins thus followed in the tradition of Morley.) In aiming to correct this omission, Shannon offers more commentary than most biographers on William's spiritual life, based largely on the diaries. He argues that Morley, Jenkins, and Colin Matthew (initially with M. R. D. Foot, the brilliant editor of the diaries, with their invaluable introductions) present a progressive 'Liberal' Gladstone while downplaying the complexities of 'Gladstonian Liberalism', which had a decidedly conservative side. Travis Crosby's uneven but illuminating biography, *The Two Mr. Gladstones: A Study in Psychology and History* (1997), draws upon stress and coping theories to explain Gladstone's controlling and self-controlling behaviour in both his public and private life.

Three twentieth-century studies directly address the question of Gladstone's religious life and ideas within particular time frames. Perry Butler's *Gladstone, Church, State and Tractarianism* (1982) focuses upon his religious ideas and attitudes up to 1859; J. P. Parry's *Democracy and Religion* (1986) discusses Gladstone and the Liberal Party, 1867–75; and Peter Jagger's *Gladstone: the Making of a Christian Politician* (1991) offers close analysis of the personal religious life and development of Gladstone up to 1832—the subject of my first chapter, which benefits from Jagger's research. David Bebbington's *William Ewart Gladstone: Faith and Politics in Victorian Britain* (1993), a miracle of compression, was a preliminary study for the scholarly monograph, not a biography, which addresses the statesman's intellectual response to the theological and ecclesiological debates of his day, *The Mind of Gladstone: Religion, Homer, and Politics* (2004), to which I and all students of Gladstone are indebted. Ruth Clayton Windscheffel's *Reading Gladstone* (2008) is an excellent study of Gladstone's long life of reading and the most perceptive account of the motives behind his establishment of St Deiniol's Library (now Gladstone's Library). William McKelvey's chapter on Gladstone and Homer in *The English Cult of Literature* (2007) is a further significant contribution to the study of the statesman's theology. Although there is important material on William's inner spiritual life scattered through the secondary material, a volume that focuses upon the heart and soul of the statesman is certainly needed, and never more so than at this cultural moment, in a Western world of 'unbelief' and biblical illiteracy that William would have found dismaying. The reader should turn to Morley, Jenkins, Matthew, or Shannon for analysis of William's parliamentary life, which is only sketched here. In focusing upon his life outside the Commons, and in a book of modest proportions, I am perforce selective, sometimes moving swiftly over a number of years in order to focus upon periods of crisis or significant development. By quoting William extensively throughout, I try to let him speak for himself.

One of Catherine Gladstone's favourite books in her widowhood was *The Life of William Ewart Gladstone* (1899), edited by Sir Thomas Wemyss Reid, which she loved to have read aloud to her. Reid included a chapter by William's protégé, Canon Malcolm MacColl, on 'Mr. Gladstone as a Theologian', a subject which David Bebbington and others were to explore in depth a hundred years later. In his introduction to the *Life*, however, Reid stated that to tell the many anecdotes that could be told concerning William's 'religion of the heart' would be 'to vulgarise a subject which may fairly be called sacred'.[7] My apologies to Sir Thomas.

Notes

1. For details of all the printed books mentioned in this introduction, see Selected Bibliography.
2. *The Prime Ministers' Papers: W. E. Gladstone, Autobiographica and Autobiographical Memoranda*, ed. John Brooke and Mary Sorensen, 4 vols. (London: HMSO, 1971–81), vol. I, p. 18.
3. Angus Hawkins, *Victorian Political Culture: 'Habits of Heart and Mind'* (Oxford: Oxford University Press, 2015), pp. 2–3.
4. *The Correspondence of Henry Edward Manning and William Ewart Gladstone: The Complete Correspondence, 1833–1891*, ed. Peter C. Erb, 4 vols. (Oxford: Oxford University Press, 2013), vol. I, p. 8.
5. John Morley, *The Life of William Ewart Gladstone*, 3 vols. (London and New York: Macmillan, 1903), vol. II, p. 186.
6. Richard Shannon, *Gladstone, God and Politics* (London: Hambledon Continuum, 2007), p. xi.
7. Thomas Wemyss Reid, ed., *The Life of William Ewart Gladstone* (London: Cassell, 1899), p. 40.

1
Walking in the light

But if we walk in the light, as he is in the light, we have fellowship one with another, and the blood of Jesus Christ his Son cleanseth us from all sin. (1 John 1.7)

The scholarly methods that William learned as a schoolboy at Eton (1821–27) and an undergraduate at Christ Church, Oxford (1828–31), stayed with him for life. They included writing lengthy essays and memoranda on a wide range of subjects, inside and outside the syllabus, in order to understand them and to clarify his own ideas. He also recorded the activities of each day, throughout the year, in a series of small notebooks which were usually marked 'private'. He was still using small notebooks for the purpose in the 1890s. Unlike the essays and memoranda, his daily diary entries were generally very brief, crammed onto the page in tiny writing, and included references to activities such as taking exercise, travelling, reading, conversing, and corresponding. Occasionally there is commentary on his own behaviour, most tellingly on his birthday, when a devout young Christian was expected to reflect on his spiritual life and moral standards over the previous twelve months. The word 'improvement' recurs in the short reflective additions to the entries for his seventeenth, eighteenth, and nineteenth birthdays, with regrets over its absence in any of its branches. The entry for 29 December 1829, however, his twentieth birthday, expands into a kind of moral balance sheet which sets the pattern for annual reviews into old age. He has to thank God for many 'signal mercies'.[1] He recognizes that his mind has 'continued strongly inclined to the Church throughout'. In 'one besetting sin', he writes,

William Ewart Gladstone. Michael Wheeler, Oxford University Press.
© Michael Wheeler 2025. DOI: 10.1093/9780191990892.003.0001

'there has been less temptation perhaps tho' not less readiness to be tempted—and though God has kept the temptation away there has been black sin on my part. Yet may I know who hath caused to be written "*The blood of Christ cleanseth from all sin*"'. The words underlined (italicized here) echo a verse from the first epistle of John, quoted above. My aim in this chapter is to examine William's attempts to 'walk in the light' of the gospel and to 'have fellowship' with his family at home, and with like-minded peers at school and university. But first, where did his acute sense of 'black sin' originate?

Family life and spiritual formation

William was born on 29 December 1809 at 62 (then number 1) Rodney Street, Liverpool, a house commissioned by his father for a growing family. The street had been laid down in the 1780s for affluent householders who could afford to live away from the old town centre. (Ten years later, the poet Arthur Hugh Clough was born at number 5.) The baby was named after his father's friend, William Ewart, when he was baptized at St Peter's, Liverpool, John Gladstone having moved away from the Presbyterianism of his Scottish upbringing to become a member of the established Church of England. John, a wealthy and powerful patriarch in the eyes of his family and the Liverpool business community, was to be the most dominant, often domineering figure in 'Willy's' educational and early professional career, not least because he provided the funds that enabled his boy to flourish in the most influential circles. But it was Anne Gladstone, John's second wife and the mother of his six children, who, together with her daughter Anne, taught the young Willy 'true religion'—how to read the bible, how to pray for forgiveness, how to listen to and recall an admonitory sermon.[2]

Anne Mackenzie Robertson was born in 1772, the daughter of a lawyer, Provost Andrew Robertson of Dingwall, who was a member of the Scottish Episcopal Church. Her personal piety, Sabbatarian views, devotion to the scriptures, and belief in God's use of suffering as an instrument to strengthen his children were characteristic of Calvinist evangelicalism in a period of fervent religious revival. She corresponded with and visited Hannah More, the famous bluestocking and writer of evangelical tracts, who presented young Willy

Walking in the light

with a copy of her *Sacred Dramas*. Like William Wilberforce, a friend of the family, and like other members of the Clapham Sect, Anne kept a diary in which she confessed her own shortcomings and recorded her spiritual struggles. Analysis of her papers has revealed that 'almost endless references are made to her utter sinfulness and unworthiness before God and in this her prayers and spiritual reflections border on obsession'.[3] Equally significant in terms of the doctrines that Willy absorbed at her knee was that of divine providence and the belief that the eye of God is always upon us. Her friend, the Revd Dr Thomas Chalmers, widely regarded as Scotland's leading moderate evangelical, wrote to her, 'It gives me pleasure to be informed of your earnest desire after that which is right—and more particularly of your own high sense of the necessity of religiously training your young family'.[4]

The eldest member of that young family was Anne Mackenzie Gladstone, born in 1802 and raised to be a model for her younger siblings, and especially Willy: she became his godmother at the age of seven. Anne was to die young, in 1829, probably from tuberculosis, having always been regarded as 'sickly', like her mother. Thomas, born in 1804, was to serve as a Tory member of parliament and inherit his father's baronetcy. Robertson, born a year later, followed Thomas to Eton but was moved to Glasgow College before joining the family business, eventually becoming mayor of Liverpool. John Neilson Gladstone, born in 1807, chose a quite separate path by training to be a naval officer; after his retirement he served as a member of parliament. In 1814, five years after Willy's birth, Helen was born. She was the unstable younger sister who was to rebel by converting to Rome, to the dismay of her brother. For William had been brought up to idealize womanhood, as represented by the two Annes who monitored his spiritual formation.

Presiding over the whole family was the paterfamilias. After his death in 1851, John Gladstone was represented kneeling at a prie-dieu alongside his devoted wife, who kneels on a hassock, in the memorial plaque to both parents in the chapel that he had built at Fasque, the Gladstones' Scottish estate.[5] His right hand supports his head, while his left rests on a book, presumably the Book of Common Prayer. Such images were familiar to those who took part in family prayers in the late Georgian period, when the practice was discussed in Jane Austen's

Mansfield Park and the Gladstone children were under instruction at home. An engraving that illustrates Morning Prayer, in a prayer book of 1811, shows a devout family of five kneeling at the breakfast table, which is covered with a dark cloth.[6] The landscape glimpsed through the open window reminds the viewer that nature is the 'second book' of God. A prosperous family, living in the country, is presented in a specifically Anglican idyll, but with an evangelical twist. The young father, in swallow-tailed coat, reads from the prayer book, which he leans upon the family bible. Mama, looking heavenward, has her arm around one of her three children. Contemporary readers would have assumed that mama's role was to supervise her children's upbringing, while papa, having presided at family prayers, was busy in his employment, or serving in public office, or overseeing the estate.

John Gladstone, born in 1764, was phenomenally busy in all these areas during his career as a merchant prince and politician. Tall, large-boned, and immensely strong, he was the eldest of sixteen children, four of whom died in infancy. Having left school at the age of thirteen, he was apprenticed to the Edinburgh Roperie and Sailcloth Company of Edinburgh until 1781, when he joined the burgeoning corn-chandling business of his Calvinist father, Thomas Gladstones, an elder of North Leith kirk. (John dropped the 's' in Gladstones.) Trading in the Baltic, he proved to be an exceptionally gifted entrepreneur. In 1787 he went into partnership with Edgar Corrie of Liverpool and made his fortune through the tobacco and grain trade in America. Breaking with Corrie in 1801, he formed a new partnership with his brother Robert and later added his five other brothers, investing in shipping, insurance, and real estate, but avoiding the new technologies that shaped the industrial revolution. He began sugar and cotton trading in the West Indies in 1803, becoming a planter and slave owner, though not a slave trader, and expanding his estates in the 1820s, facing down the anti-slavery campaigners of Liverpool and deeply embarrassing the women at home. The Gladstones' stake in the West Indies amounted to £336,000 by the time emancipation was passed: the name Gladstone is still to be found in Jamaica and Demerara.

Meanwhile, he had been church-building in the evangelical interest, in Leith, Liverpool, and Seaforth, where he built the mansion that was to accommodate his family from 1813, and establishing himself as one of Liverpool's leading philanthropists, supporting Christian charities, alongside his wife Anne. An influential figure in Liverpool politics, he worked tirelessly in support of two outstanding parliamentary candidates, both progressive Tories: George Canning and William Huskisson. In order to become a Canningite MP himself—for Lancaster in 1818, Woodstock in 1820, and Berwick in 1827—he paid out further funds. Although he made little political impact in London, beyond the circles supporting the interests of Liverpool and West Indian planters, his stature as a merchant prince was high enough, by the end of his life, to attract the attention of Samuel Smiles, who wished to write a memoir of him.[7] In 1828 he was worth about half a million pounds, roughly £35 million in today's values. His wife's ailments led to a somewhat nomadic life in the early 1830s, as they moved between spa towns in search of cures: Leamington and the famous Dr Jephson were particular favourites. In 1833 they took up residence at Fasque—the estate in Kincardineshire that John had acquired for almost £80,000—along with their daughter Helen. He was now a laird. His other ambition, to see one of his sons rise to greater things, was to be fulfilled in William. The prodigy himself was to record, late in life, that his father's was 'a large and strong nature, simple though hasty, profoundly affectionate and capable of the highest devotion in the lines of duty and of love'.[8]

William's fragments of autobiography, written in the 1890s, include a self-critical assessment of his young self that tells us more about the senior statesman than it does about the child. He has 'no recollection of being a loving or a winning child: or an earnest or diligent or knowledge-loving child. God forgive me . . . The plank between me and all the sins was so very thin . . . I was not a devotional child. I have no recollection of early love for the House of God and for divine service'.[9] But then who, apart from the infant Samuel in the Old Testament, could claim to have such an early love? And how many adults can actually remember what they were like as small children? William's mother believed that he had been 'truly converted to God' in childhood, but he was later to write, 'Of . . . any true conversion of the heart to God I do not dare and indeed I am not competent to speak'.[10] He did, however, recall the hold that Bunyan's *Pilgrim's Progress* had upon him, along with the *Arabian Nights*. A regime of family devotions, Sabbatarian observance, and constant reminders of one's Christian duty in childhood became habitual, internalized, and thus unmemorable. But its influence was profound, later in life.

Seaforth House was built in what William describes as a 'salubrious' situation, 'on the pure dry sands of the Mersey's mouth, with all the advantages of the strong tided action and the fresh and frequent north-west winds'.[11] (Those winds would occasionally break a window or bring down a chimney.) 'At five miles from Liverpool exchange', he continues, 'the sands, delicious for riding, were an absolute solitude, and only one house looked down on them between us and the town'. Among his greatest enjoyments were the annual Guy Fawkes bonfires, for which he and his brothers always had plenty of wreck timber and a tar-barrel to hand. 'Physically', he adds, 'I must have been rather tough: for my brother John took me down at about ten years old to wrestle in the stables with an older lad of that region, whom I threw'. He was eight or nine when he first saw a dead body, the child of the head gardener, Derbyshire: 'It seemed to me pleasing and in no way repelled me, but it made no deep impression'.

John Gladstone's estate of 105 acres was to include the family house, a home farm, a village of cottages, St Thomas's church, and a school. When the need for a suitable clergyman first arose, Willy accompanied his parents on a visit to Cambridge in order to consult a leading evangelical and moderate Calvinist, the Revd Dr Charles Simeon, with the result that the Revd William Rawson was appointed. Willy joined a small flock of boys who were taught at the parsonage, including members of his own large extended family. He later claimed to have learned little there, although he had begun Greek with Robertson and John at the age of eight. Willy used to teach 'pretty regularly' in the Sunday school built by his father near the Primrose Bridge. 'It was I think a duty done not under constraint', he commented 'but I can recollect nothing which associates it with a seriously religious life in myself'.

Fellowship one with another at Eton

Mrs Gladstone was aware of 'the very awful state of the Church at Eton' and the 'general indifference to religion' in the school;[12] but Mr Gladstone wanted Willy to follow his brothers there and thus to rub shoulders with the sons of the aristocracy and some of the future leaders of the nation. Tom was unhappy at the school, had pleaded to leave, and had submitted to a flogging rather than being sent home in disgrace after a row with his despised 'dame'. (His mother recorded that flogging, 'like physic, is bitter', but it is 'wholesome'.[13]) His presence softened William's arrival in September 1821, at the age of eleven. The boys shared accommodation and William fagged for his brother, while learning how to survive the more brutal side of school life, even though he was said to be the prettiest little boy that ever went to Eton. Tom progressed no further than the fifth form, and his brother missed him on returning to school the following year. But William was to thrive there. Although the classical syllabus was extremely narrow, and the boys 'knew very little indeed', they 'knew it accurately', he later recorded. Dr Hawtrey, subsequently Dr Keate's successor as head of Eton, inspired him for the first time 'with a desire to learn and to do', which he 'never wholly lost'.[14] His Eton notebooks are those of a remarkably conscientious young scholar with obsessive tendencies; and his retention of them indicates an archival instinct.[15] His later insertion of short comments on his own youthful efforts reflects a retrospective interest in his own development.

Like his brother, he was initially bemused by the lack of 'vital' religion in the school and the absence of spiritual guidance from the clerical masters. He filled the vacuum in three ways. First, he drew upon the tradition of private devotions and bible reading in which he had been raised. At Eton on 11 November 1825, he noted in his diary that he had been employed with the usual schoolwork ('Fridays business'), a French lesson, and some 'jogging about'.[16] Then he added, 'reading Bible a regular thing which however I do not put down every day'. Ten months later, during the summer holidays, he made a similar note: 'Read Bible. I do not put down in my diary my nightly reading of Bible during the week.'[17] These entries, for his eyes only, were clearly intended to remind him of his daily routine when he consulted the diary at a later date. Of the several copies of the Book of Common Prayer that he owned, one is marked 'William Ewart Gladstone, January 1821'.[18] The daily offices of Morning and Evening Prayer, said or sung in churches and chapels, were also used by Anglicans for private worship, offering the reader the complete cycle of Coverdale's version of the Psalms, read in sequence over each calendar month, and Cranmer's resonant collects, absorbed through daily repetition ('whose service is perfect freedom', 'grant that this day we fall into no sin, neither run into any kind of danger', 'may pass our time in rest and quietness', 'lighten our darkness, we beseech thee, O Lord'). William took his scissors to various copies of the prayer book and pasted short extracts into a used octavo notebook, thus covering manuscript material.[19] This personalized collection of 'Prayers for home use' contains different sequences for each morning and evening of the week, bringing variety and freshness to the owner's daily devotions. The third prayer chosen for Sunday morning, for example, is the collect for the eighth Sunday after Trinity ('O God, whose never-failing providence ordereth all things'), and the fourth is 'A Prayer for a Blessing on the Word' ('read, mark, learn, and inwardly digest'). On Wednesdays he said the litany.

Secondly, he turned to commentaries, printed sermons, and books of devotion that complemented his reading of the scriptures and the prayer book. His reading was wide-ranging. At Seaforth, on Sunday 10 September 1826, he read 'Simeons two first sermons on the Liturgy', which would have pleased his mother. He also read the sermons of other evangelicals, such as Chalmers and John Bird Sumner, a future Archbishop of Canterbury, along with standards such as Hugh Blair's sermons in five volumes, published at the end of the eighteenth century. His bible studies included the Greek New Testament and what was known as *D'Oyly and Mant's Bible*, with notes by George D'Oyly and Richard Mant, 'for the use of families' (3 vols., 1814). Sunday reading between May 1826 and March 1827 included *Psalmorum Davidicorum* (1551) by George Buchanan and dedicated to Mary Queen of Scots. At the same time he was wrestling with Sir George Pretyman Tomline's *Elements of Christian Theology* (1799), which he finished on Sunday 8 July 1827, declaring it to be 'as far as I can judge a very good & useful work'.[20] Bishop Tomline's book was designed for the use of Anglican candidates for ordination.

Thirdly, and perhaps most significantly, William attended chapel and discussed matters of faith with some of his friends at Eton, who were themselves passing through adolescence and the early, exploratory stages of their spiritual lives. Lord John Russell, writing in 1820, suggested that English public schools were part of the constitution.[21] They produced a 'democracy of the aristocracy' by giving a rough experience to those not accustomed to it, and they produced a common

Walking in the light

intellectual climate for those who would become public men: 'Upon the whole, there is perhaps no point from which a man can start in any profession or pursuit so advantageous as a complete and thorough knowledge of what is known by other young men, among whom he wishes to excel'. This was as true for future bishops as it was for aspiring politicians; and several of William's friends were to become senior churchmen. He recorded later that he went to Eton in 1821, 'after a pretty long spell in a very middling state of preparation, and wholly without any knowledge or other enthusiasm, unless it were a priggish love of argument which had begun to develop'.[22] That love of argument came out in private conversations with the other 'fellows', in debates at the Eton Society and in editorial work on the *Eton Miscellany*, of which he was the 'guiding spirit' and much of which he wrote.[23]

His closest school friend for a while, Arthur Hallam, was regarded by his peers as a potential future prime minister or archbishop. He was to suffer a fatal stroke in 1833, soon after graduating from Trinity College, Cambridge, where his friendship with Alfred Tennyson was to inspire *In Memoriam* (1850). William idolized Arthur, referring to him frequently in the diary between February 1826 and July 1827, when Hallam left Eton. Particular attention is paid to Arthur's performances in debates, where his Whig politics clashed with William's Tory views, although a fifty-year rule ensured that discussion focused upon historical questions rather than current affairs. They 'messed' together, played chess, went sculling on the Thames, went 'up Windsor', and talked on walks. Following a sermon on 'the history of Joseph' in Genesis, on Sunday 23 April 1826, William records: 'Long talk with Hallam on subjects of Trinity, Predestination, &c.'[24]

Such discussions would have arisen naturally after chapel services and in the interstices between activities associated with lessons, private study, work on the *Eton Miscellany*, and debates at the Eton Society, to which William was so committed that he sent detailed accounts of exchanges between mutual friends to William Wyndham Farr, after the latter's departure for Cambridge. In this lengthy correspondence, William Gladstone's 'priggish love of argument' is displayed in commentary on both religion and politics, which were closely intertwined when Catholic emancipation was in the air. On 22 November 1826 he wrote to Farr from Eton: 'You provoke me on the subject of Catholics to a reply, which I am persuaded to make only by the hope that the goodness of the cause itself will compensate, and even counter-balance the inability of its advocate.'[25] (In style, such bumptious statements from the sixteen-year-old Etonian anticipate the rolling periods of classical Gladstonian oratory in his maturity.) 'Many Catholic priests are bigoted and superstitious', he admits, 'many perhaps violently adverse to our Church'. Grant Catholic emancipation, however, 'and pay the Catholic clergy: you place a check on the priesthood'.

Other friends who were regular debaters in the Society included James Milnes Gaskell, later a Whig politician and already fascinated by the arcane rules of parliamentary life, whose nonconformity had a broadening influence upon William; Francis Doyle, poet and civil servant; and the Earl of Lincoln, Henry Pelham-Clinton, later 5th Duke of Newcastle, a friend for life and the epitome of the landed aristocracy that William idealized as the guardians of church, state, and constitution. The *Eton Miscellany*'s 'prime man' was another lifelong friend, George Selwyn, the future Eton beak, Bishop of New Zealand and later of Wakefield, after whom a Cambridge college is named. William was later to describe him as 'the scholar, Christian, and hero, who had Eton graven on the core of his heart and whose influence during the many years he spent there must have been very great'.[26] Selwyn and William were assisted on the *Miscellany* by Frederic Rogers, who was to be drawn to Oriel College, Oxford, by John Henry Newman, and was later to join William and James Hope in forming the 'Engagement', a group of high Anglican Oxonians in London. (Later still, in 1871, Rogers was to be the first ennobled civil servant in modern Britain, on William's nomination.) When Rogers was proposed for the Eton Society by William, in October 1827, he was elected unanimously. A year earlier, in his role as secretary, William had 'got Wellesley fined' for some minor infringement of the rules.[27] Gerald Wellesley, Wellington's nephew and a future Dean of Windsor, was to provide a crucial link between William as premier and Queen Victoria, who relied on his advice. Edward Hayes Pickering, a future England cricketer and ordained assistant master at Eton, was also fined by William in 1826, along with Doyle. Finally, there was Walter Kerr Hamilton, with whom William breakfasted on 28 September 1827. He was a moderate evangelical at this stage of his life, who, like William, moved towards a high Anglican position. He became a Tractarian bishop and a friend for life.

Here, then, was a group of Etonians who shared an interest in current affairs and in the history of a nation whose political and religious life were linked through a constitution which enshrined church and state under the crown. And they prayed together in chapel, forming a fellowship (*koinonia* in the Greek), defined as the 'living bond that unites Christians'.[28] Like several of his friends, William was aware of the possibility that God might call him to ordination, which could help to explain why there was an increase in the number of religious books that he read in 1827.[29] His confirmation on 1 February that year was also influential. On the previous Sunday he recorded in his diary,

> Grover preached—could not hear him at all. read Bible—with Mant's Compilation of Notes—will call them for brevity, Mant's Notes. They are bulky, but excellent. Read a few of Buchanan's Psalms—1 of Blair's Sermons, & some Tomline: also endeavoured to prepare myself for the sacred & awful rite of Confirmation. May it please the Giver of all good things, for the sake of His Dear Son, our Adorable Redeemer, to give unto me & my fellows the grace of His Holy Spirit, and to grant efficacy to the means which have been ordained for our assistance, in working out our Salvation [Philippians 2.12]. May He have compassion on our weakness, and remove our corruption; may He give us both the power to promise, and the strength to perform; and when we take upon us our Baptismal Vows, may we do it with a stedfast resolution to fulfil them, and an humble hope that God in His mercy will be pleased to grant to us that without which we cannot attain unto so great a glory. Tutor read to all his pupils to be confirmed, a most excellent sermon in a most impressive manner. Walk with Pickering & Doyle. Wrote to A. M. G. [his sister Anne] & J. N. G. [his brother John].[30]

The tone is that of an evangelical ('our Adorable Redeemer', 'working out our Salvation'), but the emphasis upon 'us'—he and his fellows—and upon the 'efficacy' of the presiding bishop's actions ('the means which have been ordained'), indicates that William was becoming more aware of the sacramental significance of the church, the body of Christ.

Next day, he read 'parts in the Bible relating to Confirmation, with Notes & part of Serm. on Mount, with Notes'; on the Tuesday, 'Read more of Sermon on the Mount' and heard 'another very good sermon on Confirmation' read by his tutor; and on the Wednesday, 'Read more of the Sermon on the Mount'. The entry for Thursday 1 February is headed '*Holiday for the Confirmation*': 'This day, with upwards of two hundred more, I, most unworthy of so great a privilege, was confirmed according to the apostolical rite preserved in the Church of England'. The bishop, he records, was 'not dignified in appearance—but went through the service apparently with great feeling and piety—gave an exhortation after the Blessing'. The urbane Bishop of Lincoln, George Pelham, may not have looked the part, but William appreciates the heart and soul that he put into the service.

The newly confirmed Etonians received the sacrament for the first time on Sunday 4 March 1827, thus becoming sharers in 'the fellowship of the Lord's Supper' and companions of Christ.[31] William recorded in his diary that 'it is a blessed institution indeed; a work worthy of the Divine Grace; may we, seeing his wonders not be like Capernaum & Bethsaida, lest it be more tolerable at the great day for Sodom & Gomorrah than for us' (Matthew 11.20–24).[32] Modern readers may be startled by the sudden leap from a sense of gratitude and celebration in this passage—'blessed institution', 'Divine Grace', 'his wonders'—to a reference to eternal damnation at the last judgment—'the great day'. But it was not only evangelical clergy, inside and outside the Church of England, whose sermons focused more frequently on eschatological themes—death, judgement, heaven, and hell—than any others. Rather, these were the dominant themes of most clergy and Christian commentators in the early and mid-nineteenth century.[33] And they were to remain at the centre of William's theological reflections and devotional reading for the rest of his life, as was the mystery of the holy eucharist, on which he first reflected at length in a small notebook, probably started after his confirmation and continued in his final months at Eton. In his notes on 'The Supper of the Lord, or Holy Communion', which cover thirteen folios, he writes on the 'new life' with God, adding, 'By nature we have many lusts which we like to indulge. But the grace of God teaches us to deny and abstain from all fleshly lusts because they war against the soul'.[34]

On Sunday 2 December 1827, William received the sacrament for the sixth time at Eton, 'finished Paleys Christian Evidence', read the bible, and sat down, 'with a heavy heart', to write an account of his 'last Eton day, in all probability'.[35] He prayed that his 'feeling', that the happiest period of his life is now past, may teach him to 'seek humbly, penitently, constantly, eagerly, after an eternal happiness which never fades or vanishes'. The months that followed proved to be an important bridge between school and university, during which William prepared himself for Oxford, both academically and spiritually. In late January 1828 he joined the household of the Revd John Turner, Rector of Wilmslow, along with a fellow Etonian, Horatio Powys, already a Cambridge graduate, who was preparing for ordination and would later become the Bishop of Sodor and Man. A manual of pastoralia for the active parish priest was studied alongside the Greek New Testament, Homer, Cicero, and Euclid: for William, ordination remained a future aspiration. After two months with his family at Seaforth, he took up residence at Cuddesdon parsonage in August, to continue his cramming for Oxford with the Revd Augustus Page Saunders, later to be one of his tutors at Christ Church. Again he worked alongside a fellow Etonian, Christopher William Puller (soon to join him at Christ Church), and engaged in parish life, teaching Sunday school. It was at Cuddesdon, he thought later, that he 'first learned to like *hard* work'.[36]

That August he responded to a letter from his younger sister, Helen, asking for advice on baptism, by writing her a fourteen-page reply. There he cites Anglican divines and the early fathers of the church in support of the doctrine of baptismal regeneration, marking a movement from the evangelicalism of his youth towards a more catholic Anglican understanding of the sacraments that was to deepen at Oxford.[37] He writes, 'Regeneration is a birth: the principle of life only is imparted therein: it is an admission into the covenant: continuance in its blessing being independent of it . . . I remember the time when I had a horror of anything that upheld the Doctrine of Baptismal Regeneration Fool that I was'.[38] Further reflection on the doctrine was to follow at Christ Church. During the period of study at Cuddesdon he had a long conversation with a woman, met late at night in Oxford, a harbinger of the numerous London prostitutes who were later to be approached through his 'rescue work'. He kept in touch with his family and Eton friends by post. He met John Henry Newman of Oriel, the newly appointed vicar of St Mary's, the university church, who dined with them. And he praised an *'excellent* sermon' by Edward Bouverie Pusey, Canon of Christ Church, who was about to be appointed Professor of Hebrew in the university and who, in a few years' time, would be a cofounder of the Oxford Movement, with Newman and John Keble of Oriel.[39]

William slept in Christ Church for the first time on 10 October 1828.

Fellowship one with another at Oxford

As at Eton, Tom Gladstone was the family pioneer at Oxford: he went up to Christ Church five years before William. Dogged by various complaints, which he reported back to a family preoccupied with health, he had an undistinguished undergraduate career and managed only a pass degree.[40] But his father sent him a valet and a groom, as suitable appurtenances for the future heir. Although William was a much brighter prospect, his father did not pay for him to be a gentleman commoner, whereby he would have been entitled to wear a splendid long gown and to dine at high table, privileges enjoyed by Lord Lincoln, the Acland brothers, and, nine years later, John Ruskin, another wealthy merchant's son. Indeed, William's first rooms were small and extremely dirty. The rooms became grander and he went on to enjoy a glittering career at Christ Church, becoming President of the Union in the Michaelmas term of 1830 and graduating, in November–December 1831, with a rare double first class—in *literae humaniores* (classics) and mathematics—like Peel (Harrow and Christ Church) twenty-three years earlier.

William was not alone when he followed the beaten path from Eton to Christ Church. Seven months earlier he had informed Farr in a letter that Gaskell was to be a 'fellow collegian', adding, 'This I am very glad of'.[41] On 23 October 1829, at the beginning of his second year, when 'canvassing for the projected Essay Society', he recorded that 'we met at Jim Gaskell's rooms' in the evening.[42] Known as the 'WEG', after its founder, the society was conceived as the Oxford equivalent to the Apostles at Cambridge, a secret discussion group which met in undergraduate rooms, often at Trinity College. The prospects for WEG had been 'very dark during the early part of the day—Acland & Anstice refusing even to attend the meeting—Rogers uncertain, Harrison backing out in consequence of this bad news, Seymer & Gaskell lukewarm'. When the meeting went well, however, with Gaskell elected secretary, William expressed his 'great delight', tempered by an innate spiritual wariness, verging on anxiety: 'I trust it may work well, & that nothing in it may be displeasing to our Heavenly Father, but all in strict subordination to his will'. Two other members of the informal fellowship at Eton—Francis Doyle and the Earl of Lincoln—joined William at Christ Church, became members of the WEG, and were active in the university Union, Lincoln becoming President, like William. Friendships tend to wax and wane in our youth, as in the case of Hallam and of Doyle, who fell away later in life, having been William's best man. James Hope, later Hope-Scott, arrived at Christ Church from Eton at the beginning of William's second year, but did not become his closest friend (also called 'Jim' in the diary) until 1836.

During their years at Oxford, these privileged young men witnessed a sea change in national politics. Wellington and Peel introduced Catholic emancipation in 1829 and King William IV ascended the throne in 1830, thus triggering the general election that brought in the Whig 'Reform Government' under the 2nd Earl Grey. Two decades of Tory hegemony came to an end at Westminster, but not at Oxford, where the university remained solidly Conservative, as the party was soon known, and where Christ Church controlled one of the two university seats in parliament. Many of the clerical fellows of Oxford colleges were 'high and dry' supporters of the established constitution of church and state, and adhered to the kind of orthodox Anglicanism that they inherited from their eighteenth-century predecessors—Protestant, royalist, Tory, and protective of their colleges' patronage of parish churches, and thus their schools, across the land.

During his three years at Oxford, William's own churchmanship continued its gradual evolution from evangelicalism to what Jagger labelled a 'catholic evangelical' position.[43] But while 'coming to accept a more "catholic" view of the sacraments, church and ministry', Jagger suggests, 'there were other facets of his faith which remained evangelical, including his attachment to the Prayer Book, Thirty-nine Articles, the authority and study of the bible, a "holy life-style," a personal relationship with Christ, Christian service and witness and an emphasis upon the church's function of preaching and mission'. The complexity of William's churchmanship, he adds, 'and the fact that he was never a "party man", made it difficult for others to understand him'.

On the evangelical side, we find him recording in his diary, on 1 August 1828, 'Heard Sumner was made Bp of Chester, for wh we shd I think be thankful', and in Holy Week and Easter Week 1829, when reunited with his parents at Leamington, he read Sumner's *Sermons on the Principal Festivals of the Christian Church* intensively.[44] Soon after settling at Christ Church, William met a 'new party' over wine in St Mary Hall, 'hearers apparently of Mr Bulteel at St Ebbes'.[45] One enthusiastic follower of the charismatic Henry Bellenden Bulteel, curate of St Ebbe's and a future member of the Plymouth brethren, is called 'Mr Q' in the dialogue which William records in his diary on 15 November 1828. When William explains that he is prevented from hearing Bulteel because it seems to him 'right to attend our own Church', and Bulteel's services clash with those in the university church and the chapel of Christ Church, the overbearing Mr Q tries a number of strategies to draw him into the Calvinist's fold, one of which is personal: 'Mr. Q. Unless I am disappointed in your name, I think you would like him. W. E. G. In my name, Sir? Mr Q. Yes, Sir, in the name of your family & principles'. On Sunday 15 February 1829 William did manage to hear Bulteel, having also attended two services in chapel ('Heard between the three, a great deal of admirable matter'), and on 29 March, a few weeks after the death of his beloved sister, Anne, he returned to hear him on 'I know that my Redeemer liveth' [Job 19.25] and on 'rejoining our relatives in heaven!' ('suited well to my circumstances, and touching').[46]

By keeping up chapel and/or university church attendance, while very occasionally hearing Bulteel, William was exposed to a wide range of preachers—useful, perhaps, for a future clergyman. On Sunday 28 June 1829 he records, 'Chapel mg & aft. St Ebbe's—& heard pt of Mr Newman's in aftn'.[47] (Newman's afternoon sermons at St Mary's attracted flocks of admiring undergraduates, whose motto became 'Credo in Newmanum'.) Five months later, on Sunday 15 November, he heard a sermon in chapel by 'Mr Keble (earnest on love & recollection of our Lord)'.[48] Earnestness and true feeling were crucial features of a good sermon for William, whose response to another sermon by Keble, delivered at St Mary's during his third year, was mixed: 'Are all of his opinions those of Scripture & the Church? Of his life and heart & practice none could doubt, all would admire.'[49]

When Bulteel gave his most famous sermon, on Sunday 6 February 1831, William was in the congregation. Taking I Corinthians 2.12 as his text, the Calvinist attacked the establishment's erastianism—state interference in church affairs—and its widespread rejection of the doctrine of predestination (which William had discussed with Hallam at Eton). For a young man with an acute sense of his own besetting sins, however, there was good news in the preacher's emphasis upon assurance, and his claim that 'God doth not behold our sins, because they are all behind his back', and 'because the sin of every believer was mystically put to death when Christ died'.[50] William recorded that, 'after having heard the remarkable sermon of this remarkable man, I cannot but still remember the words of St Paul, (in reference to the extent of redemption) For as by the disobedience of one *the* many were made sinners, so also by the obedience of one shall *the many* be made righteous [Romans 5.19]'.[51] Having written 'a long letter home, giving an account of Bulteel's extraordinary sermon', William sent the preacher *The Brazen Serpent* by the lay theologian Thomas Erskine, with 'a strange letter (anon.)' attached, and followed the controversy that followed the sermon's publication. During his last long vacation, he noted that 'poor Bulteel' had 'lost his Church for preaching in the open air' (an illegal act in the Church of England) and later heard him preach 'from a window in Mrs Albutt's house—congregation large & very attentive'.[52]

One of William's Oxford notebooks contains a fragment of an imaginary dialogue between a Calvinist and an Arminian, adherents of the two great branches of Protestant tradition.[53] (Wesleyan Methodists were Arminian, for example, while Calvinist Methodists were led by George Whitefield in the eighteenth century.) Memoranda of this kind indicate an inquiring mind and a desire to explore a range of beliefs and ideas for himself. While thinking about Bulteel and Calvinism, he was also reading the Anglican divines who were venerated by the establishment that Bulteel attacked. At Seaforth, during his first long vacation, he read straight through Richard Hooker's *Ecclesiastical Polity* (1594–97), a foundational Anglican text, alongside a life of Wesley. Having completed Hooker's monumental work he characteristically began an 'analysis' of it.[54] Over a period of three months in his third year he read and made notes on Bishop Joseph Butler's *The Analogy of Religion* (1736), the Anglican classic which he would study with enthusiasm throughout his life. Butler's view of the church as a 'divine society', the creation of God rather than of man, deepened William's ecclesiology at this time.[55] In the same Oxford notebook as the Calvinist-Arminian dialogue is a large 'Collection of Testimonies on Baptismal Regeneration', which draws upon a range of sources: 'I. That which is immediately deducible from Holy Scripture. II. The testimony borne by the Fathers of the Christian Church. III. The language of our authorised formularies. IV. The opinions given by the Divines of the English Church, from the Reformation till the present day', these last being presented in extensive extracts, painstakingly transcribed.[56] There is also a paper on the doctrine of conversion, dated January 1830 and written in homiletic style. Here William reflects upon the way in which an individual passes 'the limit which divides the realm of light from the pit of darkness', but not necessarily in a moment. Having recently read Bishop Richard Mant's orthodox high Anglican Bampton Lectures, he was 'beginning to identify with a new point of view'.[57] These notes are permeated with a desire to get to the bottom of a subject, as are his lecture notes on classics and mathematics. William Gladstone the undergraduate was nothing if not thorough.

All this pious reading and reflection also served as a helpful distraction from the 'fleshly lusts' that troubled him in adolescence and early manhood. In January 1831 he read and 'began an Analysis' of John Bird Sumner's *Treatise on the Records of the Creation* (1816), in which the evangelical Bishop of Chester argued that the chaste postponement of marriage would be less painful if literature and other intellectual pursuits were brought into play: 'the mind, diverted from one object, turns, without pain or convulsion, to another'.[58] William had read *Onania* (1712/16), the classic work on the dangers of masturbation, in July 1829, five months before referring to his 'one besetting sin', in the birthday diary entry cited at the head of this chapter.[59] His later diary entries of the 1840s and 1850s, examined in Chapter 4, anticipate D. H. Lawrence's description in the 1920s of the 'shame, anger, humiliation, and the sense of futility' associated with masturbation, feelings that deepen 'as the years go on, into a suppressed rage'.[60] In

'Pornography and Obscenity' Lawrence challenges his reader to 'Fight the great lie of the nineteenth century, which has soaked through our sex and our bones', and to 'fight the sentimental life of purity and the dirty little secret wherever you meet it, inside yourself or in the world outside'.[61] Writing on education in *Fantasia of the Unconscious* (1923), he argues that 'To introduce mental activity is to arrest the dynamic activity and stultify true dynamic development'.[62] By the age of twenty-one, he adds, 'our young people are helpless, selfless, floundering mental entities, with nothing in front of them, because they have been starved from the roots, systematically, for twenty-one years, and fed through the head. They have had all their mental excitements, sex and everything, all through the head, and when it comes to the actual thing, why, there's nothing in it'. The controlling 'mind of Gladstone' the intellectual provided him with a sense of order, but his 'mental excitements' also led to what Lawrence defines as self-consciousness and 'sex in the head'.

Like his 'one besetting sin', William's undergraduate reading was a private matter. But he was also overtly pious, which did not make him universally popular. (His elder brother, Tom, warned him against 'the extravagance of religious effervescence'.[63]) As at Eton, William was upset by misbehaviour at services, and on 23 March 1830 he reported 'a most disgraceful disturbance in Chapel' to a senior member of the college. That night he was beaten up by 'a party of men' in his own rooms.[64] Lengthy reflection ensues, written in a slightly larger hand than usual, perhaps indicating physical injury as well as emotional disturbance:

Here I have great reason to be thankful to that God whose mercies fail not. And for two special reasons.

1. Because this incident must tend to the mortification of my pride, by God's grace ... It is no disgrace to be beaten for Christ was buffeted and smitten—but though calm reasoning assures me of this, my impulses, my habit of mind, my vicious & corrupt nature, asserts the contrary—may it be defeated.

2. Because here I have to some small extent an opportunity of exercising the duty of forgiveness ...

> I may condemn myself, for though I soon ceased to resist, I did not behave as I ought afterwards. It was suffering but it was not endurance.
>
> And if this hostile and unkind conduct be a sample of their ways, I pray that the grace of God may reveal to them that the end thereof is death. Even this prayer is selfish. I prayed little for them before, when I knew that they were living in sin and had rejected Christ their Saviour—but this is but one small product and fruit of the state of mind which such rejection implies.

And so the self-flagellation goes on, as the victim of an assault by a group of hearties beats himself up, sifting the many subtle ways in which his own sinful nature is revealed in the event. The passage is reminiscent of puritan spiritual autobiography of the seventeenth century and of evangelical testimony of the nineteenth.

Such morbid reflections were not confined to moments of crisis: rather, they were characteristic of William's spiritual life throughout his time at Oxford. Early on, for example, on 17 November 1829, he wrote to Farr, 'The very basis of all religion as it seems to me is . . . "Lord be merciful to me a sinner" [Luke 18.13]: an earnest and humble prayer for mercy, rested on no grounds whatever excepting our lamentable, God knows most lamentable, need, and the abundance of those means which his unbought favour towards us has provided'.[65] Similarly, three months later he lamented in a diary entry that he had been 'leading a more unchristian life lately than for a long time before', one cause of which was 'a grossly careless & sinful habit of saying my prayers when half asleep at night & half awake in the morning'.[66] The crisis of March 1830 did, however, result in an intensification in his 'self-examination', the title of a section in one of his Oxford notebooks, dated June 1830. 'We speak of self examination', he wrote: 'if we practise it in addition, so much the better: but who can understand it? Who can investigate and analyse that mysterious process, in which *The understanding* sits in judgment on *the heart*, which itself so powerfully affects the source from whence the verdict is to proceed. And while the accused influences that which acts as judge & accuser, & almost forms the decisions of that tribunal before which it is arraigned, who is that third party, that mysterious "I" who watches the process, scrutinises it in all and each of its steps, and registers and records the result? O mystery of mysteries, all is mystery.'[67]

Walking in the light

In the spring of 1830 devotional texts also figured more prominently in his reading. On 9 May he reflected on the psalmist's invitation that men should commune within their heart and be still before God (Psalm 4.4).[68] His first collection of psalms, again produced with scissors and paste, began life while he was at Oxford and clearly stayed with him for years, judging by the wear on the marbled covers to the octavo notebook and by the pencil annotations alongside many of the selected verses from individual psalms. Using a number of different print editions of the Psalms, in various translations, and of hymns based upon the Psalms, William seems to have selected the verses which 'found him', as Coleridge might have put it, carefully cutting and pasting dozens of extracts which cover thirty-nine pages of the notebook. The pencil markings record the season or festival at which the psalm was said or sung, or the location of the church where William heard it, such as Winchester, Peterborough, or one of the London churches he frequented after 1832.[69] This hand-crafted collection reveals not only an obsessive commitment to record-keeping, but also a profound spiritual need.

On Sunday 30 May 1830 William read Jeremy Taylor's Anglican classic, *The Rules and Exercises of Holy Living* (1650), on which he had started soon after the previous Christmas.[70] And two days later he read the 'Introductory Essay & Preface to Thomas a Kempis'. *The Imitation of Christ*, published anonymously in the early fifteenth century, is one of the most popular yet also most astringent of all Christian meditations on human frailty and divine grace. In his introductory essay, Thomas Chalmers provided a safe way into *The Imitation* for a reader like William. 'The severities of Christian practice', Chalmers wrote, 'which are here urged upon the reader, are in no way allied with the penances and the self-inflictions of a monastic ritual, but are the essentials of spiritual discipline in all ages'.[71] William started on this strong meat on Sunday 13 June 1830 and finished it two weeks later. He was to keep the work by him for the rest of his life, in a number of Latin and English editions, often turning to it at times of stress.

William first absorbed these devotional works when actively considering the possibility of ordination. At the end of his second year, on the afternoon of 25 June 1830, he left Oxford and walked fifteen miles towards Leamington. Having sheltered from a thunderstorm overnight, he walked eight miles to Banbury, where he breakfasted, and a further twenty-two miles to his parents' temporary home at the famous spa. (The death of George IV on 26 June remains unremarked in the diary.) Just over a week later he returned to Oxford, commenting ruefully, 'so ends my Long Vacation'.[72] He now began another period of cramming with the Revd Saunders at Cuddesdon, in the company of fellow Christ Church men Joseph Anstice, a future professor of classics, and Walter Hamilton, a future Bishop of Salisbury, who was to help him in his choice of a career. While working through a fearsome reading list, he was 'up soon after six' on 6 July and began his 'Harmony of Gk Testament'. By early August he was suffering from headaches and recording in his diary a 'fearful weight' on his mind, as he reflected upon 'souls throughout the world' who were 'sinking daily' into (spiritual) death.[73] It was his 'sad and solemn conviction that a fearfully great portion of the world [was] dying in sin' that drove him to write a long and convoluted letter to his father, bringing him up to date with his current thinking about his future calling, more than eighteen months after their discussion at Seaforth, when John Gladstone recommended the law, and sixteen months before his graduation.[74] As in other communications with the paterfamilias, the primacy of parental authority almost leads to a conflation of earthly and heavenly 'Fathers' in William's mind. At a more mundane level, he shared his tormented thinking with Anstice the following Sunday, concluding that he must consider himself 'a being not yet competent for self-direction'.[75] His earthly father replied from Leamington on 10 August, reminding him that a clergyman's 'field of actual usefulness' was 'more circumscribed and limited' than that of individuals whose study of the law prepared them for public life.[76] Father had spoken and so the matter rested for the time being.

Jagger points out that many scholars have failed to recognize how seriously William considered ordination. He also argues that William never seemed to recognize that his dilemma was 'a conflict between his ultimate duty to God and his duty to his parents'.[77] Jagger wonders whether 'deep down Gladstone thought he ought to be a priest, but was secretly more attracted to politics'. He was either mistaken about his call to the priesthood and was genuinely called to be a politician, or he was 'haunted by this act of disobedience' and tried to make amends by serving God as a layman in both state and church.[78] The event which brought these questions into high relief was to occur on 17 May 1831, when William fiercely opposed the Reform Bill at the

Union, in a speech of three quarters of an hour that for some marked him out as a potential future prime minister. A fortnight later he reflected on the fact that he had received more compliments than usual on the speech. He then echoed Bishop Butler, whose chapter 'Of a State of Probation, as Implying Moral Discipline and Improvement' he had recently read: 'It has also happened that I have never had cause to feel my own utter & abandoned sinfulness before God more deeply. Oh who can look at these bitterly instructive contrasts & yet deny that there is a Providence wonderfully framing out of a seeming series of accidents the most appropriate & aptest discipline for each of our souls.'[79]

The last months of William's Oxford career unfolded at a time of political turmoil over reform. Echoing Matthew 16.3, two years after the publication of Thomas Carlyle's famous essay and Edward Irving's pamphlet of the same title and year, 'Signs of the Times', he wrote in his diary, on 22 October 1831, 'Surely the actual signs of the times are such as should make us ready for the coming our Lord'.[80] It was only after the glories of the double first at the end of the year, however, that William's own future would be decided, whether by divine providence or by parental interference we will consider in the next chapter.

Notes

1. *Diaries*, vol. I, p. 276.
2. See S. G. Checkland's ground-breaking study, *The Gladstones: A Family Biography, 1764–1851* (Cambridge: Cambridge University Press, 1971), p. 85, and Peter Jagger, *Gladstone: The Making of a Christian Politician: The Personal Religious Life and Development of William Ewart Gladstone, 1809–32* (Allison Park, PA: Pickwick, 1991), p. 21. I am grateful to the late Revd Jagger, formerly Warden of St Deiniol's Library, Hawarden, for his revisionary but somewhat neglected study which covers the same subject-matter as this chapter, albeit with a greater emphasis upon matters of theology and doctrine.
3. Jagger, *Gladstone*, pp. 7, 11–14.
4. Jagger, *Gladstone*, p. 14.
5. See Ruth Clayton Windscheffel, *Reading Gladstone* (Basingstoke: Palgrave Macmillan; New York: St Martin's Press, 2008), pp. 98–100.
6. *The Christian's best Companion, containing the whole Book of Common Prayer, and Administration of the Sacraments, and other Rites and Ceremonies of the Church* (Bungay: Brightly, 1811), n.p.

7. Smiles specialized in 'men of invention and industry'. William liked the idea in 1860, but nothing came of it because of a 'difference of opinion in the family': *The Prime Ministers' Papers: W. E. Gladstone, Autobiographica and autobiographical Memoranda*, ed. John Brooke and Mary Sorensen, 4 vols. (London: HMSO, 1971–81), vol. I, p. 18; see also *Diaries*, vol. V, p. 481.

8. John Morley, *The Life of William Ewart Gladstone*, 3 vols. (London and New York: Macmillan, 1903), vol. I, p. 10.

9. *Prime Ministers' Papers*, vol. I, pp. 18–19.

10. See Jagger, *Gladstone*, p. 20.

11. *Prime Ministers' Papers*, vol. I, p. 21.

12. Jagger, *Gladstone*, p. 18.

13. Checkland, *Gladstones*, p. 135.

14. *Prime Ministers' Papers*, vol. I, pp. 24–25.

15. See, for example, six small Eton notebooks (BL, 44,802) and the worn larger notebook that he took to Oxford with him (BL, 44,801).

16. *Diaries*, vol. I, p. 18.

17. *Diaries*, vol. I, p. 73. Seaforth, Sunday 10 September 1826.

18. See Jagger, *Gladstone*, p. 60.

19. BL, 44,832.

20. *Diaries*, vol. I, p. 125.

21. Lord John Russell's *Essay on the History of the English Government and Constitution* is cited in G. H. L. Le May, *The Victorian Constitution: Conventions, Usages and Contingencies* (London: Duckworth, 1979), p. 10.

22. *Prime Ministers' Papers*, vol. I, p. 21

23. James Milnes Gaskell, *Records of an Eton Schoolboy*, ed. Charles Milnes Gaskell (p. p., 1883), p. 71.

24. *Diaries*, vol. I, p. 43. See also Gladstone's notes on Calvinism and predestination in BL, 44,801, ff. 31r–33v.

25. *Prime Ministers' Papers*, vol. I, p. 183.

26. *Prime Ministers' Papers*, vol. I, p. 26.

27. *Diaries*, vol. I, p. 35.

28. Gerhard Kittel and Gerhard Friedrich, eds., *Theological Dictionary of the New Testament*, abridged and trans. Geoffrey W. Bromiley (Grand Rapids, MI: Eerdmans; Exeter: Paternoster, 1985), p. 450.

29. See Jagger, *Gladstone*, p. 74.

30. *Diaries*, vol. I, p. 96.

31. Kittel, *Theological Dictionary*, p. 449.

32. *Diaries*, vol. I, p. 104.

33. See Michael Wheeler, *Heaven, Hell and the Victorians* (Cambridge: Cambridge University Press, 1994).

34. BL, 44,802, notebook F, f.12.

35. *Diaries*, vol. I, p. 151. William Paley's *Evidences of Christianity* (1794) became a standard work of Christian apologetics.

36. Letter to Catherine Gladstone, Cuddesdon, 22 January 1852: GLA/GGA/2/10/1/18a.

37. See Perry Butler, *Gladstone, Church, State and Tractarianism: A Study of his Religious Ideas and Attitudes, 1809–1859* (Oxford: Clarendon; New York: Oxford University Press, 1982), pp. 23, 141; Jagger, *Gladstone*, p. 48.
38. See Butler, *Gladstone*, p. 23.
39. See *Diaries*, vol. I, pp. 193, 195, 196, 202.
40. See Checkland, *Gladstones*, pp. 164, 167.
41. *Prime Ministers' Papers*, vol. I, p. 202.
42. *Diaries*, vol. I, p. 264.
43. Jagger, *Gladstone*, pp. 136–37; also see p. 155.
44. *Diaries*, vol. I, pp. 192, 236–38. Liverpool was in John Bird Sumner's diocese of Chester.
45. *Diaries*, vol. I, p. 211.
46. *Diaries*, vol. I, p. 226.
47. *Diaries*, vol. I, p. 248.
48. *Diaries*, vol. I, p. 268.
49. *Diaries*, vol. I, p. 366.
50. Henry Bellenden Bulteel, *A Sermon on I Corinthians II.12, preached before the University of Oxford at St. Mary's, on Sunday, Feb. 6, 1831*, 3rd edn (Oxford: Baxter, 1831), p. 19.
51. *Diaries*, vol. I, p. 343.
52. *Diaries*, vol. I, pp. 374, 384.
53. BL, 44,719, f. 240.
54. See *Diaries*, vol. I, p. 261 and BL, 44,720 f. 86.
55. See Jagger, *Gladstone*, pp. 147–48; David Bebbington, *The Mind of Gladstone: Religion, Homer, and Politics* (Oxford: Oxford University Press, 2004), p. 37.
56. BL, 44,720 f. 126.
57. BL, 44,720, f. 218; see Colin Matthew, 'Gladstone, Evangelicalism, and "The Engagement"', in *Revival and Religion since 1700: Essays for John Walsh*, ed. Jane Garnett and Colin Matthew (London and Rio Grande: Hambledon, 1993), pp. 111–26 (pp. 114–16); Bebbington, *Mind of Gladstone*, p. 46.
58. *Diaries*, vol. I, pp. 336–37; John Bird Sumner, *A Treatise on the Records of the Creation*, 2 vols., 2nd edn (London: Hatchard, 1818), vol. II, p. 167; BL, 44, 721, ff. 112-15.
59. *Diaries*, vol. I, pp. 250, 276.
60. *Phoenix: The Posthumous Papers of D. H. Lawrence*, ed. Edward D. McDonald (London: Heinemann, 1936), p. 179.
61. Lawrence, *Phoenix*, p. 185.
62. D. H. Lawrence, *Fantasia of the Unconscious* and *Psychoanalysis and the Unconscious* (London: Heinemann, 1961), p. 89.
63. See Jagger, *Gladstone*, p. 219.
64. *Diaries*, vol. I, p. 290. 24 March 1830. LPL, MS 1418 ff. 28v–29r.
65. *Prime Ministers' Papers*, vol. I, p. 212. At Cuddesdon in 1830, William agonized over whether he truly knew himself to be 'the chief of sinners': BL, 44,801 f. 74.

66. *Diaries*, vol. I, p. 285.
67. BL, 44,801 f. 64. Gladstone echoes Ecclesiastes 1.2.
68. BL, 44,801.f.71.
69. BL, 44,833.
70. *Diaries*, vol. I, p. 306.
71. Thomas à Kempis, *The Imitation of Christ, in three Books*, trans. John Payne, introductory essay by Thomas Chalmers, 7th edn (Glasgow: Collins, 1830), p. xvi.
72. See *Diaries*, vol. I, p. 311.
73. See *Diaries*, vol. I, p. 316.
74. The whole letter, dated Cuddesdon, 4 August 1830, is reprinted in Morley, *Life of Gladstone*, vol. I, pp. 635-40.
75. *Diaries*, vol. I, p. 317.
76. Morley, *Life of Gladstone*, vol. I, p. 641.
77. Jagger, *Gladstone*, pp. 100, 223.
78. Jagger, *Gladstone*, pp. 224, 234.
79. *Diaries*, vol. I, p. 361. 30 May 1831. See Joseph Butler, *The Analogy of Religion* (1736), part I, Ch. 5.
80. *Diaries*, vol. I, p. 389. Irving was a famous preacher and founder of the Catholic Apostolic Church.

2
True allegiance

I solemnly swear by Almighty God that I will be faithful and bear true allegiance to Her Majesty Queen Victoria, her heirs and successors, according to law. So help me God. (Parliamentary Oath)

Having sworn allegiance to the crown as a young bachelor MP, William briefly served under Peel as a junior lord of the treasury and under-secretary for war and the colonies. He also published his most important and controversial book, *The State in its Relations with the Church* (1838). The following year he swore an oath of a different kind, this time to Catherine Glynne of Hawarden Castle, Flintshire: 'I William take thee Catherine to my wedded wife, to have and to hold from this day forward' (Solemnization of Matrimony, Book of Common Prayer). Happily married and soon a father, William sought his wife's and his father's support as Peel returned to power and promoted him to the vice-presidency and then presidency of the board of trade. This chapter traces William's spiritual life between 1832, when he committed himself to politics, and 1845, a year of crisis in which he resigned over the Maynooth grant and was then drawn back into the cabinet as colonial secretary.

I have committed myself

On 7 January 1832, William began to draft a letter to his father on the vexed question of his 'future destination', seventeen months after their previous correspondence on the matter.[1] Although living under the parental roof at the time, he found it easier to open his heart and soul to his 'beloved Father' on paper than face to face. Writing was also his way of organizing his thoughts. He posed a question: 'how shall I best be enabled to do in my sphere & calling the will of Him whose property I absolutely am, that will being, the extirpation of sin and misery from the world?' Next day he heard an 'excellent sermon' from Mr Rawson 'on the signs of the times'.[2] With these signs in mind he argued in his draft that 'the human race, or at least the civilised world, is rapidly approaching its crisis . . . no very great number of years will in their revolutions bring the time, when the whole fabric of human society shall be rocked to its very foundations, and when everywhere it shall be put to the test whether the house is built upon the rock or upon the sand, amidst the fury of the tempest and the flood' (Matthew 7.26–27). Old sympathies are 'daily falling into disrepute', he believes, and 'national expressions of religion' have adopted a 'latitudinarian tone'. So, he concludes, his own desires for 'future life' are 'exactly coincident' with his father's: 'a *profession* of the law, with a view substantially to studying the constitutional branch of it, and a subsequent experiment, as time and circumstances might offer, on what is termed public life.' After several revisions, he handed the letter to his father, who was delighted, as was his mother. Heavenly and earthly Fathers seemed to be of one mind on William's future. But subsequent events led to the vague timetable that he sketched being concertinaed into just twelve months.

Soon after taking his bachelor's degree in Oxford, on 26 January, he set off on his grand tour. He was accompanied by his beloved brother John Neilson Gladstone and, as he later put it, 'equipped as it were with a full suit of Protestantism'.[3] William was an observant and painstaking tourist, noting in a separate notebook his observations on the manners, art, and architecture of countries through which he passed, and commenting on the rites and teachings of the Roman Catholic Church from his own Anglican ('catholic evangelical') perspective. He continued to read voraciously, he corresponded with friends and family, and he kept up with news from home on the controversial reform bill that was carried in a second reading in the Lords on 14 April 1832, by which time the brothers were settled in Rome.

Like many Anglican visitors of the period, William found certain Roman Catholic observances alien and distasteful. On Palm Sunday he recorded that the priests in the Sistine Chapel moved 'with little

True allegiance 29

of interest or energy, but rather like men who did it simply because they had done it before.'[4] (Always on the search for 'vital religion', he was later to observe that a nun's initiation ceremony had 'more heart than most of them'.[5]) The washing of feet on Maundy Thursday was 'an extremely curious sight, as a relic of other times.'[6] Pope Gregory XVI, Catholicism's 'Holy Father', seemed to him 'ordinary and undignified' in appearance, although his expression was 'benign, simple, & devout'.[7] On Easter Sunday, however, among a crowd of up to 20,000 in St Peter's Square, he was deeply impressed by the grandeur of the papal benediction: 'The Vicar of Christ upon earth, in the metropolitan city of his universal Church, that city crowned with a thousand rays of glory, each bright enough to ennoble a nation's history—ascends the most gorgeous temple, peradventure, that the world ever saw, and calls down, while he authoritatively declares, the blessing of the Eternal Father upon the multitudes gathered from all quarters of the world at this holy season, crowding even the wide expanses before him, endless in variety as countless in number; essentially one fold, and visibly marshalled under one Shepherd. And how noble the terms—"urbi et orbi."'[8]

Arriving in Naples on 28 April, he saw the sights, studied the classical antiquities, took singing lessons, and witnessed the 'most indecorous' crush at the liquefaction of St Gennaro's blood at the cathedral.[9] On Sunday 13 May he examined in detail the occasional offices of the Church of England in the Book of Common Prayer. These include baptism, confirmation, matrimony, the burial of the dead, and ordination. Coinciding with his 'coming into Catholic countries', they offered him 'glimpses' of 'the nature of a Church'.[10] Six decades later he was to record that he had previously 'taken a great deal of teaching direct from the Bible', but that now, on this day,

> the figure of the Church arose before me as a teacher too, and I gradually found in how incomplete and fragmentary a manner I had drawn down truth from the sacred volume, as indeed I had also missed in the Thirty-nine Articles some things which ought to have taught me better. Such, for I believe I have given the fact as it occurred, in its silence and its solitude, was my first introduction to the august conception of the Church of Christ. It presented to me Christianity under an aspect in which I had not known

it: its ministry of symbols, its channels of grace, its unending line of teachers joining from the head: a sublime construction, based throughout upon historic fact, uplifting the ideas of the community in which we live, and of the access which it enjoys through the new and living way, to the presence of the most high.

From this time I began to feel my way by degrees into or towards a true notion of the Church. It became a definite and organised idea when at the suggestion of James Hope I read the just-published and remarkable work of Palmer. But the charm of freshness lay upon that first disclosure in 1832.[11]

William Palmer's *Origines Liturgicæ* (1832) was set reading for Anglican ordinands and his *Treatise on the Church of Christ* (1838), recommended by Hope, was the nearest that the conservative strand of Oxford high churchmanship came to a systematic theology.[12] It was in Catholic Italy, however, in 1832 that the significance of the Church of England's own identity as part of the universal catholic church, with its unending line of teachers, came home to William.

Meanwhile, back in England, Lord Lincoln suggested to his father, the 4th Duke of Newcastle, that William would be a good candidate for Newark, one of the constituencies that the family controlled. When the duke wrote to William's father, asking whether he could answer for his son's accepting such an offer, John Gladstone wrote a letter to his son which arrived in Milan on 9 July 1832, a few days after Lincoln's own letter to William, pledging his support. Stunned, confused, and intoxicated by Lincoln's letter, William once again turned to his earthly father for support. 'Happily', he wrote in his diary, 'God, who established the order of nature, and who seals parental wisdom & experience by parental authority, did by this order relieve me. To learn his will, the first human means is to refer to my parents—and this was done. It remained to add earnest supplications to the throne of grace for defence and guidance on this arduous and delicate occasion.'[13] By the following Sunday he was in Geneva and could write, 'I have committed myself . . . The resolution was taken, I trust, in a spirit not of utter forgetfulness of Him, who is the Author of all good counsels, all holy desires, and all just works.' Whether in papal Rome or Calvinist Geneva, it is the Book of Common Prayer, and here the second collect for evensong, that informs his spiritual response to an external shock.

True allegiance 31

Having returned to England, William prepared for the hustings in the general election, lamenting the fact that the urgent pleas of his agent compelled him to start his long coach journey from Newton Abbot in Devon to Newark in Nottinghamshire, via London, on a Sunday.[14] On his arrival he was soon embroiled in a sharp debate over slavery and the Gladstone family's plantations in the West Indies. During his time at Eton, his father's political career had focused upon the defence of the plantation owners who had made substantial investments and had legal rights associated with land ownership. In one of his publications on the subject, John Gladstone had acknowledged the need for improvements in the way that some, though not all, plantations were run. He also recognized that the time would come when slaves' 'acquirements' became such as would 'enable them to understand the *obligations* as well as the *advantages* of being their own masters.'[15] Like Canning, however, John Gladstone believed that the sudden freeing of uneducated slaves would be disastrous for them. He referred to 'that well-meaning, but mistaken man, Mr. Wilberforce' and added an appendix on slavery in scripture, concluding that 'Slavery being a civil institution, Christianity does not interfere with it.'[16]

These arguments were familiar to his son, who also read widely on the subject at school and at university. At Newark, where John Gladstone shared the election costs with the duke, William kept his father in touch with developments by post, writing one of his letters on the back of a foolscap printed election address dated the Clinton Arms, Newark, 9 October 1832. The address is the work of a seasoned debater in the Oxford Union whose ethics are grounded in the bible and Aristotle.[17] Four of its nine paragraphs are on slavery, at a time when gradual emancipation was the normal progressive view of the time. 'As regards the abstract lawfulness of slavery', he writes, 'I acknowledge it simply as importing the right of one man to the labour of another: and I rest it upon the fact, that Scripture, the paramount authority on such a point, gives directions to persons standing in the relation of master to slave, for their conduct in that relation: whereas were the matter absolutely and necessarily *sinful*, it would not regulate the manner.'[18] 'We are agreed', he continues, 'that both the physical and the moral bondage of the slave are to be abolished. The question is as to the *order*, and the order only: now Scripture attacks the moral evil *before* the temporal one, and the temporal *through* the moral one, and I am content with the order which Scripture has established.' A system of (Anglican) 'christian instruction' is needed for the slaves. Immediate emancipation could lead to 'a relapse into deeper debasement', if not 'bloodshed and internal war'. 'Let *fitness* be made the condition of emancipation,' he argues, 'and let us strive to bring [the slave] to that fitness, by the shortest possible course.'

In winning the election and becoming an MP, William was yet again following in the footsteps of his elder brother Thomas, whose political career as a reactionary Tory MP, initially funded by his father, was to be undistinguished. For the younger brother, his new role took on a semi-mystical significance, as he was later to recall: 'in my imagination I cast over that party [the Conservatives] a prophetic mantle and assigned to it a mission distinctly religious as the champion in the state field of that divine truth which it was the office of the Christian ministry to uphold in the Church. Nor was this mental attitude however strange it may now appear altogether unaccountable.'[19] High Christian ideals with regard to politics were not uncommon at the time. Martin Farquhar Tupper, an evangelical Oxford friend, wrote to him on 12 January 1833, 'You are called upon by the Providence of God to do what you can towards being a witness for the one Truth that it is a national as well as an individual duty to acknowledge God in all our ways and have Him in all our thoughts.'[20] Two weeks later, William wrote in a commonplace book, 'We love the *state* for the sake of the Church ... The highest light in which the State can be contemplated is as the handmaid of the Church.'[21] When he took the loyal oath, cited at the head of this chapter, he was swearing true allegiance to the supreme governor of the Church of England.

Intellectually, the relation of the state to the church was to preoccupy William Gladstone MP for the rest of the 1830s. More immediately, however, his task on taking his seat on the opposition benches, alongside his brother, was to defend the family honour in debates on emancipation. When Lord Howick denounced the manager of John Gladstone's Demerara estates as 'the murderer of slaves', William responded in his first long speech, arguing on similar lines to his electioneering address.[22] The speech was well received, but he remained troubled by what was a complex moral issue for politicians. When he attended William Wilberforce's funeral in Westminster Abbey, on 3 August 1833, he recorded in his diary that it 'brought solemn thoughts, particularly about the slaves. That is a burdensome question.'[23] (William had visited Wilberforce on his deathbed: the reformer asked after his dear mother.) When slaves became free apprentices in 1834, William recorded the event in his diary, later adding the words, 'A momentous day in the W[est] I[ndies].— May God govern it aright.'[24] Four years later he was to speak in the House of Commons for two hours in defence of continuing the apprenticeship scheme on West Indian plantations. The first of his marathon speeches was regarded as a *tour de force*.[25]

Fellow travellers

The early years of William's political career were marked by a sense of promise and momentum, as his intellectual and oratorical gifts led to junior ministerial appointments. External change and development were balanced, however, by continuities in his spiritual life, as he maintained the devotional habits and bonds of Christian fellowship of earlier years. Characteristically, the bright young MP controlled the more volatile side of his personality by attending to his duty to his family and servants, and by drawing upon the support of friends and mentors from school and university. Father paid for him to take chambers in the exclusive Albany in Piccadilly. 'For the years 1833–6', he later recorded, 'I lived in The Albany, attending St. James's Church [Piccadilly] morning and afternoon with very little variation: when at Fasque going to the Presbyterian church in the forenoon, when at Edinburgh (where my father wintered) attending St. John's, of which Dean Ramsay was the incumbent.'[26] According to G. W. E. Russell, nephew of Lord John, he read family prayers with his servants at the Albany while pursuing 'the same even course of steady work, reasonable recreation, and systematic devotion which he had marked out for himself at Oxford.'[27] On 26 March 1834 he 'wrote on the Lord's Supper', taking as his text a verse from the gospel reading set for the Wednesday before Easter in the prayer book.[28] Next day he recorded, 'read to servv. before prayers some of what I had written. Hope came to breakfast.' Citing Luke 22.19, 'This do in remembrance of me', William challenged his auditors and himself: 'Every one who claims the name of a Christian, not only *is* bound, but thereby acknowledges himself to be bound, to obey all the commands of Christ. For if

Christianity does not mean this what does it mean?'[29] 'Obedience' and 'discipline' were to be keywords in William's spiritual lexicon.

His Sunday reading in the autumn of 1834 included Augustine's *Confessions*, the 'practical parts' of which had for him a 'wonderful force, inimitable sweetness & simplicity'.[30] His notes on the Latin text are as detailed as his undergraduate notes on classical and Christian literature, and some of his short passages of precis are revealing. For a young man whose heart-searching was always intense and often troubled, chapter 5 in book X could be summarized, 'We do not see to the bottom of our own hearts but God does and this is our consolation. Cf. 1 Joh.iii.20'.[31] His comment on chapters thirteen and fourteen in book XIII resonates with the call to 'walk in the light' (I John 1.7), discussed earlier: 'Beautiful description of a Christian, once darkness, now light, yet in a residue of sin, saved by hope, and joyfully content with the earnest of salvation.'[32] Similarly, for him the core message of chapter nineteen in book XIII is 'cast away every sin, set heart & treasure in Heaven, & shine out on earth.' The second stanza of a prayer that William wrote in 1834 reads, 'When the passion-blast is rude, / Faint the flesh and all-subdued, / Weak the willing soul within, / Tyrannous the strength of sin, / Father! let my spirit flee / From its earthly coil to thee.'[33]

Early in that year he completed a total of three weeks' residence at Oxford in order to qualify for his master's degree. Keble's call to arms in his assize sermon on national apostasy was still fresh in the memory, as the Oxford Movement got underway with the publication of the first fifty *Tracts for the Times* (1833–34). On Sunday 19 January 1834 William recorded, 'Read the 1st lesson in morning Chapel. A most masterly sermon of Pusey's preached by Clarke.'[34] Next day he called on Pusey and dined at Merton as the guest of his friend Hamilton, now a fellow of the college and later Bishop of Salisbury. Further conversations with Harrison, Rogers of Oriel, and Palmer of Worcester College were followed by one with Newman at Oriel, 'chiefly on Church matters', and a conversation with Pusey of Christ Church 'on Convocation'. Ever anxious about his use of time, he commented: 'Much time now goes in conversations, yet I hope not unprofitably spent.'[35] On Sunday 2 February he 'read no 24 of the Tracts', entitled 'The Scripture View of the Apostolic Commission', returning to his London life three days later.

He need not have worried about time-wasting, as these Oxford conversations deepened his understanding of 'Church matters', the subject of his private meditations and political aspirations since 1832 and, crucially, of his future book, *The State in its Relations with the Church* (1838). Exchanges with members of the informal fellowship of Eton and Oxford days continued in London, where he kept in contact with Thomas Dyke Acland, Anstice, Doyle, Gaskell, Lincoln, and, following the death of Arthur Hallam in 1833, Arthur's father, Henry. In the spring of 1834 he read Newman on the Arians and various *Tracts*, and met and corresponded with Pusey on the question of religious tests in Cambridge. In 1836 he read Pusey's influential *Tracts* on holy baptism. But although he was regarded as a Tractarian in the 1830s and early 1840s, he never became a devotee of the leaders of the Oxford Movement. Whereas their priority was the defence of the church against the forces of a reforming government, William's was the unity of the church as a whole.[36] As David Bebbington states, William's reading of Augustine 'restrained him from going beyond what he considered the middle way of the Church of England.'[37]

In the mid-1830s William was on a journey of discovery in his thinking on the church and in finding his way as a politician. Frequent actual journeys by coach, between London, Oxford, Seaforth, Fasque, Edinburgh, and various spas, were often gruelling and occasionally dangerous. In all of this he was governed by a strong sense of providence, as when the coach in which he was travelling north was upset, on 14 February 1834 'at 7.20 A.M. 1 ½ m. S. of Leicester. Thank God, no one hurt. How small was our thankfulness! We went down gradually. God commanded it so. Instead of blessing him for that commandment, we use the fact, its result, to justify our withholding praise from Him to whom it is due.'[38] Startlingly literal as these words may appear to the modern mind, the idea that divine providence 'doth many times step in to divert the most probable event of things' had long been a strand of orthodox Anglican teaching.[39]

In November that year, King William IV dismissed the Whigs and called Peel home from Italy to form a government. When Peel arrived in London on 5 December, William was staying with his parents in Edinburgh, where he celebrated his father's seventieth birthday ('His strength & energy are wonderful') and corresponded with officials at Newark in advance of the statutory general election. On the 17th he 'went to meet the Post: found a letter from Peel, desiring to see me dated 13th.'[40] The prospect of a ministerial post led to pious reflection and an echo of William Law's famous book in his diary entry: 'This is a serious call. I got my father's advice, to take anything with work and responsibility. May God guide me: much has he done for me: surely this is providentially ordered—the call upon me comes but two days after I had made a settlement at Newark.'[41] He set off on the morning of 18 December, then 'All night on & on', 'The same again' on the 19th, and arrived in London, 'safe thank God & well 5¾' on the 20th, 'went to Peel about eleven' and was duly made a junior lord of the treasury.

When the newly appointed under-secretary for war and the colonies lost his seat in the general election and resigned, in late January 1835, Peel appointed William to the office, after just a month at the treasury.[42] The Peel government fell on 8 April that year, an event that is not presented as a crisis in William's diary, but is simply noted amidst the various speeches, dinners, and conversations that made up his busy weekday schedule, and his church-going and private reflections on Sundays.[43] In the dying days of the government, he devoted time on Sundays to writing a memorandum entitled 'Considerations upon Christian Experience', begun on 8 March and finally revised on 19 April. The purpose of life, he believes, is 'the renewal of every man in the image of his God and Father', the 'construction of this new spiritual creature, the edification of this bright and enduring temple'.[44] The passage in which he defines Christian experience is characteristically labyrinthine in construction. 'In sum', he writes, 'God acts upon the soul through the medium of those ^ mental ^ acts which have no palpable outward form ^ as much as in those which have ^, and communicates impressions to it without the subsidiary use of the senses, as well as with it. The entire substance of the inward, and the entire application of both the inward and outward teaching, constitute a discipline, which takes effect upon the heart, and is termed experience.'[45] What follows, however, is his clearest statement to date on the workings of the heart and the soul in relation to the spiritual life: 'It is amidst these inner feelings, that the warmth of religious truth is concentrated: it is here that the faculties appointed to bear it out into habitual practice are recruited and refreshed. It is here that God's truth chiefly dwells, the soul of our souls, the continual antidote to the continual bane of our corruptions, the ever restoring principle of Life against the ever corroding and destroying principle of Death within us.'

Following Peel's resignation, William had more time to focus upon church matters and particularly the relationship between church and state, a subject which also interested the young parliamentary lawyer James Hope (later Hope-Scott), like William a devout high churchman. (They were to be cofounders of Trinity College, Glenalmond, a school for Scottish episcopalians, which was part-funded by John Gladstone and opened in 1847.) Hope became the close friend to whom William often turned for professional and spiritual advice from 1836 until 1851, when 'Jim' converted to Rome. 'I rely much on your friendship', William wrote in a letter of 1839, adding, 'I hope you will never shrink from admonishing me, and that my attachment may grow with your fidelity.'[46]

During the spring of 1838 he held conversations on church matters with numerous friends and associates, including Acland, Doyle, Hamilton, Edward and Philip Pusey, Robert Wilberforce, Henry Edward Manning, William Praed, William Dodsworth, George Selwyn, Sir James Graham, and Arthur Kinnaird. As church government and the Catholic question 'fermented' in his mind in the summer of 1838,[47] he drafted *The State in its Relations with the Church*, supported by Hope, who presented him with a copy of Palmer's *Treatise on the Church of Christ*. William's argument turned upon the 'great doctrine' of Richard Hooker, whose foundational *Laws of Ecclesiastical Polity* was published in the 1590s, 'that the state is a person, having a conscience, cognisant of matter of religion, and bound by all constitutional and natural means to advance it.'[48] Invoking more recent thinkers such as Edmund Burke and Samuel Taylor Coleridge, he argued that the state was duty bound, in all conscience, to support the minority established church in Ireland.[49] Although he regarded that church as an anomaly, in representing only one ninth of Ireland's population, this did not change 'the nature of truth, and her capability and destiny to benefit mankind.' The Roman Catholic Church, on the other hand, 'we sorrowfully hold to have hidden the light that is in her amidst the darkness of her false traditions, and which adds to the evils of false doctrine those of schism.'[50]

While Hope saw the book through the press, William revisited Catholic Italy. It was here, in 1838, that he got to know and admire his future wife, Catherine Glynne of Hawarden Castle.

Purer and better

Wooing did not come naturally to William, an earnest and pious young politician who idealized his mother and his sister Anne. His campaign for the hand of Caroline Farquhar, sister of his Eton friend Walter and a member of an established landed family, came to grief in the spring of 1835. When Caroline expressed her reservations about his religious intensity, he responded in letters on the subject of moral conduct.[51] Early in 1837 he left his rooms at the Albany and moved into a substantial house owned by his father, 6 Carlton Gardens, off Pall Mall. In the autumn he opened a second campaign for the hand of Lady Frances (Harriet) Douglas, eldest daughter of the Earl and Countess of Morton, whom he had met in Edinburgh.[52] Although a week's stay at the family's great house outside the city was enough to show Lady Frances and her family that the couple were quite incompatible, William continued his heavy attempts at courtship by post after everybody else, including his friend Dean Ramsay, had drawn the inevitable conclusion. His self-assessment, in his diary for 17 January 1838, was characteristic. 'God in his wisdom', he wrote in Italian, 'afflicts me in this quarter where even more than in others I have been a sinner.'[53] Dropping into Italian, as he did during the romance with Caroline Farquhar, suggests a desire for extra privacy in a diary already marked 'Private'.

Having seen in the new year at Oakley Park, home of fellow Tory MP Sir Edward Kerrison, William had walked the seven miles into Norwich on Monday 8 January to attend the cathedral service. He had been asked to choose an anthem, but, failing to make himself 'intelligible', Mr Buck the organist 'gave one':

> It was Ps. 128—beautiful. [In Italian] Sometimes I could not tell whether the music was made on heaven or on earth, and I willingly stayed rooted to the spot. I heard it saying to me, 'Thy wife shall be as a vine, upon the walls of thine house. Thy children like the olive branches, round about thy table. And

thou shalt see thy children's children, and peace upon Israel.'
Was not this really a Providence for me? And entirely without
my playing any part. And a promise as well: not of marriage,
but—as I firmly believe—of that eternal love which hitherto
has preserved me.[54]

The anthem was probably a version of Psalm 128 which William pasted into his hand-crafted collection of psalms: 'The man is blest who fears the Lord', from Tate and Brady (1696), new version, set to the tune Hythe by the Canterbury composer and bookseller William Marsh.[55] In conveying what the psalm 'said' to him, however, he translated into Italian verses from the prayer book version. Sixteen years later he was to write, 'On most occasions of very sharp pressure or trial, some word of Scripture has come home to me as if borne on angel's wings: many could I recollect: the Psalms are the great storehouse: perhaps I shd. put some down now for the continuance of memory is not to be trusted. 1. In the winter of 37, Ps. 128. This came in a most singular manner but it wd. be a long story to tell.'[56] The long story would have included not only the pain associated with Lady Frances but also the subsequent high and low points of that formative year.

William later recalled that he had passed through 'more real depression' in the earlier half of 1838 than ever before, and that this depression was 'attended with a partial diminution of sin in some of its branches'.[57] Having given up the possibility of ordination in order to enter politics, he now found himself in a rut at Westminster. In March he drew up a memorandum on 'A Third Order' within the Church of England, designed to promote daily worship, 'divine learning', education, the visitation of the sick, and the care of hospitals, prisons, and workhouses, similar aims to those of the 'Engagement', a lay group that he was to join at Margaret Chapel in 1844.[58] In June he threw himself into writing *The State in its Relations with the Church*. He also attended the young queen's coronation in Westminster Abbey.[59] What he described as the 'noble' service included the anthems 'I was glad' (Psalm 122, King James Bible version), 'The queen shall rejoice in thy strength' (Psalm 21, adapted from the prayer book), and 'This is the day which the Lord hath made' (Psalm 118.24, prayer book).[60] 'Chanting greatly wanted', he commented. On 11 August he set off for a second extended tour of the Continent, taking his troubled sister Helen with him.

He spent almost a month at the German spa town of Bad Ems, reading Palmer, correcting his own proofs, and settling his sister, whose opium habit necessitated a break from life with her parents at Fasque. He also encountered the Glynne sisters, Catherine and Mary, whom he had met at a breakfast of Samuel Rogers's in London in July. They were travelling with their widowed mother, Lady Glynne, and their brothers Sir Stephen Glynne, Bt, owner of Hawarden Castle, and the Revd Henry Glynne, Rector of Hawarden, both of whom had been known to William at Christ Church.[61] He saw the family again on the way to Italy, where he spent time with them at Rome and Naples, before exploring Sicily and Calabria with his travelling companion, Arthur Kinnaird, Whig MP for Perth, covering about a thousand miles. Having reunited with the Glynnes at Naples, he saw much of them during Advent, Christmas, and the New Year in Rome, where he also met other compatriots, including his friend Manning and his political opponent Macaulay. On 3 January 1839 he tried to propose to Catherine at the Colosseum under a full moon, but was driven to writing another of his tortuous letters of proposal two weeks later.[62] This time he was not rebuffed. Catherine replied next day and, although she could not commit herself, he returned home a hopeful suitor. Aristocratic, warm, lively, scatty, devout, philanthropic, and 'extremely pretty and graceful',[63] she read William's book, transcribing passages for her own use. She returned to the Glynnes' London house in Berkeley Square in May and accepted William's renewed proposal on 8 June. They were married by Henry Glynne in an emotional double wedding at Hawarden parish church, alongside her sister Mary and the educationalist, George, 4th Baron Lyttelton, on 25 July. When the house and furniture at 13 Carlton House Terrace, overlooking St James's Park, had been acquired for the couple, Catherine was overjoyed.[64]

At the heart of William's halting Roman letter, a draft of which is full of erasures and superscripts, lies a statement that reflects both his ingrained sense of sin and his idealization of women in general and of Catherine in particular. 'I wait your command', he wrote, 'with the humility which I owe to a being so far purer and better than my own.'[65]

On the day on which Mary Glynne became engaged to Lord Lyttelton, William wrote in his diary, 'I now know enough to be convinced that not without the faithful Providence of God have I been reserved for access to a creature so truly rare and consummate as my Catherine.'[66] Like her betrothed, Catherine viewed marriage sacramentally. When she accepted him, at Lady Shelley's house near Fulham, she 'asked for the earliest Communion, that we might go together to the altar of Christ.'[67] Here was a true meeting of hearts and souls. William's own devotion to 'the Lord's Supper', sparked at his Eton confirmation, developed at Oxford, and expressed in his lay sermon at the Albany in 1834, deepened later in the decade, together with his understanding of the church as the body of Christ. In his personal index at the back of 'Gerbet on the Eucharist' (1839), written in pencil, he drew attention to (page) '159. The joys of Holy Communion'.[68] Failing to 'find a sermon' at Messina, in November 1838, he had 'read through Thomas à Kempis's Fourth Book on the Eucharist', concluding that 'this or parts of it might be usefully adapted for a Tract. Ours are in general but cold and come short of teaching the Church the doctrine of *food*.'[69] ('I must often approach You', à Kempis wrote in *The Imitation of Christ*, 'as the medicine of salvation, lest if I be deprived of this heavenly food, I faint by the way.'[70]) William was to acquire two copies of *Eucharistica: Meditations and Prayers on the Most Holy Eucharist, from Old English Divines* (1839), compiled by his friend Samuel Wilberforce, and in 1841 began to compile his own collection of 'private Eucharistical devotions'.[71] He went further than other members of the Engagement in their commitment to attending a daily service: he always sought a weekly communion, which was one reason for persuading his father to build an episcopalian chapel at Fasque in 1846. Like Pusey, he believed in the real presence of Christ in the eucharist, while repudiating transubstantiation. He was to argue in 1848 that the eucharist 'sums up in a manner the whole of Christianity', being associated with the doctrine of the incarnation.[72]

Catherine viewed the business of politics through a Christian lens, as her husband did. In May 1843, three years after the publication of William's *Church Principles considered in their Results* (1840), he agonized for two days after being offered promotion from vice president of the board of trade to president, with a seat in the cabinet. He was concerned about government policy on the opium trade, education, and the possible closure of two Welsh bishoprics. Catherine wrote in her diary:

> I walked with him in Kensington Gardens. He was much oppressed—the great anxiety to act rightly. He asked me to pray for him. How thankful I ought to be to be joined to one whose mind is purity & integrity itself—if I have received joy in reading Sir R P.'s letter how much more ought I to have received in seeing the way *he received* it—in witnessing that ~~even balance of~~ tenderness of conscience wh. shrinks at the base idea of any worldly gain ~~if it~~ could that in any way interfere with higher duties.[73]

In her life of her mother, Mary Drew tidied away the 'oughts' when transcribing this passage, perhaps to avoid the kind of strong reading that Joyce Marlow was to offer: 'at times even the devoted Catherine found the pure integrity of her husband's conscience a trifle irritating.'[74] Far more energetic and idiosyncratic than William's beloved mother and sister Anne, Catherine became his faithful Christian soulmate. Their daughter Mary was to write, 'To both of them religion was the master-key of life.'[75] Catherine became a busy mother and aunt, and increasingly a tireless philanthropist. Meanwhile she had to come to terms with William's workaholic tendencies. In a letter addressed to her in January 1844, he related the long hours of labour which kept him from her company to his belief that the 'final state which we are to contemplate with hope, and to seek by discipline, is that in which our will shall be *one* with the will of God.'[76] It was against this ideal that he measured his own performance in the confessional that was the diary.

William greeted the prospect of fatherhood with unalloyed joy and was present at the birth of his firstborn, William Henry, on 3 June 1840. In his diary entry that day he reflected upon Catherine's first labour: 'six times as much bodily pain as I have undergone in my whole life. "In sorrow shalt thou bring forth children" [Genesis 3.16] is the woman's peculiar curse, & the note of Divine Judgment upon her in Adam: so "she shall be saved in childbearing" [I Timothy 2.15] is her peculiar promise in Christ.'[77] He also recorded that 'Catherine's relief & delight were beyond anything . . . Her first wish after it was that I should offer a prayer.' Next day Catherine's sister Mary visited, 'without injury, wh might easily occur by the acceleration of her own confinement'. (Mary was to give birth to a 'healthy & large baby' a fortnight later.) And on Whit Sunday William attended St James's Piccadilly ('mg & aft. Holy Communion'), 'wrote on the subject of the day: & read it aloud to servants in the library so that C. (in bed) might hear.'

These intimate scenes are reminiscent of those described in the early chapters of Luke's gospel, including the Virgin Mary's visit to her cousin Elisabeth. As was expected of a devout Anglican couple, on 25 June 'Cath[erin]e went to Churching: the first time she has left her carriage—she was soothed by this short but beautiful office.'[78] In July came the office of baptism, described by a doting father who looked for physical signs of grace and believed in baptismal regeneration:

> Henry administered: Hope & Manning with Mary were sponsors. When the time came for the beloved child to be taken by the priest from the nurse, he threw out his arms towards Henry in the most touching way: surely God would not have that action be without meaning: O may he so ever prompt and draw that infant towards Himself, as today towards His sacrament of regeneration whereby he has clothed him in the white robe of righteousness. May He defend him from his father's sins . . . the solemn beauty of the office and the loveliness of the scene were not marred even to the ear by those wailings in which we often read the obstinate reluctance of the fleshly nature to receive an indwelling God.[79]

During the pregnancy, William and Catherine had read the scriptures together. At seven months, Catherine wrote to her husband, not quite grammatically, 'My very precious thing . . . Should anything happen to me & that your Baby is spared Willie, I feel that you will love & cherish it, but, more than all you will watch over its *spiritual* interest you will guard over its soul & body.'[80] She knew from her husband's recent sermon, delivered at home, that he regarded it as the duty of 'those who are placed at the head of a house, to see that God is reverently worshipped therein by all its inmates: to collect them for prayer: to lead them to an acquaintance with God's Holy Word.'[81] The 'inmates' would include any children born to them. In his first birthday meditation as a father, William confessed to being 'awfully impressed with the responsibilities of a parent: to have brought an immortal being into the conflict which must bring unspeakably whether of weal or woe! . . . But I am incessantly followed by the temporal mercies of God, in my wife & child, in competency & comfort, in the enjoyment of labour & even of in [sic] receiving praise.'[82] As young Willy grew up and other children were born, William reflected on a specific aspect of Christian parenting. In November 1844 he wrote to Catherine, 'It often occurs to me what a blessing it will be to our children if they can be brought up in the habit of constantly disclosing the interior of their minds.'[83] In the case of his firstborn son he did not wait for the disclosure, but frequently asked for it in the years that followed.[84] In this regard he was his mother's son.

At the beginning of the marriage service, in the Book of Common Prayer, the priest reminds the couple and their friends and neighbours that matrimony is an honourable estate, 'signifying unto us the mystical union that is betwixt Christ and his church' (cf. Ephesians 5.23–33). Matrimony had led to the creation of the domestic space in which William delivered his lay sermons on Sundays in the 1840s, a necessary release for such an earnest clergyman manqué. These sermons were often Tractarian in tone. The opening of his sermon for 23 February 1840, for example, could have come from Keble or Pusey: 'Our Blessed Lord, during his brief abode in that tabernacle of flesh which for a time was permitted to veil His Divine glory, had frequently instructed His disciples upon the vital subject of prayer with a frequency proportioned to its nature and importance.'[85] Distancing himself from his evangelical heritage, he says in the same sermon that 'God has called us not as individuals, but as a people, but as a fallen race: he has called us into a society, ^ namely ^ into the Church which is the body of Christ.'[86] Sunday by Sunday he highlights the seasons of the Christian year, as on the first Sunday after Trinity in 1841: 'During one half the year, between Advent and Whitsunday, our spiritual mother the Church commemorates the great events of our Redeemer's course upon earth.'[87] And the joy associated with Christmas that year is expressed in catholic Anglican terms: 'The great and joyful anniversary on which we hear these words of Holy Writ read to us in the Communion Office [John 1], may be regarded as the Festival of the Incarnation: that stupendous event which is one of the great foundation stones of the Catholic Faith, ^ in its sound ^ a mystery inscrutable, ^ in its aspect to usward ^ a mercy inestimable, a fountain alike of instruction and of consolation, whereunto upon this happy day we are especially enjoined to repair, and to drink of those waters which are in those that receive them a well springing up unto everlasting life.'[88] In their weekly church attendance, usually at St Martin-in-the-Fields from 1841, and in their daily family prayers, William and Catherine were living out their matrimonial vows.

William's voracious appetite for divine worship demanded more, however, and he often attended Margaret Chapel, just north of Oxford Circus, alone. The chapel was an undistinguished building which the Revd Frederick Oakeley, a dynamic Tractarian, transformed into a centre of liturgical and music excellence between 1839 and 1841.[89] William later recalled it being 'so filled by the reverence of Oakeley's ministrations, that its barrenness and poverty passed unnoticed', while the congregation was 'the most absorbed in devotion' of all he had seen 'in any country or communion'.[90] In 1844 he joined 'the Engagement', a lay high church group that was formed by the Acland brothers on the advice of John Keble.[91] Among the fifteen members who met in the chapel were former Oxford friends, including Frederic Rogers, future colleagues, such as Roundell Palmer, and the architect William Butterfield, who would later design the new All Saints on the site in Margaret Street. Here was another form of male Christian fellowship of the kind that William valued. His 'rescue work' among London prostitutes was initially a contribution to the social outreach of the Engagement. We will return to this theme in Chapter 4. First, however, we should consider a series of bereavements in the Gladstone family between the late 1820s and early 1850s, as these were to be important landmarks in William's spiritual life.

Notes

1. GL, GLA/GGA/2/2/1/152/1; for extracts see John Morley, *The Life of William Ewart Gladstone*, 3 vols. (London and New York: Macmillan, 1903), vol. I, pp. 82–83.
2. *Diaries*, vol. I, p. 403.

3. *The Prime Ministers' Papers: W. E. Gladstone, Autobiographica and autobiographical Memoranda*, ed. John Brooke and Mary Sorensen, 4 vols. (London: HMSO, 1971–81), vol. I, p. 150.
4. *Diaries*, vol. I, p. 473. 15 April 1832. Quotations checked against original of the travel diary of February–28 July 1832, see BL, 44,818A.
5. *Diaries*, vol. I, p. 512. 3 June 1832.
6. *Diaries*, vol. I, p. 477. 19 April 1832.
7. *Diaries*, vol. I, p. 473. 15 April 1832.
8. *Diaries*, vol. I, p. 480. 22 April 1832.
9. *Diaries*, vol. I, p. 490. 5 May 1832.
10. *Diaries*, vol. I, p. 495. This entry is from LPL, MS 1420.
11. BL, 44,791, ff. 1-19; *Prime Ministers' Papers*, vol. I, pp. 142–43.
12. See Perry Butler, *Gladstone, Church, State and Tractarianism: A Study of his Religious Ideas and Attitudes, 1809–1859* (Oxford: Clarendon; New York: Oxford University Press, 1982), pp. 57–59; Peter Jagger, *Gladstone: The Making of a Christian Politician: the Personal Religious Life and Development of William Ewart Gladstone, 1809–32* (Allison Park, PA: Pickwick, 1991), p. 149.
13. *Diary*, vol. I, p. 546. 6 and 8 July 1832. This entry is from LPL, MS 1420.
14. *Diaries*, vol. I, p. 575. 23 September 1832.
15. *The Correspondence between John Gladstone, Esq., M. P., and James Cropper, Esq., on the present State of Slavery in the British West Indies and in the United States of America; and on the Importation of Sugar from the British Settlements in India, with an Appendix; containing several Papers on the Subject of Slavery* (Liverpool: West India Association/Kaye, 1824), p. 17.
16. *Correspondence between John Gladstone and James Cropper*, appendices, p. viii. See also *The Speech of the Rt. Hon. George Canning, in the House of Commons, on the 16th Day of March, 1824, on Laying before the House the 'Papers in Explanation of the Measures adopted by his Majesty's Government, for the Amelioration of the Condition of the Slave Population in His Majesty's Dominions in the West Indies'* (London: Murray, 1824), pp. 20–21.
17. On Gladstone and Aristotle, see David Bebbington, *The Mind of Gladstone: Religion, Homer, and Politics* (Oxford: Oxford University Press, 2004), pp. 23–24, 35–36.
18. GL, GLA/GGA/2/2/1/152/16.
19. *Prime Ministers' Papers*, vol. I, p. 145.
20. See Jagger, *Gladstone*, p. 259. Tupper later became a prolific writer and poet.
21. BL, 44,815A, f. 10, cited in Bebbington, *Mind of Gladstone*, p. 54.
22. See Morley, *Life of Gladstone*, vol. I, pp. 102–5.
23. *Diaries*, vol. II, p. 52.
24. *Diaries*, vol. II, p. 121. 1 August 1834.
25. See Morley, *Life of Gladstone*, vol. I, p. 146.
26. *Prime Ministers' Papers*, vol. I, p. 144.
27. See Thomas Wemyss Reid, ed., *The Life of William Ewart Gladstone* (London: Cassell, 1899), p. 209.
28. *Diaries*, vol. II, p. 98.

29. BL, 44,779. f. 2r. For later adaptations to this 'family sermon' in 1848, see p. 00 below.
30. *Diaries*, vol. II, p. 138. 26 November 1834.
31. BL, 44,723, f. 384
32. BL, 44,723, f. 386.
33. BL, 44,723, f. 399.
34. *Diaries*, vol. II, p. 83.
35. *Diaries*, vol. II, p. 85. 30 January 1834.
36. 'For the more extreme Oxford men only the spiritual integrity of the Church mattered. Fearful though they were of 'national apostasy', they were more concerned that the Church should be free than that the nation should be Christian.' Butler, *Gladstone*, p. 89.
37. Bebbington, *Mind of Gladstone*, p. 54.
38. *Diaries*, vol. II, p. 89.
39. Martin Battestin quotes from a sermon by Archbishop John Tillotson (1630–94) in *The Providence of Wit: Aspects of Form in Augustan Literature and the Arts*, 1974; rpt. (Charlottesville: University Press of Virginia, 1989), p. 153.
40. *Diaries*, vol. II, p. 142.
41. William read an abridged version of William Law's devotional classic, *A serious Call to a devout and holy Life* (1729), over three days in October 1829.
42. General elections could take several weeks.
43. See *Diaries*, vol. II, p. 163. 'God's will be done', he wrote the previous night.
44. BL, 44,724 f. 57r.
45. BL, 44,724, f. 58r.
46. *Correspondence on Church and Religion of William Ewart Gladstone*, ed. D. C. Lathbury, 2 vols. (London: Murray, 1910), vol. II, p. 242. 11 June 1839.
47. *Diaries*, vol. II, p. 367. 1 May 1838.
48. William Ewart Gladstone, *The State in its Relations with the Church*, 4th edn, 2 vols. (London: Murray, 1841), vol. I, p. 14.
49. Gladstone, *State in its Relations*, vol. II, pp. 13–14.
50. Gladstone, *State in its Relations*, vol. II, p. 17.
51. See S. G. Checkland, *The Gladstones: A Family Biography, 1764–1851* (Cambridge: Cambridge University Press, 1971), p. 300.
52. Checkland, *Gladstones*, pp. 303–4.
53. *Diaries*, vol. II, p. 336.
54. *Diaries*, vol. II, p. 334. Checkland dismisses this episode as William's taking 'refuge in fantasy': *Gladstones*, p. 304.
55. See GP 44,833, f. 34r. Gladstone later recalled that the 'New Version was used, I think, exclusively' at Margaret Chapel: see Lathbury, *Correspondence*, vol. I, p. 409.
56. *Diaries*, vol. IV, p. 617. 9 May 1854.
57. *Diaries*, vol. II, p. 576. 6 February 1839. See also *Diaries*, vol. II, pp. 358 (30 March 1838), 367 (28 April), 375 (4 June), 380 (23 June), 381 (30 June), and William's memorandum on depression, 5 June 1838, in Lathbury, *Correspondence*, vol. II, p. 433.

58. Lathbury, *Correspondence*, vol. II, p. 434.
59. *Diaries*, vol. II, p. 381. 28 Jun 1838.
60. *The Form and Order of the Service performed, and Ceremonies observed, in the Coronation of Her Majesty Queen Victoria, in the Abbey Church of St. Peter, Westminster, on Thursday, the 28th of June 1838* (London: Prayer Book and Homily Society, 1838), pp. 3, 14, 18.
61. See Checkland, *Gladstones*, p. 290.
62. See Philip Magnus, *Gladstone: A Biography* (London: Murray, 1954), pp. 38–39.
63. Susan M. E. J. St Helier, *Memories of Fifty Years* (London: Arnold, 1909), p. 23.
64. *Diaries*, vol. III, p. 8. 8 February 1840.
65. GL, GLA/GGA/2/10/1/15/2, 3r.
66. *Diaries*, vol. II, p. 608.
67. *Diaries*, vol. II, p. 605. 8 June 1839. Lady Shelley was the Glynnes' next door neighbour in Berkeley Square.
68. GL, WEG/E 63.5/GER, O. P. Gerbet, *Considerations on the Eucharist* (1839), p. 237. See *Diaries*, vol. III, p. 432. Sunday 9 February 1845. He also owned a copy of *The Eucharist* (1846) by the controversial Ritualist, William Bennett.
69. *Diaries*, vol. II, pp. 487–88. 4 November 1838.
70. Thomas à Kempis, *The Imitation of Christ*, trans. Leo Sherley-Price (Harmondsworth: Penguin, 1952), p. 190.
71. *Diaries*, vol. III, p. 100. The devotions are reprinted in Lathbury, *Correspondence*, vol. II, pp. 421–27. William also owned a copy of Christopher Sutton's *Godly Meditations upon the Most Holy Sacrament of the Lord's Supper* in a reprint of 1839, introduced by Newman.
72. See Bebbington, *Mind of Gladstone*, pp. 94–96.
73. GL, GLA/GGA/4/9/1/10.
74. Mary Drew, *Catherine Gladstone* (London: Nisbet, 1919), pp. 58–59; Joyce Marlow, *Mr and Mrs Gladstone: An Intimate Biography* (London: Weidenfeld, Nicolson, 1977), p. 36.
75. Drew, *Catherine Gladstone*, p. 240.
76. Drew, *Catherine Gladstone*, p. 123.
77. *Diaries*, vol. III, p. 33.
78. *Diaries*, vol. III, p. 41. 25 June 1840. The office in the prayer book is entitled 'The Thanksgiving of Women after Child-birth commonly called the Churching of Women'.
79. *Diaries*, vol. III, p. 46. 16 July 1840.
80. GL, GG/609/4. 1 April 1840. Catherine signs off, 'Yours I trust in life & death prays Your Wifie'.
81. 'Duties of Masters and Servants', 22 March 1840: BL, 44,779, ff. 26-29.
82. *Diaries*, vol. III, p. 74. 29 December 1840.
83. Sunday 24 November 1844: Lathbury, *Correspondence*, vol. II, p. 259.
84. See, for example, Lathbury, *Correspondence*, vol. II, pp. 149–50, 157, 159.
85. 'Easter Day', BL, 44,779, f. 10r.

86. BL, 44,779, f. 13r.
87. BL, 44,779, f. 127r.
88. 'Christmas Day', BL, 44,779, f. 181r.
89. See Peter Galloway, *A Passionate Humility: Frederick Oakeley and the Oxford Movement* (Leominster: Gracewing, 1999), p. 46.
90. Galloway, *Passionate Humility*, pp. 63–64. See also the plate in Lathbury, *Correspondence*, vol. I, p. 408.
91. See Colin Matthew, 'Gladstone, Evangelicalism, and "The Engagement"', in *Revival and Religion since 1700: Essays for John Walsh*, ed. Jane Garnett and Colin Matthew (London and Rio Grande: Hambledon, 1993), pp. 111–26.

3
Many mansions

In my Father's house are many mansions: if it were not so, I would have told you. I go to prepare a place for you . . . Thomas saith unto him, Lord, we know not whither thou goest. (John 14.2,5)

Ruskin had the 'profoundest sympathy' with Thomas, thought that 'mansions' would suggest to most parish children 'a splendid house with two wings', and proposed 'remaining-places' as a better translation from the Greek.[1] Jesus' mysterious words to his disciples were often quoted by those who gathered around the nineteenth-century deathbed, a site of ambiguous or half-understood utterances.[2] Roy Jenkins found some truth in Richard Shannon's flippant description of Gladstone as a connoisseur of deathbeds and acknowledged that he 'dwelt on them'.[3] In order to explain why, I will consider his accounts of the deaths of his sister Anne in 1829, his mother in 1835, his little daughter Jessy in 1850, and his aged father in 1851. These landmarks in William's spiritual life receive closer attention here than they have received in earlier biographies. In 1903 Morley devoted only a single paragraph in a two-thousand-page biography to the death of William's mother. This reflects the biographer's priorities, as does the absence of references to the births of his daughters in an index which includes the boys'. And the death of Jessy at the age of four, one of the most distressing and formative events of William's life, merits only five short sentences in Morley.

Later in life, William stated that he had never 'seen one die without much of pain and struggle'.[4] 'It is a tremendous thing to die', he went on, 'from the laceration and violence done to nature, however sure one may feel that the Divine mercy and goodness which have been all sufficient *here* will suffice *there* also'. For him, the hope of future blessedness for the faithful was grounded in the bible, the psalter, and à Kempis's *Imitation of Christ*, and was bound up with his deepening sense of the sacrament of the eucharist as spiritual food. Of the two leading ideas of the nature of heaven in the nineteenth century, however—as a place of continual worship or as a home, the site of reunion—it was the latter which sustained William in his hour of need.[5]

Ordering a black coat

George Canning died on 8 August 1827, having been prime minister for less than four months. William was home for the summer holidays, in his last year at Eton, when he heard the news in Liverpool, two days later. He noted in his diary that the statesman had died 'at 10 minutes before 4': 'It has pleased God to remove him—and I trust to a better place—but the recollection of the past, and the anticipation of the future involve us in sorrow, and in uncertainty. Personally, I must thankfully remember his kindness and condescension . . . all is for the best: and I trust in God this has been to him a happy release. Read the Accounts in the papers'.[6] While the nation mourned the loss of a prime minister, the Gladstone family shared personal memories of the brilliant politician whose former Liverpool seat had been secured with John Gladstone's support. William wrote from Seaforth to his friend Farr, 'we have sustained in him a great, an almost irreparable loss. Best and greatest of the followers of "his great master, Pitt," his principles had not degenerated from the true, ancient, loyal stock of Toryism'.[7] Having returned to Liverpool to order a black coat for the day of the funeral, he attended a meeting about 'Mr Canning's monument'.[8] On 21 September he travelled all day and all night to London by coach, visiting 'poor Mr Cannings burial place' in Westminster Abbey before finally arriving at Eton, 'somewhat tired', in the evening of the 22nd.[9] Once settled back at school, he entertained Canning's youngest son, Carlo, to wine and went on walks with him. He also wrote the verse 'Reflections in Westminster Abbey' for the *Eton Miscellany*, including the lines, 'Death aim'd the stroke at him, at him alone, / Claimed him, the first, the noblest, for his own'.[10]

The seventeen-year-old's response to a public event which had strong personal associations was in certain respects conventional: the combination of closely observed external details, such as the time of death, and private reflections—thanks to and trust in God, spiritual writings—is not unusual among educated devout Christians of the period. But the considerable expenditure of time and effort recorded here—the coat, the meeting, the visit to the grave—is exceptional in one so young. It indicates a compulsive desire not only to honour the departed, but also to mark the death as an event in his own spiritual life, which was lived out with great energy and intensity.

William's first major family bereavement occurred in his first year at Oxford, when his beloved sister Anne died on 19 February 1829, aged twenty-six. Ten days earlier he had received a 'most affectionate letter' from his sister Helen, 'but sad accounts of Anne. "Sad"!'[11] His father's 'melancholy account of dear Anne' arrived on the 12th, and he later learned that 'dearest Anne' was 'alarmingly ill at night' on the 18th. His diary for the 19th includes a brief statement, set in a ruled box, which he added later: '*Thursday.* '*At 20 m. to 3, A.M.*, our dearest sister Anne breathed her last without a struggle or a groan. Present. Father & Mother—Tom & Helen—Aunts E. & J. Mr Bickersteth—& Janet'.[12] Having received a letter from his father on the 21st, announcing the 'sad & unexpected decease' of his sister, he travelled all night by coach: 'At first much dismayed: but afterwards unable to *persuade* myself of the truth of the news'. Arriving home on Sunday 22 February, he 'found all in great grief'. He 'saw the pale remains of dearest Anne, but felt in weeping over them, that my tears were entirely selfish. Blessed & praised be God's Holy Name for thus calling to Himself first from among us one who was so well prepared, so thoroughly refined, so weaned from earth, so ripe for Heaven'. His diary entry for this difficult day ends, 'Listened to the accounts given of Dearest Anne's deathbed scenes, with an interest which must be felt under such circumstances even by those whose feelings are as little tender and as much abstracted as my own'.

William's confused emotions were clearly related to the fact that he had relied upon letters that took two days to arrive for reports of her decline, and then upon oral accounts from those who witnessed 'deathbed scenes' that he had missed. The self-chastisement of Sunday, blaming himself for being 'abstracted' and lacking in tenderness, continued next day, when he wrote about his 'torpor of mind & habitual selfishness'. The further observation that he should have been reflecting on Anne's happiness in heaven, and on his duty to 'honour her memory in following (by God's grace) her footsteps', is the product of years of training by his mother and by Anne herself, both evangelicals. Morbid introspection yields to activity, however, once he is present to witness the closing of the coffin, to read the burial service to his mother, and to attend the funeral at one of his father's churches, described with an eye to external details and an ear to the liturgy:

> Breakfast early—we were all now in regular mourning—then clad in mourning cloaks—about 10 m. past 10 we left Seaforth in the following order (I believe)—
>
> Mutes.
>
> Hearse.
>
> 1st Coach. Father, Tom, John & myself . . .
>
> Soon after 12 we heard the bell of St Andrew's [Liverpool], and the burial service was read by Mr Rawson. The coffin was placed in a vault in the Church, by my Grandmothers. Surely never could mourners receive the glorious consolations which that sublime service is intended to impart, with better or surer confidence.—The day was very rainy & seemed as we left home to suit our occupation.[13]

After the death of his spiritual guide, William entered a pact with his younger sister Helen to monitor each other's conduct.[14] Inevitably, he idealized the late lamented Anne, describing her birthday as 'a sacred day at least of right' and commenting in extravagant terms when reading her letters to him: 'O is it possible that such a saint can have held communion with such a devil?'[15]

Six years later, on 23 September 1835, his mother died at the age of sixty-three. Already fragile, Mrs Gladstone had been deeply affected by two recent deaths in the family: her sister Mary, at Bath, and her brother-in-law Robert, who died suddenly during a visit to Fasque, where John Gladstone found him unconscious in the night. William Gladstone MP was living at the Albany, and dreaming of Caroline Farquhar, when news of his aunt's and uncle's deaths reached him by post on Thursday 3 September.[16] Next day a letter from Lady Farquhar seemed to put an end to his hopes, but he wrote back, 'submitting'. On Saturday 5th he departed for Scotland on the *City of Aberdeen*, feeling 'less squeamish than usual'. The fact that he could attend a service next day, conducted by a chaplain, on board a packet-boat, is a reminder of the pervasiveness of a shared Christian culture in early nineteenth-century Britain. Having attended his uncle's funeral on Monday 7th, he arrived at Fasque to find 'his dear Mother ill' and immediately started to write, initially turning his hand to verses on the contrast with the day of his brother Thomas's marriage the previous week.[17] Subsequent diary entries record the arrival of his brothers, his reading morning prayers in the household, and his reading the bible to his mother, who was suffering from erysipelas and whose symptoms, carefully monitored by two doctors, waxed and waned. His diary entry for Monday 21st, two days before his mother's death, ends, 'The events of the illness I have detailed in a separate paper'.

William intended this paper, entitled 'Recollections of the last hours of my Mother', to be his 'contribution towards a record of the circumstances attendant on the removal from this mortal life of the tenderest and best of mothers'.[18] He had read 'Accounts in the paper' when Canning died and had heard oral 'accounts' of Anne's 'deathbed scenes'. Members of his family regarded it as their duty to write letters to their relatives containing 'melancholy accounts' of such scenes, and William himself added two individuals to his list of correspondents the day before his mother's death: 'We again wrote our accounts', he recorded.[19] But his 'Recollections' were a more substantial contribution to a permanent record, and they drew upon a specific tradition of religious writing: the improving 'account' of a good death.

Charles Wesley's *A short Account of the Death of Mrs. Hannah Richardson* (1741), which ran through many editions, was perhaps the most influential of the deathbed conversion narratives that were popular during the evangelical revival. *A short Account of the Life & Death of Ann Cutler* (1796) was by William Bramwell, the most successful Wesleyan revivalist of his generation, who drew attention to 'her custom *daily* to write down the dealings of God with her soul; a custom which numbers have found to be extremely beneficial and which I strongly recommend'.[20] This was also to be Mrs Anne Gladstone's habit and, less regularly, that of her son William. The Revd Charles Jerram, a representative second-generation Anglican evangelical, wrote *A Tribute of parental*

Affection to the Memory of a beloved and only Daughter: containing some Account of the Character and Death of Hannah Jerram, who died May 9, 1823, aged 23 (1824), another work which has Gladstonian overtones. 'During the whole of her life', her father writes, 'she was ever under parental inspection; or that of pious relatives and instructors'; and she was 'diligent in self-examination'.[21] In his account of his daughter's last illness, Jerram cuts rapidly between records of pulse rates and medicaments ('I gave her a dose of James's powders') and testimony to her faith and her belief in the atonement.[22] Similar juxtapositions of the earthly and the heavenly characterize an 'account' of the death of Ann Freeman, a female lay reader, by her husband, Henry, published in 1826. 'She was attacked by violent pains', we are told, 'from the wind in her stomach'; and, 'The cold sweat then came on, and other certain harbingers of death. I said to her, "The Lord is good;" and she answered, "Yes!" and spake something with respect to the position of her body'.[23]

William drew upon diary entries and recent memories as he wrote his own day-by-day account of his mother's last days in the 'Recollections'. On 10 September she wished to discuss his courtship of Miss Farquhar, but he begged her to defer the subject until she was well. 'It was deferred', he comments, 'but until the time and place, where they neither marry nor are given in marriage' (Matthew 22.30).[24] As he recounts his mother's suffering over subsequent days, he pays particular attention to the challenges of interpretation that faced him and his family in both spiritual and physical matters. On Thursday 17 September 1835, for example, he was 'cut to the heart' when he recognized her physical decline. When she spoke of the lack of a memorial tablet for her daughter Anne, William made a remark on the 'very powerful character' of the verse which he had 'understood from her, it was Anne's wish to have inscribed, without addition, upon her tomb: and it *now* strikes me much, that she made no reply: as, in general, even the feeblest observation upon Scripture sufficed to elicit a response from a heart attuned to it like hers'.[25] Later he added a note citing Romans 8.11 and offering exegesis on the power of St Paul's hope in order to explain what he had meant in his remark to his mother. A private bereavement document takes on the characteristics of a bible commentary, itself a work of interpretation. Next day, after dinner, Dr Hunter 'announced a coldness in the feet' and a change in the pulse rate, concluding that 'we should consider the case one of extreme danger, even though not precluding the hope of her being carried through by the vigour of her constitution'. William inserted a further explanatory footnote here, this time recording how, about midday, Helen and their father had differed in their interpretations of the doctor's comments, but how 'the thought of writing to Robertson' had never entered their minds: 'John was out shooting, and I joined him'. Diagnoses and decisions relating to close relatives are carefully set out as if for a recording angel.

Three days later, William, Tom, and John 'agreed to divide the night'.[26] During William's watch 'there was a good deal of occasional pain which she seemed to bear with perfect willingness, raising up her hands to heaven with short and scarcely audible ejaculations of prayer. The suffering resulted from the action of the medicine upon the bowels'. She said to him, 'My precious, why do not you go to rest?' 'Such were the epithets', William comments, 'which she was accustomed to bestow upon her children, while she esteemed herself vile. But she is now a plant blossoming for ever in the garden of the Lord, beyond the reach of cold and storm'. The sudden shift from the temporal to the eternal is characteristic of such accounts of a situation in which stomach pains and the Christian hope are both present realities. After a further two days, 'the will of her Heavenly Father now seemed intelligibly announced' and the family dispatched their letters 'in the most desponding terms'. On the 23rd she became unconscious, every breath was laboured, and 'the chest, then the head, wrought upwards and downwards'. But then

> the muscular movement descended from its climax, and subsided into perfect, childlike, gentleness and peace. A few breaths of decreasing force, at increasing intervals—my dear father who asked anxiously if she were gone came forward—then three slight movements of the head as if meant to second the chest which had ceased to act—and all was over: we wept for her who perhaps at that very moment was employing her young immortality in bringing truths and consolation to our minds from Him who is the source of both. Tender, affectionate, unwearied in love and devotion as she was, she is perhaps nearer us than ever.[27]

Of all Christian paradoxes, this last is one of the most challenging for the sceptical mind. For William it was an article of faith that came home to him as he described his mother's death.

The 'Recollections' continue, 'She was not during her illness in a state of mental vigour to warrant its being proposed to her to receive the Sacrament. Though she was deprived of this joy, and we of this palpable manifestation of her faith, we cannot feel it a cause for permanent regret while we know that in her daily life she had realised that communion with her Lord, which the ordinance is intended to convey and assure'. While his evangelical style of 'account' was of an appropriate kind for an evangelical mother, this somewhat defensive paragraph comes from a high churchman for whom 'joy', an underused word in his lexicon, is often associated with the liturgy, and particularly the eucharist. Six months later he wrote to Manning, 'I have to convey to you what I know will be a melancholy announcement, the death of Anstice which took place on Monday morning last at Torquay'.[28] Anstice had 'received the Sacrament', he reports, and 'then appeared fatigued: but there was no pain whatever and he slept away what remained of his mortal life in perfect peace'. From a high church perspective, the ideal death.

William's 'Recollections' end with some brief general reflections upon his mother's death. The story of what followed is taken up in the diary: 'at a quarter past midnight her soul went to blessedness, her body to sleep . . . We met for breakfast at ten. Much occupation afterwards in writing: I had near 20 letters and notes. My father wonderfully sustained. In turns we went into the Chamber of Death, and kissed the claycold face. In the evg & night wrote my recollections of her last days. Bible. Long and interesting conversation with my Father'.[29] The funeral followed a week after the death: 'We laid a body in the grave; but, from whatever cause, I do not feel separated from the spirit which possessed it: and which I rejoice to think is now very near us, and associated again with that of her beloved daughter'. In a letter to Gaskell, written during the period of mourning, William echoed his 'Considerations upon Christian Experience', composed six months earlier: 'few mortals suffered more pain, or more faithfully recognised it as one of the instruments by which God is pleased to forward that *restoring* process for which we are placed on earth' (my emphasis).[30]

Recollections of her little life

William's mother did not live to see his children: Willy, born in June 1840, Agnes in October 1842, Stephen in April 1844, Jessy in July 1845, Mary in September 1847, Helen in August 1849, Henry in April 1852, and Herbert in January 1854. The children's spiritual welfare was monitored as closely as their physical and mental wellbeing. Godparents were chosen with care. When Manning stood as godfather to Willy in July 1840, he promised to pray for him 'morning & night'.[31] Five years later, in August 1845, he was consulted by William, who wondered whether baby Jessy should be baptized before the family took a railway journey, even though 'the risk of travelling be now only infinitesimal'.[32] He replied in the affirmative by return of post.

The sacrament of baptism was soon to become the subject of public controversy. In August 1847 Bishop Phillpotts of Exeter refused to institute the Revd George Cornelius Gorham as the new incumbent at Brampford Speke, on the grounds that he was unsound on the doctrine of baptismal regeneration. William was elected MP for the University of Oxford in the same month and was to follow the controversy closely as it intensified year by year. When the judicial committee of the Privy Council eventually found for Gorham, on 8 March 1850, high churchmen like William were dismayed, not least because laymen had been involved in judging an ecclesiastical case.[33] He immediately engaged in urgent conversations on this 'gigantic evil' with allies, wrote to senior clerics, and, while suffering from a cold, received Phillpotts himself in his bedroom.[34] Forty years of age and the father of six children, he had been under stress for some time, grappling with the Glynne family's acute financial difficulties at Hawarden and scourging himself, literally and metaphorically, during periods of rescue work among London prostitutes. Now the church was in danger, his two-year old daughter Mary was keeping him up at night with an ulcer on her eye, and the four-year-old Jessy's health was a 'wreck'. Having spent most of March embroiled in the Gorham controversy, William focused upon Jessy over the Easter period as her health deteriorated. On 9 April 1850 she died of meningitis. It was related in the family that, 'for some hours after her death', he was 'in a state of such violent grief as almost to frighten those around him'.[35] The depth of his grief can be gauged by the sheer quantity of documentation that followed—his diary, his long account of Jessy's life and death, his correspondence with Catherine when he took the coffin to Fasque for burial, and his correspondence with relatives and friends.

Jessy's illness began to look serious on Good Friday, with 'apparently some unconquerable obstruction in the bowels'.[36] She was much better by Easter Monday, when her father was examined for three and a half hours, 'by a most tedious process', on Lady Lincoln's 'wretched case'. (With Catherine's encouragement, William had pursued his friend's wife when she fled to Italy with her lover, Lord Walpole, in 1849, an impetuous rescue bid which failed.) Jessy's condition then fluctuated violently during the week, and on the following Sunday night, 'chiefly while watching' in her room, William began 'a sort of journal of her illness'. This later became the third section of a document begun immediately after her death. In a diary entry dated 9 April, and surrounded by a heavy black line, he echoed Julian of Norwich's famous affirmation that 'all shall be well': '(*St Anne's Soho* 8¼ *P.M.*) It is all over, and all well. The blessed child was released at two o'clock in the morning compassionately taken by her Saviour into the fold of His peace. I dwell on it no longer in this place: I must try to put together a few recollections of her little life'.

Whereas his recollections of his mother were of her last hours, those of his daughter cover her short life as well as her death. It is now William's turn to be the paterfamilias. The opening paragraph of the document entitled 'Some account of our second daughter, Catherine Jessy Gladstone' takes the long view, pointing out that the vault at Fasque in which his four-year-old is buried was dedicated by its founder, John Gladstone, at eighty-three years of age, in the reasonable expectation that he would be the first occupant, 'but God has been otherwise pleased'.[37] William begins the first section of his account of Jessy's life by explaining his purpose: 'She was great in love: and that which made her hard to part with, made her meet to go, to go to the home of love, to be folded in the arms of Love Almighty and Everlasting. It is for this cause that the record of her may do us good, when we . . . peruse it in a world where love is so sorely nipped and blighted not by sorrow which waters and feeds it, but by the sharp and burning blasts of sin. For the main thing that we have come into the world to learn, is that which she has learned already'. The text of this 'most private' document was to be engraved on Jessy's memorial stone: 'And in their mouth was found no guile: for they are without fault before the throne of God' (Revelation 14.5). The subtext, however, of an 'account' which in places is similar in tone to William's family sermons, is Matthew 18.3: 'Except ye be converted, and become as little children, ye shall not enter into the kingdom of heaven'.

As a strict but loving parent, he sifts through his memories of Jessy—memories that are stirred in the act of writing—in order to identify the first signs of her illness: 'While I write I recollect a circumstance which illustrates the change in her physical state'. Her nurses and the aptly named governess, Miss Eyre, 'loved her dearly and found her most docile', but noticed how she seemed bewildered by the slightest criticism. Her apparent obstinacy was a result of her illness, he comes to understand as he writes, adding a footnote as he agonizes over his own response to her behaviour, marked by a slight change of hand. She was a 'clinging child' who loved her father so much that she would 'kiss again and again the wretched stump of the finger' that he had lost in a shooting accident: 'upon deformity itself she would then pour out her fondness'.

'The details of her mournful illness need not be long', he announces in a new section, written with a different pen, or nib.[38] 'It pleased God that the fearful disease should grow up in the shade', he asserts. The Lord 'sent a messenger, of whose coming indeed we can now in retrospect perceive that there were true though feeble indications'. When he turns to specific symptoms, Catherine supplements his account by inserting a note on chilblains. She also adds a note on her daughter's character: 'in later months how often had it come across me that there would be a solidity of character about my Jessy'. While accepting God's will in taking her, both parents find comfort in recording details of a unique if short life.

The third section incorporates the 'kind of journal' that William wrote 'at intervals while watching in the room where she lay unconscious in our bed'.[39] On the evening of Monday 8 April he records, 'the convulsions gradually became stronger and more frequent'. The doctor advised her parents to 'pray that the passage of the departing spirit should be quickened', adding, 'This is a great grief, but there are greater: the spirit of the child is going back to God who gave it'. Although 'most private', William's intimate account of Jessy's life and death was presumably to be shared within the family. It excludes certain details recorded in his diary, intended for his eyes only, as they would have seemed inappropriate. In the entry for 8 April he wrote, 'C. and I with Mrs Baker sat in the room of death and watched the beloved child in her death battle, powerless to aid her. In the intervals of the thickening convulsions I read Mr Munroe's excellent Letter, & wrote the necessary letters for the morning: until latterly when there were scarcely any spaces of repose between the tearings and tossings of the conflict'.[40] A new forty-four-page pamphlet by a Tractarian clergyman on the main issue of the day could be slipped into the pocket and brought out in quiet moments as the three of them 'watch'. Jessy is unconscious, the Gorham crisis is at its height, and private letters have to be dispatched in the morning. One of them goes to John Gladstone: 'My beloved Father, My letters of this morning conveyed the intelligence of my little Jessy's departure from this world of sin and sorrow. Since then I have been busied in the communications and arrangements which the sad event required. We have kept Willy back from school: and his mother has the greatest comfort in him. She holds up, or rather is held up as well as I could have wished or asked'.[41]

The fourth section of William's account begins with an acknowledgement that witnessing Jessy's 'death struggle' has been a 'heavy trial to flesh and blood'. His theological reflections on the cause of her suffering reflect the strain that he has been under. Although she never 'sinned after the similitude of Adam's transgression' (Romans 5.14), he suggests, she paid the 'forfeit' of our fallen race, but 'not uselessly, unless it be our fault: for what a witness was before us to the intensity of sin and the wide range of its effects, when she was so torn by their power, though through God's grace not tainted by their pollution: what a lesson of penitence and humility, and of the better and heavenly life in Christ, which only saves us!' Their fourth child 'in the order of this world' is 'the eldest born into Eternity, whither she precedes her parents; her relation to them is reversed. The reverence she owed to them, they now owe to her, to a soul sprung of them, but taken before them to immortality, without the stain of wilful sin, and in the robe of purity, with which she rose from the bath of regeneration'. For William, baptismal regeneration, long the subject of ecclesiastical controversy, is more than a doctrine: it is a spiritual reality. The death of Jessy is not a tragedy, as Jenkins describes it, but part of a divine scheme.[42]

It was a 'great privilege', William states, to accompany Jessy's remains to Fasque by rail, taking with him 'a white pall, with hatbands, scarf, and gloves'. Omitted from his account are several significant observations in the diary, including the fact that Willy accompanied him part of the way, that Jessy seemed incessantly to beckon him during the long journey and say, 'Come Pappy Come', that he had to pay his fare in five parts and 'make three changes of carriage', and that he 'read T.A Kempis'.[43] *The Imitation of Christ*, a copy of which accompanied him everywhere, continued to sustain him each day at Fasque. Again, no reference is made to this in the account, where attention soon turns to the obsequies in John Gladstone's chapel: 'When the Coffin had been set down before the Altar, we had the morning Prayers: then the Funeral Office ^ which Helen affectionately attended ^. At the proper place She was carried out round the South side of the Chapel: and the remainder performed in the Vault: the first time it had been the scene of that solemn rite, and never I believe will its walls return the ^ sacred ^ sounds over the remains of a gentler or a purer spirit. We returned to the Chapel and the Holy Eucharist was celebrated'.[44] William's capitalization of initial letters here reflects his strong sense of the sacred in these particular rites. The account ends not in Fasque, but back in London, with reflections upon the changes that he and Catherine saw in Jessy's face after she died: 'it was holy and heavenly, and blessed the eyes that saw it'.

Another detail from the diary is missing from the account: 'I kept the key of the vault', William recorded, 'and was able to visit my Jessy there'.[45] The grieving Catherine had seen the coffin for the last time the day before, on its departure for Fasque. William wrote to her from there, using paper with wide black borders, on 13 April, describing the obsequies and letting her know that he had 'kissed the coffin where it lies'.[46] He then tried to share with her the spiritual consolation of the liturgy from which he, his father, his brothers, and the tearful family retainers had benefitted. They had done all they could for the 'holy remains: holy because what is earthly of them will now drop away and *they* will rise again a glorious body, in power and in incorruption: and praying at the Holy Eucharist that our solemn showing forth of the Lords death may be accepted for His sake, and that all his whole Church as well as ourselves may by that Death "receive all other benefits of His passion," which she is now more than us capable of enjoying, as well as "remission of her sins" which she does not need, we seem to have filled up the public duties to her, for the time, which our Faith enjoins. Sweet and fragrant is her memory!' On 16 April, the day on which William left Fasque, Catherine replied from Brighton, where she was in lodgings with her sister and the children: 'My precious one . . . 1000 thanks for y^r precious letter . . . God bless you & send you safe to me Y^r loving C. G.'[47]

He had shared another source of consolation with Catherine more directly, as he explained in a second letter of 13 April from Fasque: 'My beloved Cathie, I think that you stand in real need of a Book at this time with reference to the inward fruits of the exercise through which we have been passing: and I send you accordingly the work of Thomas a Kempis on the Imitation of Christ'.[48] (In his view, 'watching' at Jessy's bedside has been a spiritual exercise for them both.) Four days later he reached Brighton, where he wrote on the Gorham case, dined with his in-laws, the Lytteltons, and returned to town 'very reluctantly' on the 23rd in order to attend a debate in the Commons. Catherine wrote to him from Brighton next day: 'It was too dear love of you to find time to write me the sweet note & to send me that beautiful book—I have been reading in it you could not have sent me anything more soothing. To say what a blank pain absence makes is impossible I felt very low yesterday—one must expect to vary & I hope it is not a sign of anything like discontent the fact is that her dear image grows more & more as she was before her illness. . .but these are all too earthly these feelings'.[49] In a chapter on the uses of adversity, à Kempis reminds the disciple of Christ that 'he is an exile here, and that he can put his trust in nothing in this world'.[50] Humble submission to God is efficacious: 'If you learn to suffer in silence, you may be sure of receiving God's help'.[51] Sorrows are to be borne patiently, 'For though this present life is hard, yet by Your grace it is made full of merit'.[52] When William visited Fasque in September 1850, he 'read De Imitatione' and revisited the sacred spot.[53]

Heavenly messengers

Two days after Jessy's funeral, William could only pay 'one last visit' to the vault at Fasque, as he had to spend over seven hours on letters and papers for his father.[54] Unconvinced that this work was of use, he feared that Sir John was 'now under a mild form of mental disease beginning' and that his 'great study should be to keep it mild'. Just when they are busiest professionally, those of middle age are often responsible for both the young and the elderly. In William's case, the burden of the 'great study' regarding his father was to be compounded by other challenges which are discussed in Chapter 4. Our current interest, however, is in the relationship between his responses to the death of his young daughter and that of his elderly father, eighteen months later.

When William and his young family arrived at Fasque in September 1851, initially for a holiday, he found his father to be 'very deaf indeed, & uneasy though not ill'.[55] During their extended stay he often visited the vault, on one occasion taking the eleven-year-old Willy with him, 'with his own will, to see Jessy's last resting place: & the stone'. On 23 September he recorded the anniversary of his 'blessed Mother's death', adding, 'We have not needed to mourn for HER', so certain had they been of her blessed state. Concern over his father's health grew during November. By the end of the month his diary entries had largely become daily records of Sir John's final illness, reminiscent in style of his accounts of his mother's and daughter's. On 30 November—Advent Sunday, also St Andrew's day—his father's eyeballs were 'distorted' after bouts of vomiting, and 'before four he had a calomel & scammony pill given to act on the bowels if the evil were there'.[56] Next day the coachmen was sent off to telegraph for William's brothers and an Edinburgh doctor, but 'signs of movement in the intestines late in the afternoon & in the evening' gave the family hope. Days of 'watching' were subsequently shared with his brothers.

On Friday 5 December, when 'the death sweat came freely from this morning onwards', William worked on 'some little compilations from the Psalms oh! what companions at this time. Ps. 130 was my staple in my dearest Father's room: it is the Psalm of charity which puts each man in the place & self of each other man'. Coverdale's version of the *De Profundis* in the prayer book—'Out of the deep have I called unto thee, O Lord'—offers consolation for the dying and for those who watch and wait beside them: 'I look for the Lord; my soul doth wait for him: in his word is my trust'.[57] Two days later the diary entry for the second Sunday in Advent is headed 'My Father's Death'. 'At 2 A.M.', he writes, 'still the metal bed quivered to the strong heave of the chest.

But by five in the morning the greater part of his strength was gone'. There is 'an effort at breathing, weaker than a dying infant might have made', and 'the very faintest rattle, but it soon subsided. And so he died, upon the morning of the Lord's rest [Genesis 2.2]: oh what a day of meeting for him with his best beloved: his angelic daughter, his high hearted wife. My little Jessy too has she not seen them meet?' When William attended the chapel services later that day, he found the Te Deum, 80th Psalm, and 'Advent Hymn' overpowering.

His description of his father's physical decline ('weaker than a dying infant') and his vision of heaven as a place of reunion ('what a day of meeting') draw together the four family bereavements that we are considering in this chapter. As in this diary entry, the death of Jessy features in his more formal account of 'The Last Days of my Father, Sir John Gladstone', begun two days later and presented in a similar manner to his 'recollections of her little life', with its heading set in a ruled box, its day-by-day arrangement, and so on. Once again, the act of writing these 'memoranda' triggers memories, while their wider scope allows for broader reflection. In a section dated 30 November, for example, he recalls writing to one of his brothers that there was every prospect of his father surviving the winter, but adds, 'I had for the last eighteen months . . . been struck by a marked resemblance in his symptoms to some of those of our little darling Jessy who died in April 1850 of (tubercular meningitis) a disease of the brain'.[58] On 2 December his father's pulse was 'weakish or intermitted a little', although 'on the whole it held up astonishingly: another point of resemblance to our little Jessy'.[59] Three days later he recorded what was called a slight convulsion, adding, 'It was slight indeed to Catherine and me who remembered through what our little Jessy passed for hours before her frame was composed into the peace of her angel spirit'.[60] His father's last attempt at a breath was 'an effort calmer and fainter than a dying infant's', and 'all was over'.

The narrative then moves into the interrogative: 'And were there not other watchers there, heavenly messengers who filled the air? Had not God given His angels charge over this good and venerable as well as powerful-minded man, that they should bear him up in their hands, that he should not dash his foot against a stone [Luke 4.11], no not even against the stone of the threshold to the passage of death?'[61] In closing his account of the death of this husband, father, and grandfather, it is as if he were also rounding off earlier memoranda: 'He is gone to those whom he loved, to those whom he loved the best: to his angelic daughter now twenty and more years old in the peace of God, to his high and noble hearted wife. We too have a little one who, as I please myself to think, will as here on earth her remains rest in the same peaceful vault with theirs, so likewise be known and owned and cherished in Paradise among that blest society. I close this record on his 87th birthday, the 11th of December: he is keeping it in a better place. *December 11. 1851. (Fasque.)*'. Three days later he added in a postscript, 'He was laid on the upper shelf of the north side of the vault, by the coffin containing the remains of my mother'.

Diary entries for the days following his father's death reveal differences of opinion among the brothers and their sister Helen when the funeral arrangements were made with the undertaker. Once the closet drama of the deathbed is over, everyday life resumes. William thought the day chosen was too soon and was overruled when he 'proposed the Holy Communion', from fear of stronger disapproval 'elsewhere': 'I did not press it, but it is a great loss to me'.[62] On the Tuesday, when there was further disagreement, he records his hope that 'this will be for us an house of peace'. But he was then not satisfied with arrangements in the vault on the day of the funeral. The fact is that he was not in control, as he had been with Jessy's obsequies, being subject to his eldest brother, Thomas, the heir to the estate and the baronetcy, who is to hint that William and his family might leave a little earlier than they had planned. What William described as 'our final adieu to Fasque as a home', on St Stephen's day, proved to be a permanent break, distancing brother from brother.[63] And a sentence from the diary entry on the day of the funeral is chilling. 'I kissed thrice my Father's cheek & forehead', William writes, 'before & after his death: the only kisses that I can remember'.

Setting aside the hot-and-cold nature of the Gladstones' family life, however, the message of the angels to William seems to have been the universality of human suffering and the Christian's 'lively hope' of an inheritance 'reserved in heaven' (I Peter 1.3–4). On leaving Fasque, William wrote in his diary, 'the thought of it must for me ever be full of moving recollections'. The emotional and spiritual countercurrents that we have been tracing swirled around the sacred site of the vault at old Sir John's Scottish stronghold. Other countercurrents, of equal intensity, characterize his life in London in the late 1840s and 1850s, to which we now turn.

Notes

1. John Ruskin, Letter 27, *Fors Clavigera*, vol. III (1873): *The Works of John Ruskin*, Library Edition, ed. Edward Tyas Cook and Alexander Wedderburn (London and New York: Allen/Longmans, Green, 1903–12), vol. XXVII, pp. 489–90.
2. See Michael Wheeler, *Heaven, Hell, and the Victorians* (Cambridge: Cambridge University Press, 1994), pp. 31–50.
3. Roy Jenkins, *Gladstone* (London and Basingstoke: Macmillan, 1995), p. 65.
4. Letter to Catherine Gladstone, 26 September 1875, in Arthur Tilney Bassett, ed., *Gladstone to his Wife* (London: Methuen, 1936), p. 216.
5. On heaven, see Wheeler, *Heaven*, pp. 120–21.
6. *Diaries*, vol. I, p. 131.
7. *The Prime Ministers' Papers: W. E. Gladstone, Autobiographica and autobiographical Memoranda*, ed. John Brooke and Mary Sorensen, 4 vols. (London: HMSO, 1971–81), vol. I, p. 195.
8. *Diaries*, vol. I, pp. 132–34.
9. *Diaries*, vol. I, p. 138.
10. *Diaries*, vol. I, pp. 140–42; Peter Jagger, *Gladstone: The Making of a Christian Politician: The Personal Religious Life and Development of William Ewart Gladstone, 1809–32* (Allison Park, PA: Pickwick, 1991), p. 89.
11. *Diaries*, vol. I, p. 225.
12. *Diaries*, vol. I, p. 227. The editors suggest that Janet might be a servant.
13. *Diaries*, vol. I, p. 229. There were five coaches. Women were not expected to attend funerals.
14. See S. G. Checkland, *The Gladstones: A Family Biography, 1764–1851* (Cambridge: Cambridge University Press, 1971), p. 221.
15. *Diaries*, vol. II, p. 143 (24 December 1834); vol. I, p. 353 (17 April 1831).
16. *Diaries*, vol. II, p. 192; see also Checkland, *Gladstones*, p. 284.
17. BL, 44,724, ff. 49–50.
18. BL, 44,724, ff. 164–75 (f. 153); transcribed in *Prime Ministers' Papers*, vol. II, pp. 53–61 (p. 53).
19. *Diaries*, vol. II, p. 196.
20. William Bramwell, *A short Account of the Life & Death of Ann Cutler* (Sheffield: Smith, 1796), p. 3.
21. Charles Jerram, *A Tribute of parental Affection to the Memory of a beloved and only Daughter: containing some Account of the Character and Death of Hannah Jerram, who died May 9, 1823, aged 23*, 2nd edn (London: Wilson, 1824), pp. 156, 159.
22. Jerram, *Tribute of parental Affection*, pp. 180–87.

23. Henry Freeman, *A Memoir of the Life and Ministry of Ann Freeman, a faithful Servant of Jesus Christ, written by Herself, and an Account of her Death, by her Husband, Henry Freeman* (London: Harvey, Darton, 1826), pp. 107, 113.
24. *Prime Ministers' Papers*, vol. II, p. 53.
25. *Prime Ministers' Papers*, vol. II, p. 54.
26. *Prime Ministers' Papers*, vol. II, p. 58.
27. *Prime Ministers' Papers*, vol. II, p. 60.
28. *The Correspondence of Henry Edward Manning and William Ewart Gladstone: the Complete Correspondence, 1833–1891*, ed. Peter C. Erb, 4 vols. (Oxford: Oxford University Press, 2013), vol. I, pp. 14–15. 4 March 1836.
29. *Diaries*, vol. II, p. 196. Yet Travis Crosby states that 'he seems scarcely to have noticed' his mother's death and that 'the event is barely recorded in the diary': *The Two Mr. Gladstones: A Study in Psychology and History* (New Haven and London: Yale University Press, 1997), pp. 26–27.
30. John Morley, *The Life of William Ewart Gladstone*, 3 vols. (London and New York: Macmillan, 1903), vol. I, p. 131.
31. Erb, *Correspondence*, vol. I, p. 159.
32. Erb, *Correspondence*, vol. II, p. 99.
33. For William's letter of protest addressed to the Bishop of London (Blomfield), to which Rogers, James, Hope, John Manners, and others were cosignatories, see BL, 44,738 f. 119. For memoranda and correspondence on Gorham, see ff. 147–74.
34. BL, 44,738, f. 226r. *Diaries*, vol. IV, p. 192. 11 March 1850.
35. See Mary Drew, *Catherine Gladstone* (London: Nisbet, 1919), p. 73.
36. *Diaries*, vol. IV, p. 196.
37. BL, 44,738 f. 122r. The transcription of ff. 122–46 in *Prime Ministers' Papers*, vol. III, pp. 50–66 is mostly accurate, although the capitalization of sacred terms is altered.
38. BL, 44,738 f. 130r.
39. BL, 44,738 f. 133r.
40. *Diaries*, vol. IV, p. 200. The reference is to Edward Monro's *A few Words on the Spirit in which Men are meeting the present Crisis in the Church* (Oxford and London: Parker, 1850).
41. GL, GLA/GGA/2/2/1/158/83.
42. Jenkins, *Gladstone*, p. 108.
43. *Diaries*, vol. IV, pp. 201–2. 12 April 1850.
44. BL, 44,738 f. 140r. Capitalization was 'reduced and systematised' by the editors of the *Autobiographica*, thus losing the special emphasis here: see *Prime Ministers' Papers*, vol. I, p. 10; vol. III, p. 65.
45. *Diaries*, vol. IV, p. 202. 13 April 1850.
46. GL, GLA/GGA/2/10/1/17/99.
47. GL, GLA/GGA/2/7/1/11.
48. GL, GLA/GGA/2/10/1/17/101.
49. GL, GLA/GGA/2/7/1/13.

50. Thomas à Kempis, *The Imitation of Christ*, trans. Leo Sherley-Price (Harmondsworth: Penguin, 1952), p. 39.
51. À Kempis, *Imitation*, p. 70.
52. À Kempis, *Imitation*, p. 116.
53. *Diaries*, vol. IV, p. 237. 8 September 1850.
54. *Diaries*, vol. IV, p. 202. 15 April 1850.
55. *Diaries*, vol. IV, p. 357. 12 September 1851.
56. *Diaries*, vol. IV, p. 372. 30 November 1851.
57. Tate and Brady's version of psalm 130 features twice in William's 'Collection of Psalms': see BL, 44,833, ff. 12r, 23r.
58. *Prime Ministers' Papers*, vol. III, p. 86. Transcription from BL, 44,739, ff. 104–20.
59. *Prime Ministers' Papers*, vol. III, p. 93.
60. *Prime Ministers' Papers*, vol. III, p. 100.
61. *Prime Ministers' Papers*, vol. III, p. 102.
62. *Diaries*, vol. IV, p. 376. 8 December 1851.
63. *Diaries*, vol. IV, p. 382. 26 December 1851.

4
Work while it is day

I must work the works of him that sent me, while it is day: the night cometh, when no man can work. (John 9.3)

Among the verbs that recur in William's brief diary entries, such as 'saw', 'wrote', and 'read', the most telling is 'worked', a word that registers his commitment to making full use of every hour in each day, for the night cometh, when no man can work. He recommended that one of his sons at Oxford should 'keep a short journal of principal employments in each day: most valuable as an account-book of the all-precious gift of Time.'[1] In terms of his work as a career politician, he assumed one of the highest offices of state for the first time in 1852, serving as chancellor of the exchequer in Lord Aberdeen's coalition government, which he later described as a Liberal administration. In 1859 he returned to the treasury as chancellor under Lord Palmerston, following the formation of the official Liberal party. Between 1849 and 1852, he underwent a prolonged mid-life crisis that was associated with his charity work, his work on family investments at Oak Farm, and his vocation, or *métier*. He was tempted by erotic literature and attracted to some of the prostitutes he encountered during his rescue work in London's West End, accusing himself of 'adultery in the heart' (Matthew 5.28). His agony was compounded by the conversion of his closest Anglican allies to Rome, in his view an act of ecclesiastical infidelity. He recovered from these convulsions, establishing a more settled family life, centred upon Hawarden Castle, and returning to the top table of British politics, only to pass through another period of confusion after the Crimean War, when he lost his way professionally.

I have stained my memory and my soul

William's concern that his friends might abandon him for Rome emerged in 1845, that 'prodigious year of excitement and disaster', as John Forster described it.[2] Having resigned from Peel's cabinet on principle, being unable to support the enhancement of the Maynooth grant for the training of Roman Catholic priests in Ireland, he later voted for the bill as a backbencher. Meanwhile he declared his utter dependence upon the barrister James Hope, a fellow member of the Engagement associated with Margaret Chapel, for spiritual support, when he feared that Newman would convert to Rome and possibly take with him both Hope and Archdeacon Henry Manning, the friend with whom he regularly exchanged ideas on theology and ecclesiology. He further shored up his Anglican defences through intensive study of Bishop Joseph Butler, for him one of four 'doctors', along with Aristotle, Augustine, and Dante. On 9 July, in London, he recorded 'a touching conversation, not free from shame to me, with a woman from Cheshire near H[awarde]n.'[3] In September, at his father's request, he travelled to Munich and Baden in search of his sister Helen, now a Roman Catholic and struggling with her opium addiction. (She refused to return to Fasque.) Having spent four hours at the English church in Baden, on Sunday 26 October, he read the extraordinary 'self-examination' relating to his 'chief besetting sin' that he seems to have carried around in his diary.[4] Sexual arousal, often presumably leading to masturbation, is the subject of a carefully tabulated analysis of what he called the 'Channels', 'Incentives' and 'Chief actual dangers' associated with temptation, and of associated 'Remedies'. This analysis reveals a need to identify and control tendencies that he regarded as the weapons of Satan. Fully comprehensible only to its author, the document has an appended list of dates from 1845 to 1849, inscribed in different inks, indicating occasions on which he read what he regarded as pornography or had meetings with prostitutes that proved to be troubling on his side. Some incidents in both categories are marked with a sign like a whip, indicating the use of a scourge in 1849, after which the sign was used in diary entries.

During the first seven months of 1845 Catherine was expecting their fourth child, Jessy. She then nursed the baby herself. As the marriage service in the prayer book had reminded the couple, six years earlier, the 'holy estate' of matrimony was first ordained 'for the procreation of children'. Colin Matthew suggests that the Gladstones, like many Victorian religious families, may well have taken the implications of this literally.[5] Catherine was to be pregnant nine times (she suffered a miscarriage) over a period of fourteen years, during which there were lengthy periods of enforced sexual abstinence. Convention dictated that intercourse did not take place during most of pregnancy, nursing, and menstruation. Restraint was *de rigeur*, particularly among those who abominated the very idea of birth control, as William did. Both William and Catherine had a decidedly peripatetic existence and were often apart—hence the large number of daily letters between them that have survived.[6] William's conscience-stricken sexual crisis was not unrelated to these factors.

As an inveterate browser of second-hand bookshops, he was disturbed by his attraction to erotic illustrations and sexually explicit passages in the works of classical authors and English Restoration poets. In May 1848 he lamented his obsession with the bawdy tales in the so-called Fabliaux (*Fabliaux et contes des poètes françois des XI–XVe siècles*, 4 vols., 1808). Writing in Italian, he recorded that he bought the book because it contained the name of Catherine's uncle, the politician and book collector Thomas Grenville, who died in 1846. 'I began to read it', he continued, 'and found in some parts of it impure passages, concealed beneath the veil of a quite foreign idiom: so I drank the poison, sinfully, because understanding was thus hidden by a cloud—I have stained my memory and my soul—which may it please God to cleanse for me, as I have need. Have set down a black mark against this day.'[7] Psalm 51 ('Wash me throughly from my wickedness: and cleanse me from my sin', verse 2) features in William's manuscript collection of psalms.[8] And on the same folio in that manuscript are pasted extracts from Psalm 38, including a verse that he quoted two months later, on 19 July 1848, in a long memorandum expanding upon his analytical document that began life in Baden in 1845: 'my wickednesses are gone over my head and are like a sore burden too heavy for me to bear.'[9] He now looks back 'over more than twenty years since this plague began', confronts the fact that scholarly interest in historical literature is no excuse for reading 'poison' such as Rochester's 'vile poems', and again refers to the Fabliaux, which 'soon gave indication of their containing sad pollution'.

In the memorandum of July 1848 William also reflects upon his current workload in 'a year of over-pressure' upon him. His 'public & usual occupations', as one of the two MPs for Oxford University since 1847, were combined with 'a considerable weight of business in itself perplexing'—a reference to his tireless and ultimately successful efforts to rescue the Hawarden estate after the Glynne family's (and his own) ill-fated investment in the ironworks at Oak Farm, which failed in 1848. 'Under this', he comments, 'I have been sore, feeble, and worried: I have lost courage to look my daily duties in the face . . . and this . . . predisposes me to that vague habit of mind which seeks relief in some kind of counter-excitement.' Echoing the repetitions of the general confession at Morning and Evening Prayer ('We have followed too much the devices and desires of our own hearts. We have offended against thy holy law . . . '), transposed into the first-person singular, he describes the kind of coping strategy under stress that Travis Crosby regards as quintessentially Gladstonian.[10]

Such strategies were urgently needed the following year, 1849, when Catherine was pregnant again for the first eight months and William began to use the scourge. Having failed to establish a church in Leicester Square, he and his friend Sir Walter James MP diverted some of their resources into a chapel of ease, 'a mere little room' in Bedfordbury Street, by Covent Garden.[11] On Palm Sunday, 1 April, William noted in his diary, 'St Martin's 11 a.m. The new Bedfordbury Service at 7 P.M. May this seed of a new Church & flock be faithfully watered & abundantly blessed.'[12] The subsequent red-letter days of Easter, spent with the Lytteltons at Hagley, were interrupted by Oak Farm business. William took this problem back to London with him on the Wednesday of Easter Week, 11 April, when his diary entry includes the whip symbol, indicating his use of the scourge.[13] Next day he wrote, 'This week is ever a week of great temptations: I suppose there is a power of reaction': he refers to the end of Lent. Another whip sign appears in the diary on the 13th. After a week of debates in the Commons, a further whip sign was added to the entry for Saturday 21 April, but some kind of order was restored next day, the second Sunday after Easter: 'Bedfordbury evg. where I precented; all was very orderly only a select few of the ragged School being admitted. MS of 44 aloud in evg.'[14] And he wrote yet another memorandum on the 'sin of impurity', recording that this was the second Sunday on which he had abstained from Holy Communion because he had not 'shaken off the foe'.[15] The need for 'order'—increasingly a key term—was urgent.

William's Sunday reading in the autumn of 1834 had included Augustine's *Confessions*.[16] Augustine's route to faith through reading would have appealed to him, as would the long battle with physical desire that is described by the great sinner who became a great saint. In William's own memorandum on the 'sin of impurity', the richly stocked mind of an intellectual presides over this latest analysis of problems originating in the body—a classic case of 'sex in the head', as D. H. Lawrence was to put it.[17] William knows that two of the rocks on which he may 'fear to split' are '1. the allowing & entertaining positive desire: in regard to which our Lord has left us so clear and conspicuous a law. 2. that which is well called *delectatio morosa*' (enjoying thinking of evil without the intention of action, from Aquinas, who drew upon Augustine). He is aware that 'either of these is adultery in the heart'. Jesus expounds his 'conspicuous' law, that 'whosoever looketh on a woman to lust after her hath committed adultery with her already in his heart' (Matthew 5.28), with the kind of hyperbole that characterizes the parables: 'And if thy right eye offend thee, pluck it out, and cast it from thee: for it is profitable for thee that one of thy members should perish, and not that thy whole body should be cast into hell. And if thy right hand offend thee, cut it off.' William's reflections upon the rocks towards which 'the Enemy' and his own 'evil bias of habit' would draw him take no account of hyperbole. 'Man as God made him is wonderfully made', he wrote, 'I as I have made myself am strangely constituted. An ideal above the ordinary married state is commonly before me & ever returns upon me: while the very perils from which it commonly delivers still beset me as snares and pitfalls among which I walk.' His Christian idealism, 'above the ordinary married state', with its suggestion of restraint, and his reading of Christ's teaching as 'law', made his own failure with regard to 'adultery in the heart' all the more painful.

Impurity and lukewarmness

William's battle with his own lusts became more intense when he began his rescue work in earnest. When committing himself to membership of the Engagement, five years earlier, his charity work had focused upon the destitute of both sexes: the House of St Barnabas, Soho, opened in 1845. In 1848, however, he established the Church Penitentiary Association for the Reclamation of Fallen Women with Bishops Blomfield and Wilberforce. A growing awareness of the need for voluntary work among prostitutes was reflected in Dickens's collaboration with the philanthropist Angela Burdett-Coutts, later a friend of William's, and the foundation of Urania Cottage, Shepherds Bush, in November 1847. Elizabeth Gaskell consulted Dickens on creating a refuge in Manchester similar to Urania Cottage and sought his guidance on the case of a young seduced dressmaker aged sixteen.[18] Her first novel, *Mary Barton* (1848), was one of several literary works of the period that explored the problem of prostitution. William read it between 28 April and 8 May 1849. 'To whom shall the outcast prostitute tell her tale!' Gaskell writes. 'Who will give her help in her day of need? Hers is the leper-sin, and all stand aloof dreading to be counted unclean.'[19] When Jem Wilson encounters a bedraggled prostitute in the street one wet night, he is riveted by her narrative, as she is Mary Barton's aunt Esther. Like the Ancient Mariner, Esther holds him with her glittering eye.

William shared Gaskell's concern that prostitutes be heard. On 25 May 1849, when working on current legislation on the 'Law of Marriage', he wrote in his diary, 'Conv[ersation] with one of those poor creatures, a very sad case.'[20] Many one-to-one encounters followed, usually late at night, when he went in search of such cases and listened to their stories. It looked like soliciting, but when he took a commercial traveller to court for trying to extort money from him, in May 1853, *The Times* commented that the chancellor was 'addressed by an unfortunate woman, who earnestly begged attention to her story', and that he was 'listening, with his accustomed benevolence'.[21] 'These talkings of mine', he wrote in his diary at the time, 'are certainly not within the rules of world prudence: I am not sure that Christian prudence sanctions them for such an one as me.'[22] He ignored the gossip in clubland, but knew that he was putting himself in the way of temptation. Rescue work was thus a spiritual discipline.

The ambiguity inherent in his response to seduced women was not limited to those who had 'fallen' to the level of street walkers. On 20 June 1849 he learned from his friend Lord Lincoln that 'poor Lady L.' may have committed 'the last act of infidelity'.[23] Jesus' teaching on divorce is clear: 'whosoever shall put away his wife, saving for the cause of fornication, causeth her to commit adultery: and whosoever shall marry her that is divorced committeth adultery' (Matthew 5.32). Hence William's strenuous efforts to prevent changes to the divorce laws. Lady Lincoln had fled to Italy with her lover, Lord Walpole. William used the scourge on 29 June, spoke on the 'Marriage Bill' in the Commons on 4 July, and set off for Italy in search of the runaway countess nine days later. Catherine saw him off at the station. He eventually found the couple near Lake Como. In a scene fit for comic opera, he entered the grounds of the couple's villa disguised as a guitarist. Once he knew that the countess was heavily pregnant, he concentrated on gathering the evidence that his friend would need for a divorce by private legislation in parliament.[24] On his leisurely return journey, enjoying 'the delights of travelling', he attended holy communion at the English church in Lausanne, writing in his diary, 'Oh that poor miserable Lady L.—once the dream of dreams, the image that to my young eye combined everything that earth could offer of beauty and of joy. What is she now! But may that Spotless Sacrifice whereof I partook, unworthy as I am, today avail for her, to the washing away of sin, & to the renewal of the image of God'—precisely what he sought for himself when his middle-aged eye caused him new difficulties.[25]

On his fortieth birthday, in 1849, he wrote in his diary, 'The retrospect of my inward life is dark.'[26] He noted that the words 'Lead me O Lord in thy righteousness because of mine enemies: make thy way plain before my face' (Psalm 5.8) seemed appointed to be his 'continual prayer': 'Yet not only before my face but within my conscience.' As pressures upon him mounted in the first half of 1850, he responded by working harder than ever. Catherine was involved with the Clewer House of Mercy at Windsor, alongside her husband, when it opened in 1850. On Saturday 23 February, after a particularly busy week in the Commons, William attended a 'Sisterhood of Mercy meeting 2–4' there.[27] (Anglican sisterhoods were controversial innovations, founded by high churchman such as Edward Bouverie Pusey and John Mason Neale.) The Gladstones 'worked with tireless energy' in support of prostitutes: William often took them home for tea.[28] As we have seen, during little Jessy's harrowing last illness, in early April 1850, William was working intensively on a response to the Gorham judgment. (The short petition that he organized that month was drafted on mourning paper with black borders.[29]) On 25 April he wrote to his brother-in-law, Lord Lyttelton, 'The case of the Church of England at this moment is a very dismal one, and almost leaves men to choose between a broken heart and no heart at all.'[30] Furthermore, his political affiliation with the Peelites was contingent upon the state's relation to the church, as he explained in a letter to Manning, dated 29 April. 'I have two characters to fulfil', he wrote, 'that of a lay member of the Church, and that of a member of a sort of a wreck of a political party. I must not break my understood compact with the last and forswear my profession, unless and until the necessity has arisen. That necessity will plainly have arisen for me, when it shall have become evident that justice cannot, i.e., will not, be done by the State to the Church.'[31] On 2 May he recorded a 'Conv. at night with an unhappy woman'.[32] Ten days later he did not go to Holy Communion, as he reproached himself for 'much wicked negligence . . . as respects particular temptations'. By the end of May he was refining his method of recording days of shame. He thought of marking them in two classes: 'one of those of distinct offence against my rules: the other that of ill impressions without such distinctness of offence.'[33] This new rule was intended to help him 'in that important & difficult *work* keeping guard in respect of impurity' (my emphasis).

William was a master of compartmentalization, switching abruptly between different kinds of work, each of which offered him 'some kind of counter-excitement', rather as he found refreshment in moving between two or three books in his daily reading. At times of stress, however, when he concealed aspects of his tortured inner life even from those he loved, the barriers between the various domains in which he operated could be breached. After weeks of labour, his response to the Gorham judgement, entitled *Remarks on the Royal Supremacy*, was published in early June 1850. Presented in the form of an open letter, addressed to Bishop Blomfield of London, the pamphlet affirms the reformed Church of England as the guardian of the Christian faith, denies the constitutional right of the judicial committee of the privy council, which included laymen, to hear ecclesiastical cases, and claims that the church is capable of reforming the current system of appeal. Towards the end of this learned and densely argued tract of eighty-eight pages, William emphasizes the need for 'a prevailing and pervading harmony in the composition of the Church and the State respectively.'[34] The system of appeal becomes 'unchristian, and even directly immoral', however, when operated by a state 'composed in great part of those who do not own the authority of the Church at all'. If it be true, he suggests, that the Church of England has a divine commission to teach a body of revealed truth which includes the doctrine of baptismal grace, then 'to propose that the faith and its opposite in any particular article shall be placed on equal terms within the precinct and by the law of the Church, is simply to demand that she shall betray her office. It is precisely—however startling the comparison may appear—what it would be, relatively to the marriage state [*sic*], to enact that fidelity might be maintained in it, but that adultery might also be practised at the option of the parties.' William's private agonies and his 'ideal above the ordinary married state' spill onto the page of a public defence of church principles that underpin his work as a politician.

His efforts to control his private passions and to keep his friends in the Church of England redoubled in the summer and autumn of 1850. On 8 July, just a few days after the death of Sir Robert Peel, his political patron and inspiration, he saw a prostitute called South, in whose case there were 'some very touching & shaming circumstances', and read an important article on prostitution by the essayist W. R. Greg, a friend of Elizabeth Gaskell's.[35] The swindler may repent, Greg observed, the drunkard may reform, but the prostitute 'may *not* pause—*may* NOT *recover*'.[36] Over the next two weeks William continued to read up on the 'Marriage Law' and had a conversation with 'two unhappy women in the streets at night'. Having been emboldened to station himself opposite the Argyll Rooms, a notorious pick-up point, in search of cases, he got to know Emma Clifton, with whom he became obsessed. After half a dozen encounters in the street he visited her lodgings and persuaded her to visit Clewer with her child. He wrote letters on her behalf and, in early August, when the family retired to Hawarden for the recess, decided that it was his duty to return to London and to continue his efforts for her.[37] During a family visit to Fasque, in September, his conversations with Hope indicated that all his friend's 'doubts & dispositions' about the established church had revived after the Gorham judgement, but that Hope seemed 'disposed to think & act steadily'.[38] William immediately wrote to Manning, looking forward to seeing him in London the following week and offering a bed for the night to enable them to talk along the same lines.[39] Whether engaging in ecclesiastical matters with sophisticated friends at the top of the social scale, or with unfortunate women who had 'fallen' to the depths, William worked at his relationships, attempting to rescue those whom he regarded as being in danger of going further astray, as he himself was.

The work on both fronts continued when he returned to London on 2 October. Having left his brother Tom's place near Warwick at 6.15 a.m., he arrived at noon and 'Went to work on letters & papers.'[40] He then made a couple of calls, had Manning with him between 7 p.m. and 11 p.m., and finally 'Looked about for poor E. Clifton: but in vain.' Next day Manning 'came to dine & staid 7–11'. 'His conversation on these two evenings opens to me a still darkening prospect', he recorded: 'Alas for what lies before us.' As he was to learn the following day, Lavinia Glynne, wife of the Rector of Hawarden, died at 11 p.m., 'When *I* went to look for E. C.—in vain.' As the fruitless search for Emma Clifton continued, he reflected on Lavinia's death before attending the funeral. On 18 October he and the family set off for Naples, from which they were to return after four months. Many years later he was to describe 1850 as his saddest year.[41] On his forty-first birthday he described this *annus horribilis* as 'one of anxiety and labour, of the last as much and of the first more than most years of my life. I would to God I could add it had been one of progress in obtaining the mastery over my most besetting sins which I think are impurity and lukewarmness', the latter in reference to his commitment to the church.[42] Nevertheless, he could add, 'My blessings indeed in domestic life are richer still as my children grow: Both Willy & Agnes are advanced this year in all I most desire: and Jessy is advanced far more, dear dear blessed Jessy.'

In the spring and summer of 1851 William realized that his besetting sins of impurity and lukewarmness were related. In February, while at Naples, Catherine had suffered a miscarriage and William had witnessed the horrors endured by political prisoners, the subject of his *Two Letters* to the Earl of Aberdeen. On their return to London he went straight into political discussions that convinced him of the impossibility of joining Stanley's Conservative cabinet, on the grounds that a duty on corn was mentioned. Although church-going continued, including attendance at the Bedfordbury evening service, the diary contains relatively few references to private devotions. In late March his rescue work focused upon one P. Lightfoot and his discussions with Hope became increasingly alarming. On the fourth Sunday in Lent the diary reads: 'Wrote a paper on Manning's question & gave it to him: he smote me to the ground by answering with suppressed emotion that he is now upon the *brink*: and Hope too. Such terrible blows not only overset & oppress but I fear also demoralise me: which tends to show that my trusts are Carnal or the withdrawal of them would not leave such a void. *Was* it possibly from this that thinking P.L would look for me as turned out to be the fact, I had a second interview & conversation indoors here; & heard more history: yet I trusted without harm done.'[43] Next day, himself 'upon the brink' in relation to Lightfoot, he saw her again 'indoors' and said he thought it must be the last time. He concluded, 'I was certainly wrong in some things & trod the path of danger.' When what he called the 'secession' of Hope and Manning took place at Farm Street the following Sunday, 6 April, he recorded this as 'A day of pain!', adding next day, 'They were my two props. Their going may be to me a sign that my work is gone with them. God give us daily light with daily bread. One blessing I have: total freedom from doubts. These dismal events have smitten but not shaken . . . Dined at the Palace: when I had a most interesting conversation especially with the Queen about Naples.'

While fearing that his political work in defence of the established church may have 'gone with them', he acted decisively to remove Hope from his will as an executor before spending Easter caring for his father at Fasque. Looking back at this troubled time, he reflected on 'the blessings of discipline', adding that 'Whether owing (as I think) to the sad sad recent events (of the 6th) or not, I have been unmanned & unnerved & out of sheer cowardice have not used the measure which I have found so beneficial against temptations to impurity', namely the scourge (also known as a 'discipline' in the context of religious penance).[44] Characteristically, however, on 25 March 1851, when demoralized by these impending conversions to Rome, William spoke in the Commons for over two hours in opposition to the Whigs' Ecclesiastical Titles bill, a feeble attempt to undermine the re-establishment of the Roman Catholic hierarchy. He argued that the true interests of

Anglican clergy were not to be promoted by placing them 'between a large body of our fellow-subjects and the fullest enjoyment of religious equality.'[45] Rather, the government should apply the 'great principle' of 'religious freedom' to the question and 'follow that bright star of justice beaming from the heavens whithersoever it may lead.'[46] The author of *The State in its Relations with the Church* has moved on.

While capable of presenting a courageous defence of high principles in the Commons, he could not maintain his self-discipline on the streets. In May his search for prostitutes led to further encounters with P. Lightfoot. In June he read Hawthorne's novel of adultery, *The Scarlet Letter*, describing it as 'an extraordinary work full of poetry: it breaks down morally at the *end*.'[47] By then he had met Elizabeth Collins, to whom he was strongly attracted. He was to encounter her twenty times over the subsequent twelve months, and on 13 July 1851, a Sunday, recorded 'a strange & humbling scene' during a two-hour visit to her lodgings, after which he used the scourge.[48] A similar 'mixed scene', again followed by scourging, took place forty-eight hours later. The word 'scene' suggests some kind of interaction, something more than adultery in the heart, but less than penetrative sex outside marriage. This low point in the story of William's rescue work has been variously described as 'the trough of his mid-century crisis of nerves and sex', the moment when 'carnality had invaded charity', and an extreme example of a Freudian impulse to 'retrieve the mother within the prostitute'.[49] The declaration that he made at the end of his life, to the effect that he had never been 'guilty of the act which is known as that of infidelity to the marriage bed', was clearly qualified.[50] On 26 July, two weeks after Catherine and the children had left London for Hagley, William wrote to her, 'how little you know the evil of [my life], of which at the last day I shall have a strange story to tell.'[51] 'Self examination', he adds, 'is a mournful task especially in one who feels himself made up, as I do, of strange and sharp contrasts'. Meanwhile, Catherine must have conceived their son Henry in July 1851.

Hope and Manning had joined a church which practised auricular confession. William had his diary. His entry for 19 August 1851 begins 'Wrote to E. Collins', and later switches into Italian, here translated by Matthew, in a passage which alternates between confession of sins and assurance of grace:

Saw E. C. again by herself; from 9¼ until 11½. Things went partly as before. She nevertheless finds herself determined to have nothing more to do with anyone else, but to wait faithfully for Osborne [her lover]; who, according to his letters, longs to marry her the moment he returns. Now there are two whom I have seen this year, who are I hope resolved to do no more evil; and I am covered with many foul stains. If God's grace has made use of most unworthy me, with how very much new guilt for me, to help these souls, may it ever be praised on their account, and gloried eternally even in my miserable self. Oh how much have I seen of his grandeur and of his mercy, how much also of the marvels of the human heart; of him too I have a living awareness, a knowledge right in the very inmost parts of myself: that I am, even among guilty ones, the guiltiest. These two terrible years have really displaced and uprooted my heart from the Anglican Church, seen as a personal and *living* Church in the *body* of its Priests and members; and at the same time the two friends whom I might call the only supports for my intellect have been wrenched away from me, leaving me lacerated, and I may say barely conscious morally: these misfortunes have almost come upon me, or else if they have not, may it be God's grace that prevents them. They may yet succeed in bringing about my ruin, body and soul. But that grace, that love is boundless; otherwise, it would never suffice for me.[52]

The failure of the bishops to respond appropriately to the Gorham judgement had driven his friends into the arms of Rome and weakened his own commitment to the Church of England, thus demoralizing him, in several senses. Yet this passage contained a clue to his subsequent recovery, in that the 'lacerating' effect of his friends' departure can be set against his shaking off the more sclerotic aspects of Tractarianism and seeking God in the 'very inmost parts' of himself. Similarly, the death of Peel, his political father, left him with more freedom of movement as the leader of the small group of Peelites in the Commons; the death of Sir John Gladstone, at the end of 1851, freed him from the tight paternal bonds of previous decades; and the death of Lavinia Glynne made it more likely that the Gladstone side of the family would eventually inherit the Hawarden estate. New challenges and possibilities were about to open up.

My life might seem less unhopeful

When Edward Stanley, the 14th Earl of Derby, formed a minority administration in February 1852, William wanted to move across the floor of the Commons with the Conservatives, as he retained some hope of the party's revival. But the Peelites remained on the opposition benches with the Liberals. Party politics and party affiliations, unsettled since 1846, remained fairly fluid in the 1850s. In his political work, William shifted from pursuing the aims he had shared with his high church friends to a focus on the nation's finances.[53] His charity work continued as before, however, and on 30 April 1852, when he delivered a short speech opposing Disraeli's budget measures, he also saw Elizabeth Collins in the evening.[54] He saw 'another person, lightly & wrongfully', three days later. On 9 May he took up the Revd William Edward Heygate's sermons on 'some points of Christian prudence', entitled *The Care of the Soul*. He made them his Sunday reading, finishing this 'admirable book' on 4 July.

Heygate's sermons clearly made a deep impression on him. The text in sermon I, 'Self-government', would certainly have touched a nerve: 'He that hath no rule over his own spirit is like a city that is broken down, and without walls' (Proverbs 25.28).[55] Among the sentences from this sermon that he marked with a single vertical line, in the margins of his copy, some could have come from his own private memoranda: 'Every thing around us acts upon us; touches first one spring, and then another, and gives occasion of triumph or defeat; of self-victory, self-restraint, self-government; or their opposites'; ' "No hour without its line upon the soul," is a true saying'; 'It is only because we are temples of the Holy Ghost, that we can look for the beauty of holiness to be manifested in us, by jewels of graces, and ornaments of a holy life.'[56] Crucially, Heygate offers hope for those weighed down by 'Besetting sins', the subject of sermon III and one of William's key phrases in the diary. And in sermon IX, 'Religious selfishness', William inserted parallel vertical lines and a cross against Heygate's assertion that 'We must watch over ourselves for the sake of others.'[57] Such writings seem to have provided William with real spiritual support. In the 1860s he was to consult another devotional book by Heygate, entitled *The Good Shepherd: Meditations for the Clergy* (1860), at 'dressing times', morning and evening.[58]

In January 1852 William and Catherine discussed the future of the Hawarden estate with her brother, the antiquarian Sir Stephen Glynne. The house had been closed while William laboured to rescue the estate during the Oak Farm crisis. Now that it could be reopened, would it not be best if Catherine and her family were to return to her childhood home? Sir Stephen, Lord Lieutenant of Flintshire, acquiesced, kept his place at the head of the dinner table, and described William and Catherine as 'the great people'. For William, Hawarden became a haven and a home, later to be ceded to his eldest son, Willy, following the transfer of further Gladstone funds to the estate. After a busy early summer in 1852, when he offered advice to several London prostitutes and continued to find his own response to them unsatisfactory, he wound up another parliamentary session, heard that he had been re-elected for Oxford University, and took a short holiday before arriving at Hawarden on the morning of 17 July. He recorded in the diary, 'Cath. & the children arrived before four. We were all happy to meet at this sweet place with auspices somewhat less unhopeful for the family.'[59] Having acquired further land in his own name, he could write on 27 August, 'In Chester & walked back thro' my land.'[60] As he had also inherited the Seaforth estate from his father, he was now a landowner in two counties, if not the owner of Hawarden.

As he settled in, he recorded his 'extraordinary sleepiness', induced 'either from the warmth—or a reaction of nature after the closing time in London'.[61] Healing had begun. But he also needed to establish a routine that enabled him to *work* and to exercise a restless intellect. The pattern that was established would serve him well for decades. First a walk through the park to St Deiniol's church for Mattins at 8.30, followed by correspondence, reading, and often writing, even when guests were in the house. The Wilberforce brothers, Bishop Samuel and Archdeacon Robert, stayed in July 1852, discussing church business with William, including Convocation and the doctrine of the real presence ('Oh what hands are mine to be laid upon such objects!'). As his children grew up, he spent more time playing with them and observing their development. Members of the extended family were often guests, as were stray individuals such as the young Edward Stuart Talbot, a future Bishop of Winchester, who had happy memories of stays at Hawarden, where the 'fatherless boy' would walk to church with his eminent host.[62]

William's recovery from his mid-life crisis was aided not only by the peace of Hawarden but also by its necessary antithesis, the hurly burly of London life, when he again tackled the heavy workload associated with high office. On 17 December 1852 he defied parliamentary convention by leaping to the dispatch box at 1 a.m., at the end of Disraeli's budget speech, and insisting that members should hear an immediate riposte, rather than trooping wearily through the lobbies to vote. Once he had shouted down the roars of disapproval, he delivered a speech of over two hours that appeared to be spontaneous, but had in fact been 'fermenting' in him for two days, so that he felt 'as a loaf might in the oven'.[63] His attack upon Disraeli, who had been Peel's principal tormentor, was grounded in personal animosity and moral outrage. 'I vote against the Budget of the Chancellor of the Exchequer', he said, 'not only because I disapprove upon general grounds of the principles of that Budget, but emphatically and peculiarly because in my conscience—though it may be an erroneous belief—it is my firm conviction that the Budget is one, I will not say the most liberal, nor the most radical, but I will say the most subversive in its tendencies and ultimate effects which I have ever known submitted to this House.'[64] The Conservatives were defeated and within a week he had been appointed chancellor in what he called Aberdeen's 'mixed' government.

While these rapidly unfolding events kept the newspaper reporters busy, William wrote daily to Catherine down at Hawarden. On 17 December he explained that his 'great object' had been to show the Conservative party how their leader was 'hoodwinking' them.[65] Next day, however, he agonized over the impact of his speech on Disraeli: 'I am told *he* is much stung by what I said. I am very sorry it fell to me to say it: God knows I have no wish to give him pain, & really with my deep sense of his gifts I would only pray they might be well used. It is such a comfort to think there is One who sees these things not with our weak and partial eye but in perfect justice, and in boundless mercy too'.[66] Meanwhile an exuberant Catherine poured out her feelings, only to check them: she, too, had a monitorial conscience. On 18 December she wrote,

> God bless you my own loved one oh how weak are words to express the feelings of my heart—so excited & thankful have I been from the moment I with frantic eagerness claimed a Times at

Stafford—that I am all the better for being able to cry at reading Mrs Herberts letter to day—yes her description of the scene in the H of Commons quite overpowered me ^ *oh that I could have been there & with you afterwards & with you now*—God knows what I would have given but it is good for me perhaps I could not & surely with such cause for thankfulness as I have surely I should not complain ^.[67]

William continued to agonize. 'My own Cathie', he wrote on the 20th, 'It is by far my great pleasure in what happened on Thursday night as to myself that it makes your heart thrill with joy. In other respects it is perhaps dangerous: I am tempted to look back upon it whereas the true way is to look forward or only to look back for the purpose of regretting shortcomings and faults'.[68]

As Aberdeen laboured over his cabinet-making, the family at Hawarden scoured the newspapers and eagerly anticipated the arrival of William's daily bulletins. Although he despaired of getting away for Christmas and planned to attend midnight mass in London, he travelled to Hawarden through the stormy night, celebrating Christmas Day with his wife and children, 'a great treat'.[69] Having dashed back to London, he wrote, 'My own Cathie It blew a hurricane & rained considerably when I left Hawarden this morning . . . I certainly made a good bargain for myself in coming down to you, & I am not without compunction at having escaped my share of the burdens others have been bearing in my absence'.[70] On his birthday, four days later, the usual admission that he had 'made no progress against the besetting sin often mentioned' was followed by a caveat: 'Yet I trust my ultimate aim has not been wholly corrupt: & in some other matters my life might seem less unhopeful'.

Having adjusted to their country house in Flintshire, William and Catherine settled the family into their 'new abode in Downing Street' (number 11) on 3 February 1853.[71] William soon turned his attention to preparing his first budget, often working long into the night, a solitary figure with a mission. Receiving deputations, consulting colleagues, and gaining the approval of the cabinet were necessary stages in the process, but the proposals that he put before the Commons were to be his own. At the height of his preparatory work, he saw Elizabeth Collins on a Sunday, 10 April.[72] On the eve of his budget speech, although 'obliged to give several hours' to his figures, he delivered one of his sermons to the household and attended three church services. A verse of the Psalms was 'as it were given' him at Morning Prayer: 'O turn thee then unto me, and have mercy upon me: give Thy strength unto Thy servant, and help the son of Thine handmaid' (Psalm 86.16). Next day, Monday 18 April, he recorded in the diary, 'Spoke 4¾ hours in detailing the Financial measures: and my strength stood out well thank God'. The speech was a *tour de force*. Peel had encouraged him always to speak at length in the Commons and this broke records. Yet, having managed to make the national finances interesting, he was garlanded by his colleagues. As in his speech attacking Disraeli's budget, he presented his argument in moral terms. The peroration, a sentence of 334 words, ends with a vision of a just society bound together by allegiance to the Crown:

> we have felt we should best maintain our own honour, that we should best meet the views of Parliament, and best promote the interests of the country, by declining to draw any invidious distinction between class and class, by adopting it to ourselves as a sacred aim, to diffuse and distribute—burden if we must; benefit if we may—with equal and impartial hand; and we have the consolation of believing that by proposals such as these we contribute, as far as in us lies, not only to develop the material resources of the country, but to knit the hearts of the various classes of this great nation yet more closely than heretofore to that Throne and to those institutions under which it is their happiness to live.[73]

Now confirmed as a supreme master of parliamentary oratory, William took his message on tour in October 1853 with a visit to Manchester, then in his native Lancashire. He visited the Exchange, leaning on the arms of his friend, Bishop Wilberforce, and the mayor, and unveiled a statue of Peel in front of the infirmary. There was 'something yet more admirable than the immense intellectual endowments with which it had pleased the Almighty to gift him', he said, 'and that was, his sense of public virtue—it was his purity of conscience—it was his determination to follow the public good'.[74] Wrapped in the mantle of his mentor, he told the crowd on a busy thoroughfare of

Cottonopolis that it was a blessing to belong to 'a country that has a great and beneficial part to play in the designs of Providence for the improvement and advancement of mankind. (Loud cheers.)' At the town hall, with Catherine on the platform, he claimed that the present government was the least reliant on 'party connexion', and invoked 'that sense of duty as men and as Christians which makes us value peace'. With the possibility of war looming, Aberdeen considered that the speech had 'much promoted the cause of peace'.[75] For William, this provincial speaking tour, combined with corporate dinners and visits to various institutions, not only boosted his *amour propre* but also put him directly in touch with public opinion, to which politicians would have to attend more closely in the second half of the nineteenth century, when the views of 'the people' were often both shaped and articulated by William himself.

In recovery from his personal crisis, he maintained his vigilance. On his forty-fourth birthday he found a 'real joy' in the assurance of Psalm 90.8, adding, 'but even this may only be a deeper snare'.[76] In London he continued to meet prostitutes, including Elizabeth Collins, and 'lay awake till four' one night, 'counting up the numbers of those unhappy beings' with whom he had conversed over many years, 'indoors or out'.[77] He could remember 'from 80 to 90': they constituted the 'chief burden' of his soul. To his knowledge, only one of them abandoned her trade with his help. But he had listened to their stories, and his new homes, new friendships, and a new cabinet post had a stabilizing effect. During a tour of the Scottish Highlands in September 1853, William and Catherine stayed at the recently remodelled Dunrobin Castle, seat of the dukes of Sutherland. For eight or nine days, he was bedridden with a severe attack of erysipelas. Harriet, Duchess of Sutherland, read to him, 'full of the utmost kindness & simplicity'.[78] Her serious engagement with religion and politics made this formidable woman a perfect female friend in years to come. Back at Hawarden he began to arrange his books in the study-library that came to be known as the 'Temple of Peace', a room that for Ruth Windscheffel provides evidence of 'those contests between privacy and publicity, temperance and temptation, openness and obsession, which characterized Gladstone's life'.[79] As thousands of volumes were gradually transferred to Hawarden over the ensuing year, he created a space in which he could pursue his many literary and theological interests, while also dealing with huge amounts of correspondence associated with the politics of church and state, as well as personal and family matters. Separate desks were dedicated to the two kinds of work. A third was for Catherine's use.

During the disastrous Crimean War, William believed that, in principle, its cost should be borne by the current generation rather than passed on to another.[80] Funding the war through direct taxation, rather than loans, also meant that peace might come sooner. On 8 May 1854 his war budget statement lasted three and a half hours. Never, he recorded afterwards, had he 'more cause to feel the unutterable mercy of God, the strength of His sustaining arm, & the power of the vision of the great High Priest in Heaven ever offering Himself for us'.[81] Next day he noted that, as on most 'occasions of very sharp pressure or trial', some word of scripture had 'come home' to him 'as if borne on angel's wings', and particularly the words of 'the blessed, blessed Psalms!' By the end of the year, with the war going badly and the government in difficulties, William's 'feud in the Cabinet' troubled his conscience on Christmas Day.[82] Again, he experienced a sense of peace through a visitation. 'Brute passions' were in his mind at holy communion, he recorded, 'with the thought of the newborn Christ, even as the animals in the stable where He lay: but at the Altar the Son of God came to me and bid them be still'. On his birthday he referred to 'the sins of wrath, impurity, & spiritual sloth'. But the end of the year had been 'joyously marked by Willy's going to the altar', and he could close his diary entry for new year's eve with the words, 'I hope for better days & better things'.

The Peelites broke up in disarray in 1855, when William was among those who accepted office under Palmerston, only to resign it a fortnight later, as he could not support an enquiry into Aberdeen's government. Morley comments that 'the transaction gave a rude and protracted shock to his public influence'.[83] During the ensuing wilderness years, William embarked on his all-consuming work on Homer, a project which seems reminiscent of Casaubon's search for the key to all mythologies in *Middlemarch* (1871–72). Crosby describes this as one of several 'coping devices to deflect his continued political and psychological frustrations' between 1855 and 1859, while Bebbington argues that the most important of several reasons for his engagement with Homer was 'with a view to apologetic for Christian orthodoxy'.[84] In September 1855 Homer accompanied him on a family holiday in Wales, a 'pleasant sojourn', he wrote, where he had 'lived too happily for one who thinks as I do about the course of events & the responsibilities of needless war'.[85] He had been 'immersed with great delight' in Homer, 'up to my ears', he wrote, 'perhaps I should say out of my depth'.[86] With his highly tuned conscience always on the alert, he was beginning to see his newfound happiness as yet another snare. Self-scrutiny on All Saints Day revealed a 'faint improvement as compared with the last four', but also a growing 'disposition to Epicurean self-indulgence'.[87]

His rescue work in London continued in the mid-1850s, when he occasionally 'had a warning', or had feelings that he considered to be 'bad indeed'.[88] But he was no longer in thrall to particular prostitutes with whom he became emotionally involved. His annual review at the end of 1856 reveals new anxieties. On his birthday he gave thanks for the 'great spiritual mercy' of 'a long unbroken country sojourn', but lamented that his soul was 'still disturbed by the waves, & divided in the service of many masters: the anchor is not yet surely cast. Yet God still draws me to Him'.[89] On New Year's Eve he was more specific, saying that he was 'becoming alive to a new evil and danger' in the strength and the growing number of the ties that bound him to this world. He was drawn deeper into politics each year; he continued to share in the struggles of the church; literature had a 'new & powerful hold' upon him; the fortunes of the Glynne family had engaged his attention for over nine years; they had seven children growing up around them: 'what a network is here woven out of all that the heart & all that the mind of man can supply'. Once again, the ideal of the gospel, reinforced by guides such as Augustine, à Kempis, and Heygate, challenges his engagement with this world. 'How then', he asks, 'am I to have my conversation in heaven [Philippians 3.20] in the sense of having my loins girt & my lamp burning & of waiting for the Lord [Luke 12.35–38] before the morning watch? [Ps 130.6]'. Is his treasure in heaven or on earth? 'For where your treasure is, there will your heart be also' (Luke 12.34).

William's colleagues were also anxious about him. In December 1856 Sir James Graham told Lord Aberdeen that 'he writes and says and does too much'; and Aberdeen warned William that he did not 'possess the sympathy of the House at large'.[90] His detachment from party loyalties, combined with a readiness to take on causes in the name of Christian morality, made him a loose cannon in the Commons. He spoke for almost two hours in the China debate, for example, on 3 March 1857, asking whether the government had striven to put down the opium trade.[91] In the summer of 1857 he made seventy-three interventions in fierce opposition to Palmerston's divorce bill while defending 'the equality of the sexes under the Christian law', a subject developed in his essay on divorce in the *Quarterly Review*.[92] He thus laid himself open to ridicule, having previously helped Lord Lincoln to get his divorce. In May 1858 he argued that Britain should keep her promise to Wallachia and Moldavia. As in other cases, the fact that he lost the motion that he put forwards on the defence of the Romanians against the Turks and the Austrians did not detract from his high moral argument. Inevitably, he was regarded as quixotic. His *Studies on Homer and the Homeric World*, published in three volumes in March 1858, startled readers with its claim that traces of the original revelation granted to Adam and Noah were to be discerned in Homer. Two months later he took up wood-felling at Hawarden, a perfectly sensible aspect of estate management, as well as a healthy means of body-building, thus providing the cartoonists with material for decades. And then he surprised his friends and colleagues by becoming the Lord High Commissioner of the Ionian Islands, based in Corfu, a role that would be attractive to anyone engaged in classical research. He was deeply impressed by the austerity of the monastery at Platutera and caused a stir at home when it was reported that he kissed the archbishop's hand at a reception.

Later in 1859 he was entranced by Tennyson's *Idylls of the King*, on which he would write at length, and, some would say most quixotically, agreed to become chancellor under the ageing Lord Palmerston, the target of his most outspoken attacks over recent years. Wearing his new livery as a Liberal, he began the journey that was to take him to the premiership in 1868, a journey that provides the context of the next chapter.

Notes

1. John Morley, *The Life of William Ewart Gladstone*, 3 vols. (London and New York: Macmillan, 1903), vol. I, p. 205.
2. See Michael Wheeler, *The Year that shaped the Victorian Age: Lives, Loves, and Letters of 1845* (Cambridge: Cambridge University Press, 2023), Ch. 6.

3. *Diaries*, vol. III, p. 467.
4. *Diaries*, vol. III, p. 492–93. The sketch is pasted into a set of notes marked 'Secret' in a collection of MSS labelled 'Secreta Prayers' (LPL, MS 2758, ff. 21–22).
5. H. C. G. Matthew, *Gladstone, 1809–1898* (Oxford: Clarendon, 1997), p. 90.
6. In a long letter to Catherine from Baden, dated 12 October 1845, William confessed to feeling 'lawless' away from home and family: GL, GLA/GGA/2/10/1/16/62.
7. *Diaries*, vol. IV, pp. 35–36. 13 May 1848.
8. BL, 44,833, fol. 10v.
9. *Diaries*, vol. IV, p. 52; LPL, MS 2758, f. 27.
10. See Travis Crosby, *The Two Mr. Gladstones: A Study in Psychology and History* (New Haven and London: Yale University Press, 1997), pp. 52–59.
11. BL, 44,264. ff. 191, 203.
12. *Diaries*, vol. III, p. 111.
13. *Diaries*, vol. III, p. 113.
14. *Diaries*, vol. III, p. 116. A sermon of 1844 was reused for family prayers.
15. LPL, MS 2758, f. 63v; *Diaries*, vol. IV, p. 116 (22 April 1849).
16. *Diaries*, vol. II, p. 138. 26 November 1834.
17. D. H. Lawrence, *Fantasia of the Unconscious* (London: Heinemann, 1923), p. 123.
18. *The Letters of Mrs Gaskell*, ed. J. A. V. Chapple and Arthur Pollard (Manchester: Manchester University Press, 1966), p. 98.
19. Elizabeth Gaskell, *Mary Barton: A Tale of Manchester Life*, ed. Stephen Gill (Harmondsworth: Penguin, 1970), p. 207.
20. *Diaries*, vol. IV, p. 124. In the Commons he opposed marriage with a deceased wife's sister.
21. *The Times*, 12 May 1853, p. 5.
22. *Diaries*, vol. IV, p. 525. 10 May 1853.
23. *Diaries*, vol. IV, p. 131.
24. See Matthew, *Gladstone*, p. 80; Roy Jenkins, *Gladstone* (London and Basingstoke: Macmillan, 1995), pp. 93–95.
25. *Diaries*, vol. IV, p. 144. Sunday 5 August 1849.
26. *Diaries*, vol. IV, p. 175. 29 December 1849.
27. *Diaries*, vol. IV, p. 186.
28. Mary Drew, *Catherine Gladstone* (London: Nisbet, 1919), p. 250.
29. 'To the Bishop of London', BL, 44,738, f. 119.
30. See Morley, *Life of Gladstone*, vol. I, p. 381.
31. *The Correspondence of Henry Edward Manning and William Ewart Gladstone: The Complete Correspondence, 1833–1891*, ed. Peter C. Erb, 4 vols. (Oxford: Oxford University Press, 2013), vol. II, pp. 352–53.
32. *Diaries*, vol. IV, p. 207.
33. *Diaries*, vol. IV, pp. 214–15. 31 May 1850.
34. W. E. Gladstone, *Remarks on the Royal Supremacy, as it is defined by Reason, History, and the Constitution: A Letter to the Lord Bishop of London* (London: Murray, 1850), p. 76.

35. *Diaries*, vol. IV, p. 224.
36. W. R. Greg, 'Prostitution', *Westminster Review*, 53 (1850), 448–506 (454–55). William also described 1851 as his saddest year, at the time.
37. *Diaries*, vol. IV, p. 233. 15 August 1850.
38. *Diaries*, vol. IV, p. 239. 22 September 1850.
39. Erb, *Correspondence*, vol. II, p. 427.
40. *Diaries*, vol. IV, p. 241.
41. Letter to Laura Thistlethwayte, 25 October (1869?), LPL, MS 2761, f. 116r.
42. *Diaries*, vol. IV, p. 295. 29 December 1850.
43. *Diaries*, vol. IV, p. 319. 30 March 1851.
44. *Diaries*, vol. IV, p. 325. 19 April 1851. 'Discipline', OED, 1.3.
45. Hansard, vol. CXV, col. 566.
46. Hansard, vol. CXV, cols. 594, 597.
47. *Diaries*, vol. IV, p. 338. 20 June 1851.
48. *Diaries*, vol. IV, p. 344. His letter to Catherine of 14 July was scribbled and that of 15th very short, on tiny paper: GL, GLA/GGA/2/10/1/18/23-24.
49. Jenkins, *Gladstone*, p. 114; Richard Shannon, *Gladstone*, 2 vols. (London: Methuen, 1982–99), vol. I, p. 236; Crosby, *Two Mr. Gladstones*, p. 67.
50. See *Diaries*, vol. III, pp. xlvi–xlvii.
51. GL, GLA/GGA/2/10/1/18/34.
52. *Diaries*, vol. IV, p. 353.
53. See Shannon, *Gladstone*, vol. I, pp. 244–57.
54. *Diaries*, vol. IV, p. 424. On 1 July he recorded, in Italian, that she was 'half of a most lovely statue, lovely beyond measure'.
55. William Edward Heygate, *Care of the Soul; or, Sermons upon some Points of Christian Prudence* (London: Rivington, 1851), p. 1.
56. Heygate, *Care of the Soul*, pp. 11–12 (GL, F 25 He10).
57. Heygate, *Care of the Soul*, p. 143.
58. *Diaries*, vol. VI, p. 224. 6 September 1863. William later helped Heygate in his career.
59. *Diaries*, vol. IV, p. 444.
60. *Diaries*, vol. IV, p. 451.
61. *Diaries*, vol. IV, 445. 24 July 1852.
62. Edward Stuart Talbot, *Memories of Early Life* (London: Mowbray; Milwaukee, WI: Morehouse, 1924), p. 28.
63. Arthur Tilney Bassett, *Gladstone to his Wife* (London: Methuen, 1936), p. 92.
64. Hansard, vol. CXXIII, col. 1691.
65. GL, GLA/GGA/2/10/1/18/98.
66. GL, GLA/GGA/2/10/1/18/99.
67. GL, GLA/GGA/2/7/1/12.
68. GL, GLA/GGA/2/10/1/18/100.
69. *Diaries*, vol. IV, p. 483.
70. GL, GLA/GGA/2/10/1/18/105. 27 December 1852.

71. *Diaries*, vol. IV, p. 494.
72. *Diaries*, vol. IV, p. 513.
73. Hansard, vol. CXXV, col. 1422.
74. 'The Chancellor of the Exchequer at Manchester', *The Times*, 12 October 1853, p. 5 and 13 October 1853, p. 7.
75. Morley, *Life of Gladstone*, vol. I, p. 483.
76. *Diaries*, vol. IV, pp. 579–80. 29 December 1853.
77. *Diaries*, vol. IV, p. 586. 20 January 1854.
78. *Diaries*, vol. IV, p. 555. 9 September 1853.
79. See Ruth Clayton Windscheffel, *Reading Gladstone* (Basingstoke: Palgrave Macmillan; New York: St Martin's Press, 2008), p. 101.
80. In a later emergency budget, however, he was compelled to borrow: see Philip Magnus, *Gladstone: A Biography* (London: Murray, 1954), p. 115.
81. *Diaries*, vol. IV, p. 617.
82. *Diaries*, vol. IV, p. 669.
83. Morley, *Life of Gladstone*, vol. I, p. 543.
84. Crosby, *Two Mr. Gladstones*, p. 81; David Bebbington, *The Mind of Gladstone: Religion, Homer, and Politics* (Oxford: Oxford University Press, 2004), p. 154 (see also p. 176).
85. *Diaries*, vol. IV, p. 77. 27 September 1855.
86. Morley, *Life of Gladstone*, vol. I, pp. 549–50.
87. *Diaries*, vol. V, p. 83. 1 November 1855.
88. *Diaries*, vol. V, pp. 119, 137. 1 April and 30 May 1856.
89. *Diaries*, vol. V, p. 182. 29 December 1856.
90. Morley, *Life of Gladstone*, vol. I, p. 581.
91. Hansard, vol. CXLIV, col. 1799.
92. See Shannon, *Gladstone*, vol. I, pp. 343–44.

5
Manifest in the flesh

Great is the mystery of godliness: God was manifest in the flesh.
(I Timothy 3.16)

The summer of 1859 proved to be a turning point for William, both spiritually and professionally. In June, Palmerston appointed him to the Liberal chancellorship that he was to retain for seven years. This was also the month in which he fell under the spell of Tennyson's *Idylls of the King*, poems which explore two models of manhood in the self-disciplined King Arthur and the adulterous Sir Lancelot. At the end of July he became obsessed with Marion Summerhayes, an artists' model and a courtesan. In October he published a major review article on Tennyson's poems and wrote a sermon on the incarnation which focuses upon the discipline exhibited by Christ in his life on earth. Incarnational theology, the providential order, and religious freedom, subjects on which he focused intensely in his private reflections in the early 1860s, also figured in speeches that he gave in the Commons and in front of mass audiences 'out of doors'. In 1865 he lost his Oxford seat in the Commons and became MP for South Lancashire. After Palmerston's death that year, he became leader of the House of Commons under the new prime minister, Lord John Russell, and took responsibility for bringing in a reform bill. As Richard Shannon comments, however, Russell's designated heir 'envisaged not so much an inauguration of new times as a retrieval of old times. He was indeed a very odd and idiosyncratic Liberal'.[1]

Arthur or Lancelot?

As the chatelaine of Cliveden House in Berkshire, Harriet, Duchess of Sutherland, provided a haven for William, where he could escape from the dust of combat in the Commons at weekends, meet other leading politicians and intellectuals, and enjoy the support of a woman who was to lean on him in her turn from February 1861, when she was widowed. Catherine not only approved of the friendship, but actively encouraged William to rest at Cliveden.[2] The couple visited this Whig stronghold together on Saturday 4 June 1859, when William's friend and colleague, the Duke of Argyll, 'read Tennyson aloud' to them: 'very high strains indeed'.[3] Next day, the two politicians discussed public affairs and William's own position, a fortnight before both joined the new cabinet. Although the Gladstones returned from Cliveden early on the Monday, William did not attend the famous meeting at Willis's Rooms, where the reconciliation of Palmerston and Russell was formalized that afternoon. The resulting Whig-Peelite-Liberal-Radical coalition was to become the Liberal party. On Friday 17 June, the day before he was sworn in at Windsor, William was at the Sutherlands' London residence, Stafford House (later Lancaster House), where he 'heard Tennyson read his Guinevere': 'A memorable time. Up late. X' (indicating rescue work).

Memorable indeed, when one considers the personal resonances of Tennyson's recently published poem for William. While Guinevere's adultery with Lancelot is only vaguely reminiscent of Lady Lincoln's fall from grace, the malevolent Modred's quest to 'track her guilt until he found' is uncannily close to his own experience.[4] William's high ideals relating to marriage and his abomination of the new divorce laws were related in his mind to the stability of the family, of society, and, ultimately, of the state, presided over by Victoria and Albert. Guinevere's 'disloyal life' has 'wrought confusion in the Table Round'. When she first saw the King, she 'thought him cold, / High, self-contained, and passionless, not like him, / "Not like my Lancelot"'. But later, when Arthur visited her at Almesbury Abbey, she 'grovelled with her face against the floor'. He forgave her, 'as Eternal God / Forgives', but could not take her hand: 'that too is flesh, / And in the flesh thou hast sinned; and mine own flesh, / Here looking down on thine polluted, cries / "I loathe thee"'. In Victorian Britain the word 'polluted' was associated with masturbation, pornography (William had found 'sad pollution' in the bawdy *Fabliaux*), and prostitution, as in *David Copperfield*, where Martha contemplates suicide in the Thames's 'polluted stream', and in *Ecce Homo* (1865), where J. R. Seeley observes that both publicans and sinners were avoided 'as a pollution'.[5]

'Guinevere' stirred up strong feelings in William and became Sunday reading in the hot summer of 1859. 'Read Guinevere—twice or thrice over & with much emotion', he recorded on 17 July, 'Also other parts of the Idylls'.[6] Next day he delivered his budget ('1h. 40m.') and read Tennyson, 'who has grasped me with strong hand'. He read 'Guinevere' again the following Sunday. Sales of the *Idylls* indicate that thousands of other readers were reading them that July, and at least one reader conflated poetry and politics in his mind. It was reported in 'Punch's Essence of Parliament' that Mr Punch had passed four days 'on his back on his lovely lawn', reading Tennyson's new poems, one each day, and had then returned to town to hear the chancellor open his budget. He found that the 'Tennysonian music clung to his brain', to the extent that he was moved to verse when writing a long *resumé* of the speech, which begins: 'Gladstone the good, Gladstone the eloquent, / Gladstone the Chancellor of the Exchequer, / Rose in the chamber on the Moon's warm night, / And gave long talk to the perspiring throng'.[7]

On the day that this article appeared in *Punch*, Saturday 30 July 1859, William read an account of the foundation of the Royal Academy of Arts. (He rarely missed a private view at the Academy's summer exhibition, and he visited art dealers as he gradually built up a sizeable collection of pictures, displayed at Carlton House Terrace.) His diary entry ends, 'Saw Somerhayes: full in the highest degree both of interest and of beauty. (22)'.[8] His intense interest in Marion Summerhayes is reflected in thirty-nine references to her in the 1859 diary. He introduced her to his friend William Dyce, a high church Aberdonian whose religious paintings owe as much to German sacred art as they do to Pre-Raphaelitism.[9] *Lady with the Coronet of Jasmine* is an idealized rendering of Beatrice, Dante's guide to paradise in *La Divina Commedia*, the masterwork that had been venerated by William, as it had by Tennyson, since adolescence. 'Saw Summerhayes resp[ecting] picture &c.', he recorded on 6 August: 'That is a very peculiar case: & merits what I wrote of it to Mr. Dyce'.

August and September were devoted to the move to 11 Downing Street, to work on his review (he 'Read Tennyson, Tennyson, Tennyson' at Cliveden),[10] and to Marion. On returning to Hawarden on 18 August, having said goodbye to Marion, he found 'all the children well. Is there not a rod in store for me? We had some family singing'.[11] Catherine was indisposed: she was passing through the menopause. When he returned to London for a cabinet meeting on the 27th he missed Marion, but kept in touch with her by letter. Work on Tennyson continued during the family holiday at Penmaenmawr, which was again interrupted by government business. On Friday 16 September he wrote on Tennyson, bathed in the sea, and set off for London at 2 p.m. Arriving at Downing Street at 10.30, he 'Read Tennyson's Princess 11–3½ with M S: much & variously moved'.[12] Next day he attended a cabinet meeting in the afternoon and 'Saw M. S. a scene of rebuke not to be easily forgotten. 10–1¾'. 'Put me not to rebuke, O Lord, in thine anger', cries the psalmist, in a passage that meant much to William.[13] Although more than adultery in the heart is implied by the word 'scene', as in 1851, there is no sign of the scourge this time. On Sunday he recorded, 'St James's mg.—Chapel Royal aft. Wrote to Duchess of Sutherland ... Read ... Tennyson Idylls, parts ... Saw ... M. S. further', and on Monday 19th, 'Saw ... M. S. 6½ and 7½ and at 11 brought d[itt]o to D.St for 1 hour, esp[ecially] to see the pictures', presumably of interest to an artist's model. When a further cabinet meeting called him back to London from Penmaenmawr, on the 24th, he took his meals at the Oxford and Cambridge Club (preferred for its library) and in the evening was with Marion for two hours, 'winding up'. Yet he saw her again for an hour after a further cabinet meeting on the 26th, commenting, 'all is there on the way, if there be no illusion, to order & good: the case is no common one: may God grant that all go right. To me no trivial matter, for evil or for good. Off by Mail at 9'. For William, 'order' and 'good' are virtually synonymous.

The details of the case remain a mystery, but clearly the Arthurian William was troubled by feelings more commonly associated with Lancelot. As he wrote in his anonymous review of Tennyson's poems in the *Quarterly Review*, 'the Romance of the Round Table bears witness to a more distinct and keener sense of sin'.[14] Guinevere, he suggests, 'prefers the inferior man; and this preference implies a rooted ethical

Manifest in the flesh 101

defect in her nature'.[15] (Six years later, when he 'saw H Hastings', a prostitute, in London, he 'read the whole of Guinevere aloud'.[16]) While drawing parallels between Tennyson and Homer, his highest praise for the *Idylls* sequence is that 'It is national: it is Christian', a combination of epithets most often applied to the Church of England. His argument in the review that 'the life of our Saviour' was 'in principle a model for all' was repeated in his sermon for Epiphany that October, taking John 8.18 as his text and focusing upon a subject that lay at the heart of Tractarian theology—the mystery of the incarnation.[17] He is characteristically cerebral in the sermon, spelling out the 'three main departments' of Christ's manifestation as man that have to be 'carefully separated in our minds'.[18] He argues that the key to our salvation lies in Christ's physical suffering, and that 'in what He suffered, in His experience, lay the discipline which made that Body fit and ready for its function, as the mould and model of the human race'. The biblical passage that lies behind this sentence reads, 'Who in the days of his flesh . . . though he were a Son, yet learned he *obedience* by the things which he suffered; and being made perfect, he became the author of eternal salvation unto all them that obey him' (Hebrews 5.7–9, my emphasis). William's substitution of 'discipline' for 'obedience' reflects his belief in what he called 'the blessings of discipline' in the 1850s, when using the scourge, or 'discipline'.[19]

His rescue efforts with Marion continued in October. On the 14th he records, 'X. . . . I got to D. St. at 10¼ [pm] . . . Saw M. Summerhayes: for whom I wish to exert myself'.[20] Further meetings follow. Then a new dimension comes to light on the 28th, when he writes, 'Saw M. Summerhayes with much interest & satisfaction. We were on poor Mrs Pearsall's case, a most moving one'. So Marion appears to have assisted William on this occasion. Catherine was away from London that day, but was with William in late November and early December when he saw Marion again and read H. G. Jebb's novel about the rescue of a prostitute, *Out of the Depths: The Story of a Woman's Life*, 'a most remarkable book'.[21] On Advent Sunday he had a conversation with Catherine 'on State of the departed—on "Out of the Depths" & kindred subjects'.[22] But there is no evidence that he discussed Marion with Catherine. In the print edition, the entry for Sunday 18 December ends 'Conv[ersation] with C. resp[ecting]

Herbert. Considered the case of M. Summerhayes'.[23] In the original MS diary, however, a dash below the first sentence quoted marks a change of subject on the tightly written page of his small notebook, a convention which is not indicated in the edited version.[24] William seems to have considered the case alone. He wrote to Marion two days later. In the second half of 1859, William's rescue work had continued and was at certain stages shared with his wife. The quality newspapers were reticent about such matters, to a degree that would baffle modern journalists. It is tempting, however, to find a sly hint about William's activities in a piece that he would have read: the 'Imaginary Conversation' between himself and Disraeli which *Punch* published on 26 November 1859. As they chat in Hyde Park, feigning friendliness, Disraeli refers to the 'pretty ancle' of a passing woman.[25]

William's reflections on his fiftieth birthday should be quoted in full:

Behold me then arrived at the close of half a century in this wayward world. Half a century! What do those little words enfold! Grace & glory, sin & shame, hopes, fears, joys, pains, emotions, labours, effort; what a marvel is this life, what a miracle the construction of it for our discipline? And when will it end? When thou willest O Lord: Amen. But though I can say this, & can hope it is the truth of my heart, I have more than ever cause to hang down the head. More than ever have my besetting & peculiar dangers gathered around me during the past year. Yet as I think in a wondrous manner it has pleased the Lord whose eye slumbereth not [II Peter 2.3] to bring me in His own way towards a place of safety.

And what cause I have to be thankful! This morning came into my room my wife and seven children, all well, in body & in soul, all full of love. If God counts up His benefits what a reckoning it will be.

Yet there is in me a resistance to the passage of Time as if I could lay hands on it & stop it: as if youth were yet in me & life & youth were one.

But there are darker things than this: only I hope that the Image of the bound and stricken Saviour may hold me, and the desire never to bring the shadow of sin over the mind & heart of a fellow creature.[26]

'Gladstone the good, Gladstone the eloquent' has retired to his closet to write his humble confessions. Echoes of the Epiphany sermon drafted in October indicate a settled view that it is only through discipline of the kind that was modelled by 'the bound and stricken Saviour' that he can be rescued, as he in turn attempts to rescue others less fortunate than himself, who have sinned 'in the flesh'. More immediately, it is the love of his wife and his children that sustains him on the journey.

The rescue work continued in the 1860s, supported by Catherine. His many letters to her furnish occasional glimpses of the technicalities involved. On 30 July 1863, for example, he wrote from 11 Carlton House Terrace:

My own C. . . . I am also occupied today with a *case* of which I became aware some time ago, during the last recess ^ (but it slumbered until 3 days ago) ^ of a woman who has gone astray and is disposed to go to Clewer—am just going to see Mrs Monsell to ascertain further about it—She is aged 20 & was married I believe at 15: is at the very top of the tree, tells me she has driven her open carriage & pair daily all this year in the Park & the streets. She seems very firm in her intention, but with a certain leaning for the idea of a nunnery—I scarcely know how it will turn out but the character is singular & I believe quite true. Mrs Monsell, I ought to have explained, happens to be in town today on business. I saw yesterday what they call Sister Anne, I believe she is Miss Thorn: and I liked her. Ever afftn WEG'.[27]

William's diary for the next day reveals some of the practical details involved in such cases: 'At 12¾ E. Cowper came & I took her to Mrs Monsell in Rose Street. I saw Mrs M. first, then both. Afterwards she brought me her King Charles Spaniel wh[ich] I promised to take care of. This was her great anxiety. All seemed to go well: & she is to go to Clewer with one of the Sisters on Monday'.[28] He attended a cabinet meeting in the afternoon and then travelled to Hawarden, arriving at 11 p.m., 'all well there D[eo].G[ratias]'.

Three years later, William described another case to Catherine. A prostitute had come up to him 'when out' to assure him, '(a most curious thing) that an Engineer Mr Wynne had a perfectly blameless regard for her and had bought & started her in a shop with a little boy to help in looking after it. That she had tried hard & lived sometimes on 5/ a week—& wholly eschewed doing wrong. I advised her to write to Mrs Monsell and ask for ideas which she declared she would do: I promised to inquire more after some days when she would probably have an answer . . . I think if she could satisfy them at Clewer it would be a great help, & as I told her they might ultimately be a "reference" for her to obtain employment'.[29] In his view, this case also confirmed all that he had feared about the recently introduced divorce laws, which he had strongly opposed. 'Incidentally', he continues, 'she gave me a proof of the way in which that bad Divorce Act has acted on the general idea of marriage—She said that Wynne was quite ready to pay £100 to her husband to get a divorce from her, in order that he might marry her! You see a traffic in this way arises. Before 1857 the very idea was unknown to all but the "higher" classes'.

Meanwhile, probably in 1864, William had met Laura Thistlethwayte, the married lay preacher and former courtesan who was soon to be working among London's 'sick and dying', and with whom he formed a friendship that would last for three decades.[30] The voluminous correspondence between them will be discussed in the next chapter, when we consider the prime minister's response to her intimate memoirs. Gossip among politicians concerning this close relationship began to circulate in June 1866. On 2 July William discussed Mrs Thistlethwayte with both the Duchess of Sutherland and the Duke of Argyll at Cliveden.[31] Four days later he left the keys to Downing Street, having resigned from Palmerston's newly formed cabinet, commenting in the diary, 'Somehow it makes a void'.

The providential order

Back in May 1831 William had had mixed feelings about the positive reception of his anti-reform speech at the Oxford Union, commenting in the diary, 'Oh who can look at these bitterly instructive contrasts & yet deny that there is a Providence wonderfully framing out of a seeming series of accidents the most appropriate & aptest discipline for each of our souls.'[32] Divine providence and the discipline of the soul were to be associated in his mind for the rest of his life. Similarly, his interpretation of apparent accidents remained unchanged three decades later. Compare, for example, his descriptions of the coach overturning in February 1834—'We went down gradually. God commanded it so'[33]—and of Queen Victoria sustaining only minor injuries when 'shot out of her carriage' in October 1863: 'The Queen has had a most Providential escape', he informed Catherine from Balmoral, 'those who value the Queen's life and limb may thank God for having preserved them'.[34]

The providentialist interpretation of accidents was commonplace in Augustan thought. In the *Essay on Man* (Epistle I), Pope wrote, 'All Nature is but Art, unknown to thee; / All Chance, Direction, which thou canst not see'.[35] Not long before giving the Oxford Union speech, William had read Bishop Butler's chapter 'Of the Government of God by Rewards and Punishments' in the *Analogy of Religion*.[36] The divine government of mankind remained central to his theology. In a characteristically convoluted private reflection of October 1859 he wrote, 'Command & prohibition, promise and threat give us one aspect of the various sides of the Divine method for the government of man. Of the two great forms in which it is exhibited will and law they belong more to the former than to the latter. For law is embedded in the providential order & works out its own results: will apparently a power standing outside it though in truth exactly parallel with it'.[37]

An important but hitherto unnoticed feature of William's major speeches out of doors in the 1860s, speeches that made his name as a national public orator, is the manner in which he drew upon his own 'Christian experience', as he had defined it in 1835, and upon the private reflections that we have considered in earlier chapters— on discipline, order, law, spiritual renewal or restoration, and, above all, providence. Take, for example, his Manchester address of April 1862, delivered during the American civil war, when the unemployed workers of his native Lancashire were suffering acute distress owing to the cotton famine. Catherine had become deeply involved in the nationwide effort to support them, keeping the Queen informed of conditions on the ground.[38] As the context of William's speech was to be particularly sensitive, he worked on it for several days before reading it aloud to Catherine, 'by way of trial'.[39] *The Times* reported that 'from 3,000 to 4,000 gentlemen and ladies' cheered the chancellor when he arrived at the Free Trade Hall on the evening of 24 April to present the prizes for the last examination of the Association of Mechanics' Institutes of Lancashire and Cheshire.[40] The mayors of several towns, together with worthies who included William's brother-in-law, Sir Stephen Glynne MP, were on the platform to witness the prize-giving and to hear the address by the apostle of free trade.

William began by acknowledging that the situation was dark, and that the immediate future 'may seem darker still'. But the unemployed operatives and their families were not alone in their suffering. The nation had been in mourning for his ally at Court, the Prince Consort, who died prematurely on 14 December 1861, and whom he now eulogized. 'Perhaps in the wise counsels of Providence', he said, 'it was decreed that that crushing sorrow which came down as sudden as the hurricane, scarcely yet four months ago, upon the august head of our sovereign, should serve, among other uses, that of teaching and helping her subjects to bear up under the sense of affliction and desolation'. At a time like this in Manchester, he continued, we look around for consolation and support, part of which is knowing that severe trials are 'not of one station only but of all'. William, who venerated the aristocracy and was no egalitarian, regarded a person's 'station' or 'estate' as part of the providential order, a position that would have been shared by many who heard or read the speech. The notorious verse in Mrs Alexander's popular hymn 'All things bright and beautiful' (1848)—'The rich man in his castle, / The poor man at his gate, / God made them, high and lowly, / And ordered their estate'—remained in general use until it was omitted from *The English Hymnal* in 1906 by Percy Dearmer, a Christian Socialist.

The 180 prize-winners, however, some as young as twelve, and twenty or thirty of whom were young women, demonstrated that self-improvement was possible within the classes. Here in Manchester, William proclaimed, where 'you know what order is, and what a power it holds', we 'see at work the vast systems of machinery, where ten thousand instruments are ever labouring, each in its own proper place, each with its own proper duty, but all obedient to one law, and all co-operating for one end'. A similar order and obedience to one law is essential for the moral health of the individual:

> In beseeching, especially the young, to study the application to their daily life of that principle of order which both engenders diligence and strength of will, and likewise so multiplies their power, I am well assured that they will find this to be not only

an intellectual, but a moral exercise. Every real and searching effort at self-improvement is of itself a lesson of profound humility; for we cannot move a step without learning and feeling the waywardness, the weakness, the vacillation of our movements, or without desiring to be set up upon the rock that is higher than ourselves. (Applause.) Nor, again, is it likely that the self-denial and self-discipline which these efforts undoubtedly involve will often be cordially undergone . . . An untiring sense of duty, an active consciousness of the perpetual presence of Him who is its author and its law, and a lofty aim beyond the grave—these are the best and most efficient parts, in every sense, of that apparatus wherewith we should be armed, when with full purpose of heart we address ourselves to the life-long work of self-improvement.

He is sharing with his audience beliefs that are the fruit of his devotions and his own sense of waywardness, weakness, and vacillation. This becomes even clearer when he describes what God has 'ordained' for humanity, through divine providence:

Our life from day to day is a true, powerful, and searching discipline, moulding us and making us, whether it be for evil or for good. (Applause.) Nor are these real effects wrought by unreal instruments. Life and the world, their interests, their careers, the varied gifts of our nature, the traditions of our forefathers, the treasures of laws, institutions, usages, of languages, of literature, and of art; all the beauty, glory, and delight with which the Almighty Father has clothed this earth for the use and profit of His children, and which evil, though it has defaced, has not been able utterly to destroy; all these are not merely allowable, but ordained and appointed instruments for the training of mankind,—instruments true and efficient in themselves, though without doubt auxiliary and subordinate to that highest instrument of all which God has prepared to the means of our recovery and final weal by the revelation of Himself. (Applause.)

Here he echoes his private reflections upon the discipline of Christ's body being the 'mould and model of the human race', and the purpose of Christianity being the recovery or 'renewal of every man in the image of his God and Father'.

William took his audience out of themselves and their pressing concerns at a time of trial, culminating in a vision of what he was later to call 'divine learning', relating self-improvement to the building of the spiritual temple, and ultimately to the hope of salvation through Christ's incarnation. But after this glimpse of the promised land, he had to come down from the mountain and discuss the mundane theme of competitive examinations. A late reference to that bible of self-improvement, Samuel Smiles's *Lives of the Engineers*, raised a cheer, and he sent his audience home with a Smilesean message: 'May you live the life which on your deathbed you might desire to have lived; and may you attain all that which merit, industry, and ability may justly deserve! (Cheers.)'

This address was widely reported in the press, was published as a pamphlet, and reprinted in William's later *Gleanings of Past Years* (1879). But its impact was felt most powerfully by the live audience, who were ready to cheer Smiles, and to applaud the workings of almighty God, as the rolling periods were delivered. Here was a famous politician, widely regarded as a future prime minister, speaking to them from the heart, with sincerity and authenticity, and as a Christian who could appeal to nonconformist and churchman alike. They were not to know that the speaker had undergone half a century of 'grace & glory, sin & shame, hopes, fears, joys, pains, emotions, labours, effort', as recorded in his private diaries. But perhaps they sensed it.

Having returned to Hawarden that night, he was back in Manchester next day to receive an address at the town hall, visit the cathedral, and attend 'a luncheon followed by more speeches'.[41] Like Palmerston, William had made a provincial visit with multiple engagements in the 1850s. In subsequent decades the pace quickened. His visit to Bolton and Manchester in October 1864 occurred at a doubly sensitive time. Not only was the American civil war still raging, but he had just written a letter to Palmerston on the defence estimates, a subject on which he and the prime minister profoundly disagreed. Having angered his chief in May by appearing to support universal suffrage in a speech in the Commons, he now promised to 'endeavour to observe caution' in his speeches in Lancashire, where it might be possible to gauge public opinion on taxation and expenditure.[42]

On Tuesday 11 October he was greeted by a 'public reception' at Bolton station, before visiting 'Buildings & Institutions' there, speaking to a 'dense assembly' in the 'stifling atmosphere' of the temperance hall, and retiring to a private house 'to meet a large party'.[43] Next morning, Wednesday, he and Catherine set off in a procession of three hours to 'Mr Barnes's Park' in Farnworth, which he was due to open 'before a mass of 20000 or 30000 people'. (A general holiday had been declared.) He then spoke for forty-five minutes with some difficulty, praising Barnes as a representative philanthropist and commenting more broadly on relations between master and man in the factory system. 'It is offending against the will and designs of Divine Providence', he said, 'if we refuse to recognize the fact that moral associations and social and endearing ties of affection belong to, and ought never to be severed from, the relation between the master and the workman. (Cheers.)'[44] Quoting this passage the following morning, a *Times* leader-writer commented archly, 'To the disciples of Mr. Mill this language must savour of heresy, for it certainly is suggestive of patriarchal tutelage on the one side and dutiful attachment on the other. Yet, after all, it expresses little more than what all must admit to be desirable, at least until society is completely re-organized'.[45]

As the leader-writer also pointed out, these provincial speaking tours were 'new duties' for leading public men. And, as the paper's reporter commented, the chancellor's engagements during his visit to Lancashire were 'rather formidable'. His address was followed by a banquet, with more speeches, and departure for his native Liverpool, where he held business meetings and spoke after the mayor's evening banquet. With Robertson, his supportive brother, in the audience, he warned against 'over-extended responsibilities' with regard to the colonies, saying, 'What we have now to do is, I think, to cultivate what Providence has given us, but not to seek any addition to the sphere of our labours . . . (Hear.)'[46] The leader-writer thought that he handled the subject with 'great tact and caution'. Next day, Thursday 13 October, he returned to Liverpool, where he held a number of meetings, spoke for an hour at St George's Hall, visited the Free Library and Museum, and dined out: 'A hard days work'. On Friday the 14th he received an address at Manchester's town hall, where he spoke for an hour, visited the 'beautiful Assize Courts' and met its architect, Waterhouse, 'said a word' to 3,000 persons at the Exchange, then attended the mayor's luncheon, and at 2 p.m. distributed prizes at the Free Trade Hall in front of 6,000 or more persons, speaking for about forty-five minutes 'with considerable effort from the vastness of the crowd'. With Catherine alongside him, he revisited the theme of his inspiring speech of 1862. Only the cheers distinguished his peroration from that of a sermon:

> It is more than ever necessary that the powers of the Christian revelation—of the Christian faith—should be exercised and felt over the whole surface of society and down to its profoundest depths. (Cheers.) But that Christian revelation has not been only a revelation of Christian truth, it was a revelation in which Christian truth was designed to carry with it and to draw after it the perfect development of every human excellence. (Cheers.) The soaring faculties of the imagination, the searching powers of the mind, that which has made philosophers, artists, and poets, who are the glory of mankind—these things were not prescribed by Christianity. They were elevated into a higher sphere.

This had been a gruelling triumphal tour. How did William assess it? He reached Worsley Hall, the home of the Dowager Lady Ellesmere, at 5 p.m. on the Friday, 'and so ended in peace an exhausting, flattering, I hope not intoxicating circuit', he wrote in the diary.[47] 'God knows I have not courted them', he added, 'I hope I do not rely on them: I pray I may turn them to account for good. It is however impossible not to love the people from whom such manifestations come, as met me in every quarter'. The diary entry ends, 'Somewhat haunted by dreams of halls, & lines of people, & great assemblies'. Having spent the weekend recovering at Worsley, he returned to Hawarden, where he sorted his letters and wrote to Catherine. Two days later, on 19 October, came news from Clumber: 'Newcastle's death removes the very last of those contemporaries who were also my political friends. How it speaks to me! "Be doing: and be done"' (Matthew 7.12). The unhappily married 5th Duke, his friend at Eton, Oxford, and Westminster, was fifty-three. Other Peelite deaths had loosened his political moorings earlier in the decade: the 4th Earl of Aberdeen in 1860, Sidney Herbert in 1861, and Sir James Graham Bt the same year. The loss of his Oxford seat in July 1865 would distance him still further from his Tory years. For the moment, however, he had to deal with the prime minister.

On 19 October 1864, Palmerston finally responded to William's Balmoral letter of the 6th. The 'present State of Things in the various Parts of the world', he explained, made it impossible to reduce defence expenditure.[48] William replied from Hawarden, 'in a rather decisive tone', on 22 October: 'My belief is that our expenditure for defence is larger than the reasonable wants of the country require'.[49] When Palmerston's reply arrived, William forwarded it to Catherine with a letter dated 9 November, Carlton House Terrace:

> My own C. After more than a fortnight's delay, I received yesterday evening the enclosed very unfavourable letter from Lord Palmerston. I send with it the draft of my reply. Please to return them tomorrow by Willy—for they ought not to be even for that short time out of my custody but I do not like to keep you in the dark until next week . . . This *sort* of controversy keeps the nerves too highly strung, and makes me sensitive, fretful, & impatient. I am not by nature brave, I am always between two fears, and I am more afraid of running away than of holding my ground. But I do not quite forget how plentifully I am blessed & sustained.[50]

Writing privately to his devoted wife, he can attribute his public stance in the masculine arena of politics to the second of two kinds of fear experienced by soldiers under fire. He speaks from the heart.

Following Palmerston's death, on 18 October 1865, William's new parliamentary duties increased his workload. As always, however, other duties also called, and on 3 November he delivered his valedictory address as Rector of Edinburgh University. 'My address occupied rather over 2 hours', he recorded: 'audience 2000: much kind feeling. I omitted 40 or 45 minutes worth of matter. But I could not deliver the text exactly'.[51] His appreciative audience were spared, as extensive passages in the printed text were somewhat plodding, like many of his publications on Homer and the classics. At the core of his address, however, was an arresting argument. The Greek religion and Christianity are often seen as rivals, but 'God has been and is the God and Father and Governor of the whole human race'.[52] He continued, 'The real paradox then would be not to assert, but to deny or even to overlook, the part which may have been assigned to any race, and especially to a race of such unrivalled gifts, in that great and all-embracing plan for the rearing and training of the human children of our Father in heaven, which we call the Providential Government of the World'. Towards the end of the address, William summarized his argument, that 'Besides the loftiest part of the work of Providence entrusted to the Hebrew race, there was other work to do, and it was done elsewhere', and related it to the state in which he and his audience found themselves.[53] 'We live in times', he declaimed, 'when the whole nature of our relation to the unseen world is widely, eagerly, and assiduously questioned', and he challenged all who are 'called in any manner to move in the world of thought' to adopt 'a chivalry of controversy like the ancient chivalry of arms'.[54] (For William, part of the attraction of Tennyson's chivalric vision in the *Idylls* lay in the poet's belief in the 'unseen world'.) The distance that he had travelled from his time in Tractarian Oxford is evident in these words: 'Let us avoid the error of seeking to cherish a Christianity of isolation . . . It must be filled full with human and genial warmth, in true sympathy with every true instinct and need of man'. John Beer traces a growing awareness in the second half of the nineteenth century that belief in providence was waning, and argues that the ideal of Romantic love tended to serve as a substitute.[55] For William, however, whose ecclesiology was widening, a providentialist understanding of the 'rearing and training' of humanity remained a central pillar of his theology.

The universality of Christianity

In the nineteenth century, the 'many mansions' text from the fourth gospel (John 14.2), discussed in Chapter 3, was applied not only to the hope of heaven, but also to the universal scope of the gospel, transcending the boundaries that separated nations, races, and traditions. In one of his Oxford notebooks, William had written, 'Among the brightest of the glories of the Christian religion, is its universality. Nor is it a doctrine less consoling to man, than indicative of the grandeur of the Sacrifice of Christ, to reflect that it embraces all the degrees, and by Consequence as well as by direct Revelation, all the subjects of sin'.[56] And in an adjacent note, 'In my Father's house are many mansions. Surely then there is room for some of a more placid, and some of a more excitable temperament: for an impassioned fervour, and a quietude the result of deliberate persuasion, without advancing against the one or the other respectively the ungenerous charges of fanaticism or formality'. His book on *Church Principles* (1840) is 'surprisingly eirenic', attempting to reconcile different traditions or sects.[57] A degree of disillusionment with Tractarianism after Newman's conversion to Rome in 1845, and with the Anglican bishops after the Gorham judgment in 1850, accelerated his movement towards a broader understanding of the Church of England and of other traditions.

In his tombstone biography, John Morley offered this rare observation on William's religion: 'His persistent incursions all through his long life into the multifarious doings, not only of his own anglican communion, but of the Latin church of the west, as well as of the motley Christendom of the east, puzzled and vexed political whippers-in, wire-pullers, newspaper editors, leaders, colleagues; they were the despair of party caucuses; and they made the neutral man of the world smile, as eccentricities of genius and rather singularly chosen recreations. All this was, in truth, of the very essence of his character, the manifestation of its profound unity'.[58] William's stance on the providential government of the world was inclusively Anglican, rather than specifically 'broad church' Anglican.[59] For although the Church of England was often internally divided on party lines, usually crudely defined as evangelical, high church, and 'broad' church, or liberal, the very breadth of the established church made it possible to be hospitable to other communions, and even other faiths, in principle at least.

Among the Lancashire audiences that William addressed in the 1860s, a large proportion would have been nonconformists. Their positive response to his speeches clearly moved him. Perry Butler states that he was the most devout high churchman among the Liberal alliance of 1859, and that although in certain ways he remained extremely conservative, as in his refusal to sanction the abolition of university tests, in others 'he was coming to share the outlook of nonconformists': 'Both now tended to believe that the promotion of moral regeneration would be advanced most efficiently by increasing the freedom of competition between the various sects'.[60] Similarly, Colin Matthew argues that, although William's personal beliefs remained 'resolutely "catholic"', he enlarged his experience in the 1860s by a series of meetings with 'dissenters', organized by the congregationalist minister, Christopher Newman Hall.[61] These meetings 'did not encourage intimacy, but they developed respect on both sides'.

William's conservative and liberal sides are both in evidence in his political life and his churchmanship. While engaging in discussions with nonconformists, he ensured that his children were brought up as committed high Anglicans. He took Willy to the early service at Margaret Chapel (All Saints) in April 1859, for example, and arranged for Stephen to be confirmed by his friend Samuel Wilberforce, Bishop of Oxford, two weeks later.[62] He had lunch in Willy's undergraduate rooms at Christ Church the day after the confirmation, before embarking on a round of visits in Oxford that culminated in his induction as a fellow of All Souls, a high point in his love affair with the university. Yet his parliamentary divorce from the university began in 1859, in Roy Jenkins's view: he was 'sore' about the constituency's nomination of a candidate to oppose him (unsuccessfully) that year, and he visited Oxford only three times in the remaining six years of his tenure as a burgess.[63] His responses to events, people, and institutions were often multifaceted, as contrary forces within him were in play. He was indeed a man of strange and sharp contrasts.

Earlier in this chapter we considered his sermon of October 1859, where he argued that in what Christ suffered, 'in His experience, lay the discipline which made that Body fit and ready for its function, as the mould and model of the human race'. Having declared that love is the 'alpha & the omega of the gospel', he ended the sermon with a crucial statement on the Christian's hope of resurrection: 'for each of His followers it [is] not what we think, it is not ^ even ^ what we do, but it is what we are, upon which our all, yea our all in all depends' (I Corinthians 15.28).[64] The ever active 'mind of Gladstone' (what we think) is frequently engaged in theological reflection. The imitation of Christ in what we do (Thomas à Kempis) is his ideal in private and public life. Yet, he believes, it is the existential reality of 'what we are' that will come to judgement. Five years later, on 7 February 1864, he wrote in a sermon on 1 John 4.2–3: 'Every spirit, that confesseth that Jesus Christ is come in the flesh, is of God; And every spirit that confesseth not, that Jesus Christ is come in the flesh, is not of God: and this is that spirit of Antichrist'. 'Upon this religion', he wrote, 'the sublimest intellects have wrought . . . Yet like the huge earth on its axis, so this mighty system hangs upon a simple central truth, which may be spoken in one word, and that word is Emmanuel, God with us [Matthew 1.23]. Christianity is Christ: and Christ is the Eternal Son of God, made flesh for us'.[65] This incarnationalist sermon complements that of 1859 in its return to the fundamentals of the faith. It represents William's private response to an extraordinary set of ecclesiastical controversies that raged between November 1863 and July 1864.

Biblical criticism was first widely discussed by non-specialists in Britain in the 1860s, following the publication of *Essays and Reviews* (1860), a collection of papers by clergy and laymen that became notorious after it was attacked by Bishop Wilberforce. Debate crystallized around the final contribution, 'On the Interpretation of Scripture', by Benjamin Jowett, professor of Greek at Oxford and a liberal broad churchman. Two years later, the English bishops met to discuss the publications of Bishop Colenso of Natal, which some of his colleagues in South Africa considered to be heretical. Once again, Wilberforce led the attack, and the two controversies came to be lumped together in many of the countless pamphlets and articles that were published over the ensuing months. William, who followed every twist and turn in these debates, was particularly impressed by his friend the Bishop of St David's charge to his clergy in 1863. Connop Thirlwall, a bishop of independent mind and establishment spirit, explained that he and his colleagues had censured *Essays and Reviews* because 'its contents *were* repugnant to the doctrine of the Church'.[66] Similarly, in the case of Colenso he concluded that it was wrong for a bishop to announce 'opinions contrary to those which were generally received in the Church'.[67] Thirlwall ended by encouraging each of his brethren to 'ripen' his 'inner life', and to discharge his pastoral duties assiduously.[68] William described the charge as 'a great production'.[69]

One Sunday evening in July 1864, as the arguments continued to rumble on, William read aloud to the household ('with an explanation') Archbishop Longley's pastoral letter to the clergy and laity of the province of Canterbury, and an address, 'for signature', thanking the archbishops for their pastorals on *Essays and Reviews*.[70] Like Thirlwall, Longley focused upon the way in which 'Holy Scripture is held by our Church'.[71] One essayist seemed to mean that 'the Word of God' and 'God's Word written' was in fact the 'work of Man', while another maintained that some parts were not authentic. Although William was one of 137,000 signatories to the address to the archbishops, he made no public pronouncements on the matter himself. His sermon of the previous February focused upon the incarnation, rather than the scriptures.

During a weekend at Cliveden, in April 1864, he met Sir John Acton Bt, a thirty-year-old cradle Catholic and the stepson of his friend and colleague, the second Earl Granville. They immediately took to one another. Acton wrote to their mutual friend, Ignaz von Döllinger, now sixty-five, from Cliveden, saying that William had 'explained with rare trust his whole policy', including the disestablishment of the Irish church.[72] 'My hopes for his future ministry are much increased', he declared: 'I discovered an energy of the will, a resolve and an indignation . . . that were salutary and that foreshadow consequences for world history'. William recorded that he returned to town with Acton, 'whom the more I see the more I like. *Si sic omnes*' (if only everyone were like that).[73] It was almost a repeat of his response to meeting Döllinger in Munich in 1845, when he 'lost his heart' to 'one of the most liberal and catholic in mind of all the persons of his communion' whom he had known.[74]

Döllinger and Acton, each in his generation, opposed from within the Catholic fold those aspects of their communion which William attacked from outside, Vaticanism and ultramontanism, both of which were strongly supported by his former ally, Henry Manning. As we have seen, in 1851, the year of Manning's conversion, William had defended the right of 'our Roman Catholic fellow-Christians' to religious freedom and equality. He argued in the Commons that 'We cannot change the profound and resistless tendencies of the age towards religious liberty'.[75] Now, in 1864, he is deeply disturbed when Pius IX's Syllabus of Errors anathematizes the proposition that the pope should adjust to 'progress, liberalism and modern civilization', thus destroying the hopes of his liberal Catholic friends for intellectual independence.[76] William's heart is as engaged as his mind in his deeply personal response to events which, like Manning's and Hope's conversions, are landmarks in his own spiritual life.

The same was true of his reaction to Newman's own personal history, the *Apologia pro Vita sua*, published serially in 1864 in response to Charles Kingsley's insinuations about him. Whereas William and Newman, eight years his senior, had followed similar paths as young men, the future cardinal's apostasy in 1845 had created a permanent rift. At Windsor in November 1859, William had met and liked Charles Kingsley, another passionate, sometimes headstrong man, who constantly fought to keep his emotions in check. In the first half of 1864 he refers in the diary to the *Apologia*, and the pamphlets from which it sprang, no fewer than nine times. His reading of Newman can best be described as 'strong'. One Sunday in April, at Cliveden, he wrote in his diary, 'Read Newmans (trumpery) Letter'.[77] Whereas his extensive marginalia in his copy of Part III of the *Apologia* are mainly sympathetic, quietly marking parallels between Newman and himself, those in Part VI, where Newman describes his conversion of October 1845, indicate a distinct quickening of the pulse.[78] While strenuously defending the right of all Christians to exercise freedom in their religious beliefs within their own traditions, he continued to regard a conversion to Roman Catholicism as an act of infidelity.

He himself remained deeply committed to the Church of England, drawing strength from its liturgy in regular, often daily church-going. On losing his Oxford seat in 1865, he attended morning and evening services at St Deiniol's Church, Hawarden, commenting in his diary, 'Always in straits the Bible in Church supplies my need. Today it was in 1st Lesson I. Jer. 19. "And they shall fight against thee: but they shall not prevail against thee: for I am with thee, saith the Lord, to deliver thee" '.[79] Next day, Monday 17 July 65, he wrote, 'Ch 8½ A.M. Again came consolation in the Psalms 86.16: it did the same for me Ap. 17 1853.' Here he referred to the support that he had found in the same verse from the Psalms on the eve of his first budget speech, then, as now, carefully logged in his daily diary as a providential sign and a resource for future years.

If such continuity reflects William's conservative side, his review of J. R. Seeley's *Ecce Homo* (1865), a controversial 'survey of the life and work of Jesus Christ', represents a surprisingly liberal position. The book was widely condemned, often without being read, for its apparent failure to acknowledge Christ's divinity (the subject of Henry Parry Liddon's Bampton Lectures of the following year). 'Supposing, then', William wrote in his review, 'that the author of that work has approached his subject on the human side, has dealt with our Lord as with a man, has exhibited to us what purport to be a human form and lineaments, is he therefore at once to be condemned? Certainly not at once, if it be true, as it seems to be true, that in this respect he has only done what our Lord himself, by His ordinary and usual exhibition of Himself, both did, and encouraged the common hearer of His addresses, and beholder of His deeds, to do'.[80] When William argues that 'through the fair gloss of His manhood, we perceive the rich bloom of His divinity', he cites a text that we have encountered before: 'And they shall call his name Emmanuel, which being interpreted is, God with us' (Matthew 1.23). Seeley was pleased with the review, and Connop Thirlwall declared that it was 'a very manly act, though only a tribute of justice to a much-wronged book'.[81]

On his fifty-sixth birthday, at the end of 1865, William commented in the diary that he had begun the year 'again more heavily weighted than ever, more likely than ever, unless God defend me, to lose the balance of the soul. I trust to acquire more of the faculty & habit of throwing myself continually upon God and His inexhaustible mercy'.[82] In October, further parliamentary duties had weighed him down to earth even more, drawing his attention away from the 'unseen world'. So how would the balance of his soul be in three years' time, when he became prime minister?

Notes

1. Richard Shannon, *Gladstone*, 2 vols. (London: Methuen, 1982–99), vol. II, p. xii.
2. See, for example, GL, GLA/GGA/2/7/1/14. 20 May 1861?
3. *Diaries*, vol. V, p. 398.
4. *The Poems of Alfred Tennyson*, ed. Christopher Ricks (London and New York: Longman/Norton, 1969), p. 1727 (line 59). Subsequent quotations are from lines 217–18, 402–4, 412, 541–53.
5. *David Copperfield* (1849–50), Ch. XLVI; J. R. Seeley, *Ecce Homo: A Survey of the Life and Work of Jesus Christ* (London and New York: Macmillan, 1900), p. 255.
6. *Diaries*, vol. V, p. 410.
7. *Punch*, 37 (July–December 1859), 50.
8. *Diaries*, vol. V, p. 413.
9. On William's friendship with and patronage of Dyce, see *Diaries*, vol. III, pp. 116, 329; vol. V, p. 131; Marcia Pointon, *William Dyce, 1806–1864: A Critical Biography* (Oxford: Clarendon, 1979), pp. 55, 58, 66, 131, 166.
10. *Diaries*, vol. V, p. 416. 13 August 1859.
11. *Diaries*, vol. V, p. 418.
12. *Diaries*, vol. V, p. 424.

13. See his collection of Psalms (BL, 44,833, f. 10r) and, for example, *Diaries*, vol. IX, p. 585.
14. 'Tennyson's Poems', *Quarterly Review*, 106 (July–October 1859), 454–85 (468).
15. 'Tennyson's Poems', p. 478.
16. *Diaries*, vol. VI, p. 342. 16 March 1865.
17. William had read Robert Isaac Wilberforce's *Doctrine of the Incarnation* (1848) and *Sermons on the new Birth of Man's Nature* (1850), where Christ as the 'pattern man' is discussed. See Bruce D. Griffith and Jason R. Radcliff, *Grace and Incarnation: The Oxford Movement's Shaping of the Character of Modern Anglicanism* (Cambridge: Clarke, 2022), pp. 104–19.
18. BL, 44,781.f.124r. For further commentary, see David Bebbington, *The Mind of Gladstone: Religion, Homer, and Politics* (Oxford: Oxford University Press, 2004), p. 137.
19. The word 'discipline' occurs only once in the King James Version, at Job 30.10.
20. *Diaries*, vol. V, p. 431.
21. *Diaries*, vol. V, p. 442. 26 November 1859. He sometimes gave copies of the novel to prostitutes.
22. *Diaries*, vol. V, p. 442. 27 November 1859.
23. *Diaries*, vol. V, p. 447.
24. See LPL, MS 1435, f. 65.
25. *Punch*, 37 (July–December 1859), 213.
26. *Diaries*, vol. V, p. 450. 29 December 1859.
27. GL, GLA/GGA/2/10/1/21/118, quoted in part in Arthur Tilney Bassett, *Gladstone to his Wife* (London: Methuen, 1936), pp. 145–46.
28. *Diaries*, vol. VI, p. 217.
29. GL, GLA/GGA/2/10/1/23/3. 12 January 1866, Carlton House Terrace.
30. See Jenny West, 'Gladstone and Laura Thistlethwayte, 1865–75', *Historical Research*, 80, 209 (August 2007), 368–92 (371). West detects 'a pronounced tendency . . . to seek to protect his reputation', even in modern biographies (p. 370).
31. *Diaries*, vol. VI, pp. 448–49.
32. *Diaries*, vol. I, p. 361. 30 Mary 1831.
33. *Diaries*, vol. II, p. 89. 14 February 1834.
34. GL, GLA/GGA/2/10/1/22/8. Letter from William to Catherine, 8 October 1863.
35. *Pope: Poetical Works*, ed. Herbert Davis (London: Oxford University Press, 1966), p. 249.
36. Joseph Butler, *The Analogy of Religion natural and revealed to the Constitution and the Course of Nature*, intro. Henry Morley, 4th edn (London: Routledge, 1890), pp. 28–40.
37. *Diaries*, vol. V, p. 430. Hawarden, Sunday 9 October 1859.
38. See Mary Drew, *Catherine Gladstone* (London: Nisbet, 1919), pp. 95–98.
39. *Diaries*, vol. VI, p. 117. 23 April 1862.

40. 'Mr. Gladstone upon competitive Examinations', *The Times*, 25 April 1862, p. 7.
41. *Diaries*, vol. VI, p. 117. 24 April 1862.
42. *Gladstone and Palmerston: being the Correspondence of Lord Palmerston with Mr. Gladstone, 1851–1865*, ed. Philip Guedella (London: Gollanz, 1928), pp. 281, 292.
43. *Diaries*, vol. VI, p. 306.
44. *The Times*, 13 October 1864, p. 7.
45. *The Times*, 14 October 1864, p. 6.
46. *The Times*, 13 Oct 1864, p. 7.
47. *Diaries*, vol. VI, p. 306.
48. Guedalla, *Gladstone and Palmerston*, p. 300.
49. *Diaries*, vol. VI, p. 308. Guedalla, *Gladstone and Palmerston*, p. 305.
50. GL, GLA/GGA/2/10/1/22/64, misquoted in Bassett, *Gladstone to his Wife*, p. 164.
51. LPL, MS 1439, f. 18. *Diaries*, vol. VI, p. 394, wrongly gives 'on' for 'over' in the original.
52. *Address on the Place of ancient Greece in the providential Order of the World, delivered before the University of Edinburgh, on the Third of November, 1865*, 4th edn (London: Murray, 1865), p. 5.
53. *Place of ancient Greece*, p. 57.
54. *Place of ancient Greece*, pp. 64–66.
55. See John Beer, *Providence and Love: Studies in Wordsworth, Channing, Myers, George Eliot, and Ruskin* (Oxford: Clarendon, 1998).
56. BL, 44,719, f. 200.
57. Perry Butler, *Gladstone, Church, State and Tractarianism: A Study of his Religious Ideas and Attitudes, 1809–1859* (Oxford: Clarendon; New York: Oxford University Press, 1982), p. 64.
58. John Morley, *The Life of William Ewart Gladstone*, 3 vols. (London and New York: Macmillan, 1903), vol. I, p. 152.
59. Cf. Bebbington, *Mind of Gladstone*, pp. 137–39.
60. Butler, *Gladstone, Church, State and Tractarianism*, p. 37. He supported the burials bill (1862), often demanded by nonconformists.
61. H. C. G. Matthew, *Gladstone, 1809–1898* (Oxford: Clarendon, 1997), p. 138.
62. *Diaries*, vol. V, pp. 388, 392.
63. Roy Jenkins, *Gladstone* (London: Macmillan, 1995), p. 209.
64. BL, 44,781, f. 127.
65. BL, 44,781, f. 172.
66. *Remains, Literary and Theological, of Connop Thirlwall, late Lord Bishop of St. David's*, ed. J. J. Stewart Perowne, 3 vols. (London: Daldy, Isbister, 1877–78), vol. II, p. 12.
67. Thirlwall, *Remains*, vol. II, p. 62.
68. Thirlwall, *Remains*, vol. II, p. 87.
69. *Diaries*, vol. VI, p. 239. 22 November 1863.
70. *Diaries*, vol. VI, p. 288. 10 July 1864. For the address, see BL, 44,599, f. 89.

71. Charles Thomas Longley, *A pastoral Letter to the Clergy and Laity of the Province of Canterbury* (London: Clowes, 1864), p. 2.
72. See Roland Hill, *Lord Acton* (New Haven and London: Yale University Press, 2000), p. 94.
73. *Diaries*, vol. VI, p. 267. 4 April 1864. William recommended Acton for a peerage in 1869.
74. See Morley, *Gladstone*, vol. I, p. 319.
75. W. E. Gladstone, *Speech on the Ecclesiastical Titles Assumption Bill, 25 March 1851* (London: Bradley, 1851), pp. 29, 28.
76. See Bebbington, *Mind of Gladstone*, pp. 223–24.
77. *Diaries*, vol. VI, p. 271. 24 April 1864.
78. For further details see Michael Wheeler, 'Gladstone Reads his Contemporaries', in *The Edinburgh History of Reading: Modern Readers*, ed. Mary Hammond (Edinburgh: Edinburgh University Press, 2020), pp. 83–103 (pp. 86–90).
79. *Diaries*, vol. VI, p. 370. Sunday 16 July 1865.
80. W. E. Gladstone, *'Ecce Homo'* (London: Strahan, 1868), pp. 108–9.
81. See GL, GLA/GGA/2/10/1/23/44; *Letters to a Friend, by Connop Thirlwall, late Lord Bishop of St. David's*, ed. Arthur Penrhyn Stanley (London: Bentley, 1881), p. 132.
82. *Diaries*, vol. VI, p. 406. 29 December 1865.

6
Fight the good fight

Fight the good fight with all thy might!
Christ is thy Strength, and Christ thy Right;
Lay hold on life, and it shall be
Thy joy and crown eternally.

J. S. B. Monsell[1]

On 7 April 1871, William's reading for Good Friday included 'Dr Monsell's Hymns', the most famous of which is based upon 1 Timothy 6.12.[2] It was not until October that year that he could take a holiday of 'two whole days' for the first time since becoming prime minister, so intense had been his battle for justice in Ireland.[3] His cabinet had been sworn in at Windsor Castle on 9 December 1868, following a general election dominated by the Irish question. Three other battles were also to be fought between his sixtieth and seventieth birthdays. The first was related to his intense relationship with Laura Thistlethwayte, a married lay preacher, said to have been a former courtesan, whom he described as 'a prominent object' in his annual review of 1869.[4] The 'great battle', he reminded her in October that year, is fought 'in soul and spirit' against 'the Evil One'.[5] Secondly, on 6 April 1874, two months after the government's resignation, he wrote to Catherine from Hawarden Castle, 'I am convinced that the welfare of mankind does not now depend on the State or the world of politics: the real battle is being fought in the world of thought, where a deadly attack is made with great tenacity of purpose and over a wide field upon the greatest treasure of mankind, the belief in God, and the Gospel of Christ.'[6] Providence, he believed, had equipped him to fight the good fight in defence of the Church of England, part of the holy catholic church, as a bulwark against 'unbelief'. His main weapon was the pen. Thirdly, having taken up arms in the national debate on the Eastern question, he reflected that he had passed through an unprecedented period of parliamentary history, 'when the battle to be fought was a battle of justice humanity freedom law, all in their first elements from the very root, and all on a gigantic scale.'[7] In this chapter we begin with the extraordinary first year of his premiership, when his public mission to pacify Ireland coincided with yet another private struggle with temptation.

The great battle against the evil one

William's *Chapter of Autobiography*—a defence of what appeared to be a change of mind on Ireland—was published on 23 November 1868, the day before he lost his seat in South-West Lancashire. (He was, however, elected by the constituents of Greenwich.) The principles behind his Irish policy had been explained in a series of speaking engagements out of doors. 'There is the Church of Ireland', he thundered at Wigan, 'there is the land of Ireland, there is the education of Ireland . . . they are all so many branches from one trunk, and that trunk is the tree of what is called the Protestant ascendancy . . . It is upon that system that we are banded together to make war.'[8] Referring obliquely to the Upas tree, he told the large crowd that the ascendancy was 'still there like a tall tree of noxious growth, lifting its head to heaven and darkening and poisoning the land so far as its shadow can extend.' During the election campaign, John Tenniel caught William's chivalric idealism in full-page *Punch* cartoons, portraying him as a knight in shining armour, jousting with Disraeli in a tournament.[9] By February 1873, however, after many gruelling sessions in the Commons, the premier was seen by Tenniel as a determined jump jockey who, having cleared stone fences labelled 'Irish Church' and 'Irish Land', 'came a cropper' at the third, 'Irish Education'.[10]

Five days after delivering the Wigan speech, William heard that his beloved friend and confidante, the Dowager Duchess of Sutherland, had died. His pained reflections on this loss have chivalric and eschatological overtones. 'Why this noble and tender spirit should have had such bounty for me', he recorded, 'and should have so freshened my advancing years, my absorbed and clouded mind, I cannot tell. But I feel, strange as it might sound, ten years the older for her death.

May the rest and light and peace of God be with her ever more & more until *that day*.'[11] None, he believed, would 'fill her place' for him. Twelve months later he would confess that friendships with women had 'constituted no small portion' of his existence, and that in every 'principal case' they were women older than himself.[12] But the woman in whom he confided, and whom he now addressed as 'Dear Spirit', was his junior by almost twenty-two years.

According to an article of 2004 in the ODNB, Mrs Laura Thistlewayte was born at Kevin Street barracks, Dublin, the daughter of a Captain Bell and his second wife. After an 'unsupervised' childhood, she became a shopgirl and prostitute in Belfast, before moving to Dublin and then London, where she was 'protected' by wealthy lovers as a courtesan. In 1852 she married a wealthy subaltern whose brother had been one of her clients. Frederick Thistlethwayte had a house in Grosvenor Square and preached to large audiences in Hyde Park. Laura, herself a fervent convert, preached in London and Dingwall, declaring herself to be a Methodist. The marriage between these unusual individuals was not a success. Thistlethwayte denied responsibility for her huge debts, was not always present when she entertained prominent men, and died in 1887 from a self-inflicted shot wound.

In 2007 Jenny West published a substantial revisionary paper in which she argues that the evidence relating to Laura's career as a courtesan contains inconsistencies and inaccuracies, as William himself believed.[13] More significantly, West questions the tendency of biographers to protect William's reputation. They suggest that he was tempted into a friendship in which he became bound. Quite the reverse: the friendship was conducted at considerable intensity and risk during his first administration, and he made no serious attempt to withdraw from it. Although we have William's letters to Laura, the precise nature of the relationship, she concludes, remains a mystery, not least because, late in life, he burned her autobiographical writings and her early letters to him.

He met her in 1864, possibly through their mutual friend the Duke of Newcastle, and formed a relationship that became the subject of rumour two years later. As usual, he ignored the tittle-tattle. Unlike some of his political colleagues, he continued to believe that she was innocent of the charges levelled at her by polite society.[14] After his Irish Church bill had received the Royal Assent, on 26 July 1869, the friendship intensified and became sexually charged. His diary entry for 2 July ends, 'Dined with the Thistlethwaytes. She promised me some personal history. Saw Ramsay X.'[15] The 'X' clearly refers to Ramsay, but there were also to be many 'Xs' associated with Laura. Having reminded her of her promise, in a letter dated 25 August, he was reading 'Thistlethwayte MS' at Hawarden Castle five weeks later.[16]

The arrival of the MS in instalments upset the sense of order that William tried to maintain through his Hawarden routine—attending church at 8.30 a.m., keeping abreast of voluminous correspondence on matters of state and church, working on the Irish Land bill, reorganizing the books. 'My dear Mrs Thistlethwayte', he wrote on 1 October, 'I mean to read all in sequence, when it is complete, & this is at the risk of being put a little past my sleep as I found last night.'[17] We are presented with commentary but no text, so the little that we know of Laura's history can only be gleaned from sporadic and often obscure references to past events in William's letters to her. Much more is to be learned there about his own spiritual life. In this same letter, for example, he writes, 'I do not see that your ardour "for the Protestant faith" was not a true loving faith in Christ'. This rather vague statement is followed by one that makes his own position perfectly clear: 'The Church is or ought to be the continued manifestation of the Incarnation of Christ: and of this idea "Christendom", and all that it imports, is a noble, though a most imperfect expression.' It later became apparent that they should avoid discussion on 'church matters'.

Encouraged by William's sympathetic response, Laura quickly dispatched further instalments. By 5 October he had received numbers 11–13, while his thanks for numbers 8–10 were yet on their way to her. Six days later he received and read instalments 14–17. Letters are always vulnerable to misinterpretation, and her response to his letter of 7 October represented her as unhappy and William as angry. On the 11th he declared himself to be 'for many purposes the stupidest of men', adding, 'Now the truth is this. When I read your papers . . . I feel myself a spoilt child: and therefore, when you spoke of a weariness coming on you I could not in honour but absolve you from continuing to minister to me matter of so much interest.'[18] For whom was she writing, herself, or her demanding and powerful friend, the prime minister, who currently had their mutual friend Arthur Kinnaird staying

Fight the good fight 127

with him? (Kinnaird had given him 'a charming account' of her 'abode' and 'an excellent report too of Mr. Thistlethwayte's health', William declares in a postscript.) When he wrote on the 15th from Chester, where he was caught up in the 'tumult' of a visit by the Prince of Wales, he managed to upset Laura again, later asking the 'Dear "Broken Reed", and Wounded Spirit' to send him the 'naughty letter back', so that he could 'see *how* bad it was'.

Whereas the daily letters that William wrote to Catherine when they were apart focused mainly upon logistics, with news of family and friends, politicians and churchmen, his almost daily letters to Laura at this time concerned her self-writing, their relationship, and, increasingly, his own spiritual journey, to which hers provided a fascinating foil. 'Do not be afraid of egotism in what you write', he advises her on 18 October, when she has still only covered her first fourteen years: 'An autobiography . . . is never egotistical, and is invariably interesting. Yours is more. It is like a story from the Arabian Nights, with much added to it.'[19] Like the many sad narratives that he had heard through his rescue work, Laura's was a story of abuse: William acknowledged the suffering of 'the poor dear child', who was then 'driven out upon the wide and wild expanse of life'. He then began a new paragraph about himself:

> But now I *am* going to be egotistical, in clearing up the part-reply I have given to your question. The slow instinct, the want of perception, that I so often deplore, are partly to be explained by reference to the master-pursuit of my life. It is a life of mental & moral excess. In me you see a weak man bearing a load under which strong men might totter. Do not take this for complaint. I may tremble indeed, but not complain, when I think that God has been pleased to lay upon me no small part of the peace, happiness, true well-being, of many of the creatures whom He so much loves. In the thought of this, in the study to do as well as I can for them by His help, I am and ought to be absorbed.

The burden of office had been laid upon him through the workings of providence.

Four days later, on 22 October, he wrote one of the most revealing letters that ever came from his pen. He begins, 'Thanks, dear spirit, wounded no longer', and assures her that, 'face to face', he is sure that they 'shall never misapprehend'. Again, a new paragraph turns the spotlight upon himself and his own (unwritten) life story:

> But now, have you well considered what and to whom you give? Do you think you *know* me? I do not think you do, or can as yet . . . If I were to send you the *counterpart* of what you have sent me, I should certainly repel you. But to do it would be beyond my power. I must in honesty say to you, probe me deeper; I will conceal nothing, falsify nothing consciously; but I return to my point, *make sure* that you know me. Do not take me upon trust. I have not sought to deceive you, but I am a strange mixture of art and nature. All this is egotism, but it is also duty.

By inviting Laura to probe him, William is creating the narrative space in which he might begin what he believes to be beyond his power. That space opens up in the paragraph that follows, where we hear echoes of his mid-life crisis, twenty years earlier:

> You must also learn to know the circumstances of my life; how my country is my first wife, and the exacting one, & and how unequal I am in all things to doing what I ought to do, and being what I ought to be. You do not know the ill consequences of the exhaustion following on mental strain: how it disturbs the balance, to what evils it opens the door, how sometimes it seems to leave religion itself a name, a sound, a shadow. The 'storms' of your life have been far beyond mine . . . but . . . infinitely less formidable, because your mind is less entangled . . . your nature less complicated, because you are better than I am, because you love God more. Nor is that saying much for you! I could almost end with 'beware of me'.[20]

The spur to this confessional writing was Laura's declaration of love, as William acknowledges in his letter of 23–24 October: 'Dear Spirit Yesterday, although I wrote much, I did not touch the *core*. It is difficult. Let me try to do it now, and gently. The word you have (on paper) spoken is a great, deep, weighty word. Are you sure that it is a safe word—on the one side, and on the other.' As to 'keeping, and burning' letters, he adds, 'I think burning dangerous. It removes a bridle: it encourages levity in thought.' By Monday 25 October he had received instalments 21–23, which astonished and bewildered him. His comment about his friendships with women, quoted earlier, is followed by an acknowledgement that 'apparent weakness is real power', and that, quite apart from her letters, the '*covenant*' with which she began her tale, '(I must use a man's fencing phrase) got within my guard.' But his diary entry for that day is at once cool and chivalric: 'Narrative and letters taken together I am indeed astonished, though interested, & bound in honour to do the best I can for her if she really needs it.'[21]

Having returned to London for a cabinet meeting, he wrote to say that he would return the presents that she had sent him. He may have been uneasy that gift-giving of this kind was habitual to a courtesan like the 'pretty horsebreaker', Catherine Walters, or 'Skittles', whose affair with Lord Hartington in the early 1860s was common knowledge.[22] He did, however, retain a ring that he would have engraved 'L. T. to W. E. G': 'A ring is a bond.'[23] (He wore it for the rest of his life.) He adds, 'What a singular accumulation within the last seven weeks the post between us has supplied!' Next day he wrote to the Archbishop of Canterbury, to Archbishop Manning, and, 'in great gravity of spirit', to Laura, noting in his diary, 'Duty and evil temptation are there before me, on the right & left. But I firmly believe in her words "holy" and "pure", & in her cleaving to God.'[24] A week later he wondered in a letter whether he could be worthy of any 'boon' she offered him, a faint Tennysonian echo of the chivalric 'bounty' that he had received from his beloved duchess.[25] Perhaps the ring represented his lady's chivalric favour in the mind of one who described himself as a strange mixture of art and nature?

The battle with 'evil temptation' intensified over the weekend of 11–13 December 1869, when William cancelled a cabinet meeting in order to accompany Kinnaird, Laura, and her party to the Thistlethwaytes' house at Boveridge. On arrival, he 'saw Mrs Th. several times' and had 'much conversation with Mr Carnegie the Vicar who dined'.[26] Next day, the third Sunday in Advent, 'Mr T. read a Sermon of over an hour', in lieu of an afternoon service, and 'Mrs Th. came to my rooms aft[ernoon] & at night. Walk with her. Miss Fawcett let down her hair: it is a robe. So Godiva "the rippled ringlets to the knee" '.[27] Miss Fawcett was probably Laura's maid, but nothing is certain apart from the erotic charge associated with Tennyson's poem. On the Monday, Laura accompanied her guests to Fordingbridge station, and William noted in his diary, 'How very far I was at first from understanding her history and also her character. Came up with A. Kinnaird. Arrived at 7¼. C[atherine] G[ladstone] here.' The strange blend of piety and sexual attraction that characterized the weekend is reflected in the letter he sent her on 16 December, where he regrets having been unable to visit Lord Shaftesbury at St Giles during his stay, but also recalls having thought of her all the way to London while he '*made up* for sleep', and adds, 'in this tumult of my life I may be or may not be able to arrive at a clearer comprehension of relations and duties in the intimacy which now prevails between us.'[28] He trusts that she will tell him if he causes her harm. He is infatuated.

William's 'duties' extended to his long-suffering and currently somewhat neglected wife, to whom he had spoken 'weeks ago' on the misconceptions regarding Laura's reputation. On 18 December he sought Laura's permission to 'say this more definitely' to Catherine, as he did not want such misconceptions to 'linger however faintly in such a pure and generous mind as hers'. In the same letter he refers to the 'little group of images' of Laura that dwell in his memory: 'L. driving, L. riding, L. in red, L. in red & black as she walked on Sunday. All these pictures are pleasant. I could expand them in detail.' There is moral confusion in this account of adultery in the heart, or Laurentian sex in the head. A turning point seems to have been reached, however, on his sixtieth birthday, when he writes in his diary: 'My review this year includes as a prominent object L T: the extraordinary history, the confiding appeal, the singular avowal. It entails much upon me: and as I saw most clearly of all today, first to do what in me may lie towards building up a true domestic community of life and purpose there.'[29]

This resolution was clearly on his conscience when he wrote in his diary, on 19 January 1870, 'Finished the L. T. MS. and reviewed my unsent letter of the 6th which expresses the firm desire of my better mind to build up her marriage life into greater fulness and firmness not withstanding the agonies out of which it came & in which it grew.'[30] Three months later, when the Irish Land bill was 'not yet out of danger', he recorded a visit to Laura in the afternoon: 'She is indeed an excepted person: & strangely corresponds with me in some of the strangest points.'[31] When writing to her on 22 April, he announced that 'this is to be a letter about self', and asked her, 'by an effort of the mind', to place herself in his position: 'become, for a moment, me. What would you think and feel? Would it not be something like this [?]'[32] What follows is reminiscent of the evangelical tradition of spiritual autobiography that he had adopted at times of family bereavement (discussed in Chapter 3), and that she followed in her MS:

> 'It is difficult to repel, nay to check or to dissuade, the attachment of a remarkable, a signal, soul, clad in a beautiful body. It is a call for recollection as in the sight of the Most High, and for self-command. No matter, that the attachment is upright. Whatever be the intention that it shall ever remain so, and if that intention be nobly fulfilled, still the hold taken is deep. Should I not beseech her to have a care? It may be that so doing will look to her like indifference . . . If I feel for her, with her, in her, must I not desire that her life may be free, long, happy, holy, finished & accomplished in all womanly and noble gifts?'
>
> These, remember, are your thoughts, under your momentary transformation, estimated and conjectured by me. I now go back to the first person direct. Who & what am I? . . . the fire burns in me yet . . . My profession involves me in a life of constant mental and moral excess . . . all this is a descending course . . . But your sun is yet mounting the sky. Even in the body, your youth is not yet ended.

Laura annotated the missive in her sprawling hand: 'This letter gave me new [?] Life [,] more feeling in it [.] oh! my Life!'

A year later, William's equilibrium in relation to Laura was such that he could write a beautiful but coolly rational account of the nature of human attachment:

> For all forms, & all degrees, of attachment between human beings, be that attachment friendship, love, loyalty, or what it may, have this common and indispensible basis, that there must be a sincere interest, and a desire coming from the heart, for the welfare, and the best welfare, for the peace & calm & joy, of the person who is the object of it. How then can I promote these in & for you? How can I promote them ever so little? It is this which

I would wish, in every way, & every degree, open to me. And first I must ask myself, how it can best be done?

Now in honesty & honour I cannot doubt what would be, what is, best for you. You have an incomplete life. A life incomplete in its basis—in marriage, which is the basis of married life . . . the truest steps towards completeness of life for you would be any steps that could be made *towards* a fuller communion in your married life.[33]

In the summer of 1871, as his friendship with Tennyson deepened, he returned to the *Idylls* that had so impressed him twelve years earlier. On 15 September he wrote asking Laura, 'Have you read Tennyson lately, I mean the Idylls of the King? If not shall I send you my copy of the Book? There is so much in them that is noble, pure, lofty and broadly true—Read Lancelot's words at p. 215 "Not at my years, however it hold in youth". But he also said p. 192 "And loved her with all love except the love / Of men & women when they love their best, / Closest, & sweetest, & had died the death / In any knightly fashion for her sake". It is a wonderful book and the man who wrote it a great man.'[34] Significantly, he steers her towards 'Lancelot and Elaine' rather than 'Guinevere'.[35] A week later he wrote, 'I send you my Tennyson. The marks on it were made in reading for myself. Keep it if you like, and read it all over again. It touches much of woman's nature, and I think nobly & well.'[36]

This particular battle with the evil one was almost over. However, while staying for four days at Oakley Park, Lord Bathurst's estate, in October 1875, the sixty-five-year-old William found that Laura was a fellow guest, a fact that he did not mention in letters to Catherine.[37] He recorded three 'visits' to or from Laura in the diary.[38] As West points out, there was a depth of shared emotion in these visits, but the rest remains a mystery. In a letter written on his return to Hawarden, William asked her to accept his 'acknowledgement of the rare truthfulness of spirit and courage' which she had shown.[39] He objected, however, to her use of the word 'humbling', suggesting that 'There may be something humbling when that is withheld, which it is optional to give, but not when there is, in honour and faith, no option.' Only he and Laura knew precisely what he meant. Clearly, however, 'honour and faith', two key terms in his and Tennyson's lexicons, remained his touchstones in this complex relationship, however far he fell short of the ideal. His correspondence with Laura, now 'Mrs. Thistlethwayte' again, continued until her death in 1894. Catherine, who had met her in 1887, occasionally wrote on William's behalf towards the end. What Catherine made of her husband's inscribed ring is unrecorded.

The real battle against unbelief

Although William and Laura remained far apart on questions relating to the church, they shared a 'true living faith in Christ'; and William admired her for 'cleaving to God', and indeed, loving God more than he did. During his first premiership, these two strands of religious life, ecclesiology and the nurturing of faith, became interwoven in major speeches out of doors. Since 1838 he had been an influential member of the council of King's College, London, the Church of England's answer to University College, proverbially the Utilitarian home of the godless young men of Gower Street. On 14 May 1872 he and Catherine were 'loudly cheered' on their arrival at Willis's Rooms for a fund-raising event in support of King's.[40] With the Archbishop of Canterbury, Archibald Tait, in the chair, he 'spoke at some length'.[41] The role of religion in the education of schoolchildren had dominated the political agenda in 1870, the year of Forster's education act; and King's currently educated about 450 boys, as well as 900 'adult students'. William expressed his own 'strong personal conviction that no education that attempted to do its work without religion could thoroughly effect its end, and that there was no real hostility between real science and religion. Upon that principle King's College had been founded and had been conducted; and, true to its motto, *Sancte et Sapienter*, it had always united the two principles, which were nowadays so often set by shallow thinkers in array against each other.'

While staying at Sandringham on Advent Sunday that year, 1 December 1872, he started Strauss's new book, *Der alte under der neue Glaube: ein Bekenntniss* (The Old Faith and the New: A Confession), and continued with it until the 16th, when he also reread Comte's *Catechism of Positive Religion*.[42] On 21 December he travelled from Hawarden to the Anglican Liverpool College, where he had delivered the inaugural address, thirty years earlier. Now he warned his audience of 2,700, gathered for prize day, of the 'correlative class of dangers and temptations' in a 'wealth-making age', including a particular 'mischief': 'I refer to the extraordinary and boastful manifestation in this age of ours, and especially in the year which is about to close, of the extremist forms of unbelief. (Applause.)'[43] In addressing those preparing for 'the combat of life', he was not going to discuss the Church of England vis-à-vis other churches. Religion itself was being undermined. 'The spirit of denial is abroad', he proclaimed, 'and has challenged all religion, but especially the religion we profess, to a combat of life and death'. While paying due respect to the intellect and earnestness of Dr Strauss, he presented his book as a deeply disturbing sign of the times.

As prime minister, the high church William had to submit to the low church Queen Victoria the names of suitable candidates for senior clerical appointments in the established church of which she was supreme governor. Conversations and correspondence on the subject could be difficult. On 22 January 1874, suffering from chest problems, and with the dissolution of his government in prospect, William responded to the queen's concern about 'the present excesses of Ritualism in the Church of England'.[44] He acknowledged that he himself was 'from time to time denounced, in some quarters, as a Ritualist, as a Papist, and also as a Rationalist', but stated that he had never 'assumed for himself, or admitted rightly to belong to him, any designation whatever in religion.' He then advised Victoria that there were other clergy 'in respect to whom the mischief, less apparent, is more subtle'. There is 'not a doubt', he writes, that 'a certain number of clergymen not only deny the Authority of the Holy Scriptures and of the Church whose Ministers they are, but disbelieve the Deity of our Saviour, His Incarnation, and His Resurrection.' He 'holds them all to be altogether beyond the limits from within which alone it is his duty to recommend to Your Majesty with a view to ecclesiastical preferment', a sentence that can only be described as 'Gladstonian'.

When reflecting upon specific dangers to the established church, such as Ritualism and latitudinarianism among the clergy, William tended to broaden the agenda and reconsider the claims of Christianity itself. He consulted not only Anglican friends on such matters, but also liberal Roman Catholics such as Professor Döllinger and Lord Acton, and his friend Sir Anthony Panizzi, formerly Principal Librarian of the British Museum, who still identified as a Catholic. In a letter to Panizzi dated 8 February 1874, he argued that 'Christianity *established*—(1) Generally speaking, the moral and social equality of women; (2) the duty of relieving the poor, the sick, the afflicted; (3) peace, instead of war, as the ordinary, normal, presumptive relation between nations . . . It taught the law of mutual love. It proscribed all manner of sin.'[45]

Nine days later William and his cabinet resigned. He had long relished the thought of retirement from the premiership, and always thought of his first ministry as his last. In a letter dated 6 April 1874, cited at the beginning of this chapter, he made it clear to Catherine that he would now engage in the 'real battle' being fought in 'the world of thought' over belief in God and the gospel of Christ. When he later resigned as leader of the Liberal Party, on 14 January 1875, the lengthy memoranda that he insisted on reading to his colleagues included this statement: 'My object is to labour for holding together the Church of England. This purpose has involved & probably will involve pleadings for sufferance as to what cannot be defended on its merits, & what is intensely unpopular with the constituents of Liberal members' (many of whom were nonconformists).[46] For William, holding together the Church of England and fighting 'unbelief' were closely related.

On 30 March 1875 he had 'several conversations with C.' on a range of matters relating to their changed circumstances, including the sale of 11 Carlton House Terrace, over which they 'rubbed a good deal'.[47] Over the previous twelve months he had begun to reinvent himself as a writer and essayist, publishing two books (or long pamphlets), two review articles in Murray's *Quarterly Review*, and four articles (three of them on Homer) in James Knowles's *Contemporary Review*. Now he 'endeavoured to lay out before C.' his views about the 'future & remaining section' of his life, when his 'prospective work' was not to be in parliament. Divine providence had been at work in making him prime minister, and now seemed to be guiding him again. 'There is much to be done with the pen', he writes in the diary, 'all bearing much on high & sacred ends, for even Homeric study as I view of it [*sic*] is in this very sense of high importance: and what lies beyond this is concerned directly with the great subject of belief . . . God has in some measure opened this path to me: may He complete the work.' Over the next five years, leading up to his second administration in April 1880, he was to publish sixty-three books, pamphlets, and articles, including ten pieces in the *Contemporary* (on Homer and on Christian thought), and twenty-two in Knowles's new journal, *The Nineteenth Century*, mainly on the Eastern question, but also on church history, Homer, and ethics.[48]

Once free from heavy political responsibilities, William also became briefly involved in Knowles's other enterprise, the Metaphysical Society. He had dined with the society at the Grosvenor Hotel in November 1869, but had 'only listened to the discussion raised by Professor Huxley', as it fatigued his 'poor brain sadly'.[49] Although he read many of the papers that were circulated to members in advance, it was not until 1875–76 that he agreed to chair discussions on topics such as mysteries as defined by Newman, miracles, and the 'persistence of the religious feeling'.[50] Six meetings out of the ninety-five held by the society (1869–80) is not a high tally. Although the society offered a forum for the intellectual battle over belief in God, he seems to have preferred one-to-one discussions at this stage of his life. Visitors to Hawarden included Tennyson, whom Knowles had in mind when planning the society. On 2 November 1876, William recorded in his diary, 'Conversation with Tennyson on Future Retribution, and other matters of Theology: he has not thought, I conceive, systematically and thoroughly upon them, but is much alarmed at the prospect of the loss of belief.'[51]

Here was a much more serious cause for concern than the excesses of Ritualist clergy, against whom Archbishop Tait attempted to legislate in his Public Worship Regulation bill. William felt 'dragged' from his retirement to oppose the bill in the Commons on 9 July 1874.[52] His opposition was on the ground that the state should not interfere in the internal life of the church, rather than because he endorsed Ritualism. Having defended 'a certain degree of liberty' that had been permitted in congregations, and acknowledged that 'great diversity' existed in different parts of the country, he argued that the Church of England had improved radically over the previous half century, and that it was 'almost a moral certainty that whenever you go into a parish you will find the clergyman a man who, to the best of his ability and with little sparing of his health and strength, is spending morning, noon, and night, upon the work of his calling.' His comments carried the authority of a politician known to be a peripatetic and observant worshipper, and an attentive reader of the religious press. After the bill was passed, he developed these themes in an article for the *Contemporary*, where he criticized Ritualism as an 'unwise, undisciplined reaction from poverty, from coldness, from barrenness, from nakedness; it is overlaying Purpose with adventitious and obstructive incumbrance; it is departure from measure and from harmony in the annexation of appearance to substance, of the outward to the inward; it is the caricature of the Beautiful; it is the conversion of helps into hindrances; it is the attempted substitution of the secondary for the primary aim, and the real failure and paralysis of both.'[53]

In July 1875, when the furore over the bill had died down, he wrote a further piece on Ritualism with the startling title 'Is the Church of England Worth Preserving?' Here he emphasized that, although a wide variety of beliefs were held by Anglicans, they shared a 'common Manual of worship'; that the church fulfilled a 'national office'; and that 'she alone, of all Churches, has points of contact, of access, of sympathy, with all the important sections of the Christian community.'[54] The English Church was thus uniquely positioned to resist the spread of unbelief that was discernible across Europe. Three years later, on 3 November 1878, William read an article citing three 'candid Roman Catholics'—Pugin, Newman and the Abbé Martin—who acknowledged that the Church of England, 'whatever its defects may be, was *the* great "break-water" against the progress of infidelity in this country', and was thus 'discharging an important national work much more successfully by far', than the Latin Church was doing in France, Spain, and Italy.[55]

A battle of justice, humanity, freedom, law

William agreed with these candid Catholics on the 'national work' of the Church of England. Over the previous decade he had also developed a clear idea of the international role of the nation itself as a moral force. At the height of the Franco-Prussian War (1870–71), when he was prime minister, he had written an anonymous article for the *Edinburgh Review*, in which he concluded that a 'new law of nations' was 'gradually taking hold of the mind, and coming to sway the practice, of the world; a law which recognises independence, which frowns on aggression, which favours the pacific, not the bloody settlement of disputes . . . above all, which recognises, as a tribunal of paramount authority, the general judgment of civilised mankind. It has censured the aggression of France; it will censure, if need arise, the greed of Germany. *Securus judicat orbis terrarum.*'[56] (Matthew points out that St Augustine's famous maxim—'The verdict of the world is conclusive'—'which drove J. H. Newman to Rome, resurrects the image of a Christian, homogeneous Europe'.[57]) And the anonymous author predicted that 'the foremost among the nations will be that one, which by its conduct shall gradually engender in the mind of the others a fixed belief that it is just. In the competition for this prize, the bounty of Providence has given us a place of vantage; and nothing save our own fault or follow can wrest it from our grasp.'

As we have seen, in February 1874 he wrote of Christianity's gift of 'peace, instead of war, as the ordinary, normal, presumptive relation between nations.' By the end of the decade, following his triumphant first Midlothian campaign (November–December 1879), he could look back on the battle that he had fought over the previous three and a half years 'of justice humanity freedom law', and 'all on a gigantic scale'.[58] 'The word spoken', he added in the diary, 'was a word for millions, and for millions who themselves cannot speak. If I really believe this then I should regard my having been morally forced into this work as a great and high election of God. And certainly I cannot but believe that He has given me special gifts of strength, on the late occasion especially in Scotland.'

In specifying three and a half years, William was referring to the Eastern question and events of May 1876, when the Turks crushed a poorly planned insurrection by Bulgarian nationalists. Some 15,000 largely unarmed Christians were slaughtered. Although such atrocities were not unusual in the Ottoman Empire, the Bulgarian massacre provoked a huge protest campaign in England. Yet it was not until early September that William published his celebrated pamphlet, *The Bulgarian Horrors and the Question of the East*. Richard Shannon argues that the pamphlet 'succeeded so completely because it concentrated into a single utterance a profoundly excited public mood struggling for articulation'.[59] The essential point is that 'it was far less a case of Gladstone exciting popular passion than of popular passion exciting Gladstone.'

In May and June 1876 William established order in his new London home, 73 Harley Street, chaired two meetings of the Metaphysical Society, and read Tennyson's 'Guinevere' aloud, 'with undiminished admiration', at a friend's dinner party.[60] Although he did not attend a protest campaign meeting in Willis's Rooms on 27 July, he read belated government reports and kept up with the extensive press coverage on the massacre. On 31 July he 'got up the Turkish papers and question', and addressed the Commons on the 'common concert of Europe' for over two hours.[61] On 18 August, when at Hawarden, he read in the *Daily News* that a major rally in Hyde Park was planned. Realizing that the pro-Turkish Conservative government was vulnerable, he noted privately that 'the game was afoot and the question yet alive.'[62] On Monday 28 August he set aside a paper on 'Future Punishment' in order to work on 'a possible pamphlet on the Turkish question'.[63] Racked by lumbago, brought on by 'physical exertion' on the estate, he found it more comfortable to work in bed that week, and by Friday he could send off 'more than half to the Printer'. Having worked furiously, and been relieved by hot baths, he departed for the overnight journey to London on the Sunday, 'pamphlet in hand', as his daughter Mary recorded, 'beyond anything agog over the Bulgarian horrors, which pass description. The whole country is aflame, meetings all over the place.'[64] After a short sleep, he spent six or seven hours in the British Museum on Monday 6 September, checking sources and correcting proofs, before dining with Granville. Having incorporated changes suggested by his host the following day, he 'received complete copies' by early evening and sallied forth to the Haymarket Theatre with Granville and Hartington, the current leaders of the Liberal party. William enjoyed the farce, while Harty-Tarty 'never even smiled'.[65] How would the former premier's attack on the Conservatives affect public opinion regarding the Liberal leadership?

Having first exposed the weakness of the government's position on the Eastern question, William argued that the Turks were not like other 'Mahometans': 'They were, upon the whole, from the black day when they first entered Europe, the one great anti-human specimen of humanity. Wherever they went, a broad line of blood marked the track behind them . . . For the guide of this life they had a relentless fatalism: for its reward hereafter, a sensual paradise.'[66] Recent reports in the *Daily News*, which William singled out for praise in the pamphlet, included harrowing accounts of sexual abuse in Bulgaria to which he referred without quoting. Debate surrounding the atrocities was sexualized, with agitation leaders in England exploiting accounts of rape and the Turkish reputation for pederasty.[67] James Fitzjames

Stephen, a prominent member of the Metaphysical Society, privately commented that the protest campaigners 'tickled' John Bull's prurience with 'good circumstantial accounts of "insults worse than death" inflicted on women.'[68] Sir Charles Trevelyan wrote a letter to *The Times* on 'Turkish Terrors', in which he suggested that history was repeating itself. After the Greek war of independence, children had been sold into slavery by the Turks, 'girls for seraglio use, and the boys, for a still more shameful destiny, to *khanjees*, and other keepers of low houses of entertainment.'[69]

William begins his much quoted peroration with an appeal: 'An old servant of the Crown and State, I entreat my countrymen . . . to insist, that our Government, which has been working in one direction, shall work in the other.'[70] He then plays into John Bull's distaste for heathenish foreign terms: 'Let the Turks now carry away their abuses in the only possible manner, namely by carrying off themselves. Their Zaptiehs and their Mudihrs, their Bimbashis and their Yuzbachis, their Kaimakams and their Pashas, one and all, bag and baggage, shall, I hope, clear out from the province they have desolated and profaned.' (Consider the lame alternative: 'their police officers and local governors, their majors and captains, their deputy governors and senior officers.') He continues, 'This thorough riddance, this most blessed deliverance, is the only reparation we can make to the memory of those heaps on heaps of dead; to the violated purity alike of matron, of maiden, and of child.' The air is 'tainted with every imaginable deed of crime and shame'. No door must be left open to allow a recurrence.

William's terms in the pamphlet—'abuses', 'desolated', 'profaned', 'violated purity', 'tainted', 'crime', 'shame'—were privately associated with his rescue work, where a Christian duty to help abused women is itself tainted by his own prurience and adultery in the heart. For the man who was terrified of hurting Laura Thistlethwayte,[71] the Bulgarian horrors were a living nightmare. He continues, 'Better, we may justly tell the Sultan, almost any inconvenience, difficulty, or loss associated with Bulgaria, "Than thou reseated in thy place of light, / The mockery of my people, and their shame."' The source is identified in the pamphlet as Tennyson's 'Guinevere', where King Arthur tells his adulterous wife, grovelling in her 'shame', that she cannot return to the court, as she is like a 'new disease'.[72] A quotation from the poem that William heard read aloud by Tennyson on the eve of his swearing in as chancellor in 1859, that he obsessively reread as he became involved with Marion Summerhayes, that he read in its entirety to one of his rescue cases in 1865, and that he read aloud at a dinner party just recently, evokes a chivalric response to the fallen and the corrupt. Bulgaria, like Camelot, is a polluted site that must be cleansed.

Having written to his Greenwich constituents on 18 August, agreeing to address them, he appeared before a vast crowd on Blackheath Common on 9 September. In a personal anecdote he referred to his overnight dash to London 'on Monday morning last'.[73] 'Between 4 and 5 o'clock', he said, 'I was rattling through the calm and silent streets of London, without a footfall to disturb them, and every house looked so still that it might have been a receptacle of the dead. But as I came through them I felt it to be an inspiring and noble thought that in every one of these houses there were intelligent human beings, my fellow-countrymen—who, when they woke, would give many of their earliest thoughts, and, aye, some of their most energetic actions to the horrors of Bulgaria. (Hear, hear.)' Like Wordsworth on Westminster Bridge in 1802, he is awake, while the city sleeps. A lone crusader, he carries the document that will articulate the sleepers' thoughts and speak the word 'for millions who themselves cannot speak'.[74]

Shannon regards William's seizing of the hour as a 'nakedly opportunist' act, but one that transcended the political plane: it was a response to 'truly popular moral passion'.[75] That passion was demonstrated during a subsequent private tour of hospitable houses in the north-east of England. Although William tried to 'fight off' several invitations to speak and receive loyal addresses, he and Catherine were 'enthusiastically drawn in by a large number of most hearty people' at Castle Howard.[76] He addressed one of the widely reported meetings at St James's Hall in London on 8 December 1876, describing them as 'great, notable, almost historic'.[77] In his annual review in the diary, he reflected that his 'desire for the shade, a true and earnest desire', had been 'rudely baffled' since August: 'retirement & recollection seem more remote than ever. But [it] is in a noble cause, for the curtain rising in the East seems to open events that bear cardinally on our race.'[78]

A month later, *The Times* reported that William had been sent a pamphlet by Robert Roberts, a Christadelphian lecturer, 'showing that the present crisis in the East is a fulfilment of Biblical prophecies.'[79] He had replied saying that he would read it with great interest, 'for I have been struck with the apparent ground for the belief that the state of the East may be treated of in that field where you have been labouring.' He also came to think of his own contributions to the debate, inside and outside the Commons, in prophetic terms. Having lost sleep on the night of 23 March 1877, for example, after addressing the House for over an hour on the Eastern question, he added in the diary, 'Much came home to me Ps. XXIII.5.'[80] Coverdale's version in the Book of Common Prayer reads, 'Thou shalt prepare a table before me against them that trouble me: thou hast anointed my head with oil, and my cup shall be full.' On 31 December he was visited at Hawarden by the diplomatist and journalist Grenville Murray: 'Correspondent of Times & Scotsman came, fresh from Bulgaria; & spent the afternoon 1-6½ . . . the part assigned to me in the Eastern question has been a part great and good far beyond my measure.'[81]

Throughout the year 1878 William continued to play that part in a series of articles and speaking engagements, emphasizing the role of providence and the vulnerability of women in international affairs. In an article on 'The Peace to Come', following the Russo-Turkish war, he wrote, 'The war has been warred; the scales of the supreme Arbiter have been shown on high; and, as far as a judgment can now be formed, the scale of Turkey, after a valorous resistance, has kicked the beam.'[82] In attacking the pro-Turkish policies of the Beaconsfield government and the Court, 'the traitor Gladstone' made enemies as well as friends. On Sunday 24 February 1878, 'three parties of the populace' arrived in Harley Street, 'the first with cheers, the two others hostile': 'Windows were broken & much hooting . . . mounted police in line across the street both ways . . . This is not very sabbatical.'[83] A fortnight later he went to the levee and was snubbed by senior male members of the royal family, commenting in the diary, 'This is not very hard to bear.'[84] In his next piece in *The Nineteenth Century* he affirmed that 'the security of life, liberty, conscience, and female honour, is the one indispensable condition of reform' in all the Slav provinces in the Ottoman Empire.[85] His most supportive audience was one made up of nonconformist ministers.[86] Looking back on a year in which he had returned to the 'cares' of political combat, he commented that 'this retroactive motion has appeared & yet appears to me to carry the marks of the will of God ... In the great physical and mental effort of speaking, often to large auditories, I have been as it were upheld in an unusual manner and the free effectiveness of voice has been given me to my own astonishment.'[87]

Never was that voice more severely tested than during his first Midlothian campaign in November and December 1879, when, on his own calculation, he addressed 86,930 people in thirty speeches.[88] His purpose was to present himself to the constituency, well before a general election, and to reassert his political position nationally by a call to arms on moral grounds, in speeches that would inevitably be widely reported. In Edinburgh he challenged each 'gentleman' present to 'resolve in his inner conscience, before God and before man', to have no share in the activities of the current majority in the Commons.[89] Having addressed 3,500 gentlemen at the Corn Exchange, Dalkeith, he went to the Forester's Hall, where 750 unenfranchised women were waiting. Having thanked them for their gift to Catherine, he said, 'I speak to you, ladies, as women; and I do think and feel that the present political crisis has to do not only with human interests at large, but especially with those interests which are most appropriate, and ought to be most dear, to you. The harder, and sterner, and drier lessons of politics are little to your taste.' His position is chivalric, and far from that of the *Westminster Review* circle. On foreign affairs, he argues, 'if peace be our motto, we must feel that a strong appeal is made to you as women—to you specially, and to whatever there is in men that associates itself with what is best and most peculiar in you.' Significantly, it is in the company of women that he makes his finest prophetic statement on the Eastern question. 'Remember', he says, 'that the sanctity of life in the hill villages of Afghanistan among the winter snows, is as inviolable in the eye of Almighty God as can be your own. Remember that He who has united you together as human beings in the same flesh and blood, has bound you by the law of mutual love; that that mutual love is not limited by the shores of this island, is not limited by the boundaries of Christian civilisation; that it passes over the whole surface of the earth, and embraces the meanest along with the greatest in its unmeasured scope.'[90]

Shannon presents William as a politician who had 'little understanding of and less sympathy with all the tendencies characteristic of the period after 1870. He was moving not from right to left in the conventional manner, but rather into a lofty station of his own, remote from the main political course.' His politics had become, in fact, 'sublimely self-centred'.[91] Similarly, in his correspondence with Laura Thistlethwayte and in his battle against unbelief, his activities were centred upon the self. On Sunday 28 December 1879, in the 'last minutes' of his seventh decade, he reflected on the biblical 'three score years and ten' (Psalms 90.10), and longed for 'spiritual leisure' before passing into the 'unseen world'.[92] 'But perhaps this is a form of selflove', he went on, before reviewing 'the last 3½ years' and the course of the Eastern question. God has given him 'special gifts of strength', especially in the first Midlothian campaign. 'But alas', he writes, 'the poor little garden of my own soul remains uncultivated, unweeded, and defaced.' Sublimely centred upon the self in his spiritual life, as well as in his political career, he had reviewed the state of his heart and soul annually since adolescence—the work of a highly tuned conscience, acutely aware of sin. Yet he was also an idealist in both private and public spheres. The painful tension that resulted would be recognized by many Christians. 'Fight the good fight with all thy might.'

Notes

1. *Hymns Ancient and Modern*, Standard Edn (London: Clowes, 1916), p. 637.
2. *Diaries*, vol. VII, p. 476.
3. See Arthur Tilney Bassett, *Gladstone to his Wife* (London: Methuen, 1936), pp. 192–93.
4. *Diaries*, vol. VII, p. 206. 29 December 1869.
5. *Diaries*, vol. VIII, p. 560. 5 October 1869.
6. Bassett, *Gladstone*, pp. 201-2.
7. *Diaries*, IX, 471. 28 December 1879.
8. 'Mr. Gladstone at Wigan', *The Times*, 24 October 1868, pp. 5–6 (p. 6).
9. *Punch*, 55 (July–December 1868), 216–17, 228–29 (21, 28 November).
10. *Punch*, 64 (January–June 1873), 68–69, 120–21, 131 (15 February, 22, 29 March).
11. *Diaries*, vol. VI, p. 632. 28 October 1868. The reference is to the day of judgement.
12. LPL, MS 2761, ff. 116r, 134r. 25 October, 4 November 1869.
13. See Jenny West, 'Gladstone and Laura Thistlethwayte, 1865–75', *Historical Research*, 80 (2007), 368–92. http://onlinelibrary.wiley.com/doi/10.1111/j.1468–2281.2006.00397.x/full.

14. See, for example, letter of 3 January and diary entry of 19 August 1870: *Diaries*, vol. VIII, pp. 346, 583.
15. *Diaries*, vol. VII, p. 90.
16. See *Diaries*, vol. VIII, p. 557; vol. VII, p. 139 (30 September 1869).
17. *Diaries*, vol. VIII, p. 558.
18. *Diaries*, vol. VIII, pp. 561–62.
19. *Diaries*, vol. VIII, p. 563.
20. 'Evils' is wrongly transcribed as 'dangers' in *Diaries*, vol. VIII, p. 568.
21. *Diaries*, vol. VII, p. 155.
22. See Henry Vane, *Affair of State: A Biography of the 8th Duke and Duchess of Devonshire* (London and Chester Spring: Owen, 2004), p. 55.
23. *Diaries*, vol. VIII, pp. 572–73. 27 October 1868.
24. *Diaries*, vol. VII, p. 158. 28 October 1869.
25. *Diaries*, vol. VIII, p. 576.
26. *Diaries*, vol. VII, p. 197.
27. 'Anon she shook her head, / And showered the rippled ringlets to her knee; / Unclad herself in haste'. 'Godiva' (1842), *The Poems of Alfred Tennyson*, ed. Christopher Ricks (London and New York: Longman/Norton, 1969), p. 734. William also wrote to Catherine on the Sunday.
28. *Diaries*, vol. VIII, p. 580.
29. *Diaries*, vol. VII, p. 206. 29 December 1869.
30. *Diaries*, vol. VII, p. 223.
31. *Diaries*, vol. VII, p. 272. 8 April 1870.
32. *Diaries*, vol. VIII, p. 585.
33. *Diaries*, vol. XII, pp. 442–43. 26 March 1871.
34. *Diaries*, vol. XII, p. 448.
35. 'Lancelot and Elaine' (1859, as 'Elaine'), *Poems of Tennyson*, pp. 1656, 1645 (lines 1287, 863–66).
36. *Diaries*, vol. XII, p. 448. 21 September 1871.
37. See GL, GLA/GGA/2/10/1/25/47, 48.
38. *Diaries*, vol. IX, p. 71. 1–5 October 1875.
39. *Diaries*, vol. XII, p. 475. 6 October 1875.
40. 'King's College, London', *The Times*, 15 May 1872, p. 10.
41. *Diaries*, vol. VIII, p. 152.
42. *Diaries*, vol. VIII, pp. 251-57.
43. 'Education: Mr. Gladstone', *The Times*, 23 December 1872, p. 8. See also *Address delivered at the Distribution of Prizes in the Liverpool College, Decr 21, 1872* (London: Murray, 1873). 'Unbelief' occurs fifteen times in the New Testament (KJV).
44. Philip Guedalla, *The Queen and Mr. Gladstone*, 2 vols. (London: Hodder, Stoughton, 1933), vol. I, p. 440.
45. *Correspondence on Church and Religion of William Ewart Gladstone*, ed. D. C. Lathbury, 2 vols. (London: Murray, 1910), vol. II, p. 99.
46. *Diaries*, vol. IX, p. 5.
47. *Diaries*, vol. IX, p. 25.

48. Listed in *Diaries*, vol. IX, pp. 659–60.
49. *Diaries*, vol. VII, p. 173. 17 November 1869.
50. See *Diaries*, vol. IX, pp. 4, 42, 79, 104, 124, 133.
51. *Diaries*, vol. IX, p. 167.
52. Hansard, vol. 220, col. 1373.
53. 'Ritualism and Ritual', *Contemporary Review*, 24 (June–November 1874), 663–81 (668).
54. 'Is the Church of England Worth Preserving?' *Contemporary Review*, 26 (June–November 1875), 193–220 (205–7). Both essays were revised and published as *The Church of England and Ritualism* (London: Strahan, 1876).
55. *Diaries*, vol. IX, p. 359; Richard F. Littledale, 'Why Ritualists Do Not Become Catholics: A Reply to the Abbé Martin', *Contemporary Review*, 33 (August–November 1878), 792–824 (816).
56. 'Germany, France, and England', *Edinburgh Review* (October 1870) . . . reprinted in *Gleanings of Past Years, 1843–78*, 7 vols. (London: Murray, 1879), vol. IV.
57. Colin Matthew, *Gladstone, 1809–1898* (Oxford: Clarendon, 1997), p. 184.
58. *Diaries*, vol. IX, p. 471. 28 December 1879.
59. Richard Shannon, *Gladstone and the Bulgarian Agitation 1876* (London: Nelson, 1963), p. 110. The essential source.
60. *Diaries*, vol. IX, pp. 124, 125, 133. William dined frequently with his confidant, Sir Walter James Bt, a former Tory MP.
61. *Diaries*, vol. IX, p. 144.
62. Shannon, *Gladstone and the Bulgarian Agitation*, p. 100.
63. *Diaries*, vol. IX, p. 150.
64. *Mary Gladstone (Mrs. Drew), her Diaries and Letters*, ed. Lucy Masterman (London: Methuen, 1930), p. 109.
65. See Shannon, *Gladstone and the Bulgarian Agitation*, p. 109.
66. W. E. Gladstone, *The Bulgarian Horrors and the Question of the East* (London: Murray, 1876), pp. 12–13.
67. Shannon, *Gladstone and the Bulgarian Agitation*, pp. 34, 66.
68. Fitzjames Stephen to Lord Lytton. See Shannon, *Gladstone and the Bulgarian Agitation*, p. 66,
69. *The Times*, 11 August 1876, p. 10,
70. Gladstone, *Bulgarian Horrors*, p. 61.
71. See, for example, *Diaries*, vol. XII, p. 459.
72. *Poems of Tennyson*, p. 1738 (lines 522–23).
73. 'The Atrocities in Bulgaria: Mr. Gladstone at Greenwich', *The Times*, 11 September 1876, p. 10.
74. Cf. Houghton to Henry Bright, 11 February 1877, 'I met the great Crusader (Mr. Gladstone) at dinner on Friday': Thomas Wemyss Reid, *The Life, Letters, and Friendships of Richard Monckton Milnes, first Lord Houghton*, 3rd edn, 2 vols. (London: Cassell, 1891), vol. II, p. 358.
75. Shannon, *Gladstone and the Bulgarian Agitation*, p. 101.
76. *Diaries*, vol. IX, p. 161. 7 October 1876.

77. *Diaries*, vol. IX, p. 176.
78. *Diaries*, vol. IX, p. 181. 29 December 1876. Unusually, a violet ink is used for this retrospect in LPL, MS 1445, f. 122.
79. *The Times*, 27 January 1877, p. 5. Robert Roberts, *Prophecy and the Eastern question*, London and Birmingham: Pitman/Roberts, 1877.
80. *Diaries*, vol. IX, pp. 205–6.
81. *Diaries*, vol. IX, p. 279.
82. *The Nineteenth Century*, 3 (January-June 1878), 209-26 (231).
83. *Diaries*, vol. IX, p. 293.
84. *Diaries*, vol. IX, 297. 11 March 1878.
85. 'The Paths of Honour and Shame', *The Nineteenth Century*, 3 (January–June 1878), 591–604 (599).
86. See 'Mr. Gladstone and the nonconformist Body', *The Times*, 18 April 1878, p. 6.
87. *Diaries*, vol. IX, pp. 373–74. 29 December 1878.
88. *Diaries*, vol. IX, p. 466. 11 December 1879.
89. W. E. Gladstone, *Political Speeches in Scotland, November and December 1879, with an Appendix, containing the Rectorial Address in Glasgow, and other non-political Speeches, the Speeches revised by the Author* (London: Ridgway, 1879), pp. 50, 57–58.
90. Gladstone, *Political Speeches*, pp. 90–94.
91. Shannon, *Gladstone and the Bulgarian Agitation*, p. 11.
92. *Diaries*, vol. IX, p. 471.

7
Athirst for God

Like as the hart desireth the water-brooks: so longeth my soul after thee, O God. My soul is athirst for God, yea, even for the living God: When shall I come to appear before the presence of God? (Psalm 42.1–2, Book of Common Prayer)

During a visit to Keble College, Oxford, in April 1888, William seized the opportunity to discuss *Robert Elsmere*, the best-selling novel of the hour, with its author, Mary Ward, who was forty-one years his junior. Mary recorded his comments on religion in a letter to her husband, Humphry: '"I don't believe in any new systems," he said smiling. "I cling to the old. The great traditions are what attract me. I believe in a degeneracy of man, in the Fall,—in *sin*—in the intensity and virulence of sin. No other religion but Xtianity meets the sense of sin, and sin is the great fact in the world to me."'[1] In a second letter, Mary described the 'strenuous argument' that lasted an hour and half next morning, when 'the great man got quite white sometimes & tremulous with interest & excitement'. 'The new lines of criticism are not familiar to him', she commented, '& they really press him hard. He meets them out of Bishop Butler & things analogous.' But the Grand Old Man's autobiographical reminiscences were 'wonderfully interesting, & his repetition of the 42nd psalm "like as the hart desireth the water brooks"—*grand*'.[2]

Athirst for God, he wrote on the last day of 1883, 'My political or public life is the best part of my life: it is that part in which I am conscious of the greatest effort to do and to avoid as the Lord Christ would have me do and avoid, nay shall I say for this is the true rule as He would Himself in the like case have done. But although so far itself taken up out of the mire, it exhausts and dries up my other and more personal life, and so to speak reduces its tissue, which should be firm and healthy, to a kind of moral pulp.'[3] He was now seventy-four. Earlier in the year his drawn white face had featured in William Frith's group portrait of *A Private View at the Royal Academy, 1881*, showing a large gathering of celebrities, most of whom he knew, or had at least met. Among the black-coated politicians, lawyers, clergy, and doctors, and the colourfully dressed ladies, aesthetic and otherwise, he looks the oldest and most strained person in the room. (He faced the daunting prospect of eulogizing Lord Beaconsfield, his recently departed political enemy, whose portrait was exhibited at the private view of 1881 by royal command.) The leading actors in the painting—Henry Irving, Ellen Terry, and Lillie Langtry—were admired acquaintances, and his children encouraged his frequent visits to the Lyceum Theatre. Mary, now his London hostess, secretary for ecclesiastical patronage, and principal cheerleader, shared his enthusiasm for music and the theatre, and often read the same books, so that they could discuss them.

During the 1880s William compared his own long life with those of deceased contemporaries, recorded in their lives and letters, and with certain figures in fiction. While aligning himself with a younger generation of liberal catholic Anglicans, he reviewed the history of Tractarianism, with which he had been associated forty years earlier. Planning for retirement in the late 1880s, he established the institute that was to become St Deiniol's Library, Hawarden, a centre for 'divine learning and worship' and his legacy to the Church of England. (It flourishes today as Gladstone's Library.) Undergirding all these activities was a settled belief in divine providence and a desire to discern the will of God at work in his own public and private life. He registered a deepening sense of God's guidance in the Commons and out of doors, as the words were given to him in major speeches, along with the strength to deliver them. While campaigning in the present, with a view to the future, he frequently related his current struggles to those of the past.

Lives and letters

In the diaries, and in private letters to his wife and to Laura Thistlethwayte, William's commentary on his past life was fragmentary and occasional. Why had he not turned to autobiography, rather than Homeric studies, during those long recesses at Hawarden? The question was discussed with Lord Acton, twenty-four years his junior, but by now one of his closest friends and advisors, in the summer of 1887. 'Attended C.s garden party at five', William recorded at Hawarden on 27 August, adding, 'Ld Acton came: much conversation with him on a certain work.'[4] Acton had written to William on the 16th, encouraging him to take up 'that American proposal which you spoke of at Grillion's'.[5] An autobiography, possibly published by Putnam, would in Acton's view be 'the greatest force sustaining and guiding the Liberal party in the next generation.' Nothing came of the offer, either in 1887 or four years later, when Andrew Carnegie also encouraged him, saying that he could make £50,000 by writing his autobiography and suggesting that he dictate material to a stenographer. Work on his 'Autobiographica' did finally begin in July 1892. In the 1880s, however, his retrospective reflections were stimulated by reading the lives of others.

As with other enthusiasms, this activity sometimes came in a burst of focused attention. In October 1884, for example, when urgent government business included the franchise bill (which the Lords had rejected), General Gordon's defence of Khartoum, and the question of coercion in Ireland, William shuttled between Hawarden and London, always with some recently published biographical material to hand. On 6 October he wrote paragraphs for a Queen's Speech en route to London and started on Lord Malmesbury's *Memoirs of an Ex-Minister* (2 vols.), a book to which he was to return in November.[6] Back at Hawarden he alternated between S. J. Reid's *A Sketch of the Life and Times of Sydney Smith* and the 'astonishing memoirs' of the German actress Karoline Bauer (vol. 1), on which he wrote a short unpublished review.[7] He then took up John Bowling Mozley's *Letters*, to which he returned early in 1885, adding numerous marginal marks and comments, particularly where Mozley refers to 'WEG'.[8] On the way back to London on 21 October he read H. J. Jennings's biographical sketch of Tennyson and next day started on the second part of Froude's controversial life of Carlyle. Having spoken on the franchise bill on the 23rd, he continued with the Froude over the subsequent fortnight, before turning to the three-volume Croker papers, which he finished on Christmas Eve, by which time he had also read Max Müller on Bunsen.

Many of these lives and letters had personal resonances for William and were sufficiently engaging to lure him away from the daily political drudgery. He had been involved in the preparation of John Morley's *The Life of Richard Cobden* (2 vols.), both as a correspondent and as a trustee of Cobden's MSS. When his copy arrived, on 24 October 1881, he wrote to Morley, 'I am obliged to say that if not, like Socrates, a corruptor of youth, you are at any rate a corruptor of old age, for you seduce greybeards into a neglect of duty. I have spent my morning on your second volume . . . It is one more added to the not very long list of our real biographies.'[9] Tellingly he adds, 'The climax of Cobden's illustrious life was that which brought him into the closest connection with me, & I have naturally turned to the Treaty period. It was the most laborious time of his life, the most searching & trying of mine.' (While the Cobden-Chevalier Treaty was being negotiated with France in 1859–60, William was finding his way as Palmerston's chancellor and wrestling with his conscience over Marion Summerhayes.)

In Colin Matthew's view, it was William's response to *The Life of Samuel Wilberforce* (1879–82) that perhaps marked the beginning of his 'seeing himself as a chief actor in the published biographies of the day, and watching the intimate personal and religious crises of his youth replayed before his own and the public's gaze.'[10] Using a pencil, as usual, William indexed a wide range of 'facts' that interested him in each of the three stout volumes, the last of which also contains handwritten additions to the references to himself in two columns of the printed index.[11] He inserted marginal notes alongside transcriptions of his own letters to Wilberforce in the printed text, having first approved their publication. In August 1879 Canon Ashwell, the author of volume I, sent him the chapter on 'The Hampden Controversy'.[12] A month later, William noted in the diary, 'reviewed letters to Bp Wilberforce sent for my permission to publish,' adding that 'They are curiously illustrative of a peculiar and second-rate nature.'[13]

Athirst for God 153

This self-deprecating remark set the tone for later pained responses to biographical and autobiographical writing of the 1880s, when William was frequently caught up in exhausting political manoeuvering, particularly over Ireland, which reduced the tissue of his personal life to 'a kind of moral pulp'. On 23 April 1886, Good Friday, his reading included E. L. Hicks's recently published biography of *Henry Bazeley: The Oxford Evangelical*. 'What a lesson for a wretch like me,' he wrote in the diary, echoing John Newton's hymn, 'Amazing Grace'.[14] Here was a nonconformist minister who preached in the open in Oxford, often at the Martyrs' Memorial, sold his possessions to help the poor, and ploughed an inheritance into building the first Church of Scotland church in the city.

A year later William read *The Life and Works of the Seventh Earl of Shaftesbury*, in which Edwin Hodder quotes a reference in the earl's diary to his 'greed of place and salary and power'. William recorded in his own diary, 'The Shaftesbury book is an excellent discipline for me: it forces me to compare his nobleness with my vileness, his purity with my foulness.'[15] Although he later published corrections to inaccuracies in the book, he also wrote a private memorandum that expanded upon this penitential theme, with echoes of the poem that still enthralled him, Tennyson's 'Guinevere'. 'The Biography has certainly elevated and deepened all my appreciations of this noble character,' he wrote. 'I felt myself soon after the commencement simply grovelling in the dust before him. Not until I made some progress was I aware that while thus down I was to be hit so frequently, may I say so violently, by his broad and unreserved condemnations. I could not have believed from the constantly kind relations between us that I could have presented to one sustaining those relations a picture of such unredeemed and universal blackness.'[16] Often extreme in his self-condemnation, he is hurt and confused by the equally extreme comments of an eminent diarist who remained an evangelical throughout his life.

Like William, John Ruskin had moved on from his upbringing as a devout evangelical. England's greatest art critic visited Hawarden in January 1878, shortly before his first major mental breakdown, after which he returned for a second visit. Mary Gladstone kept in touch with the 'dear old blessed man',[17] and on Sunday, 21 June 1885, when the family were about to move out of Downing Street, her father read the first part of *Præterita*, Ruskin's fragmentary 'outlines of scenes and thoughts perhaps worthy of memory in my past life'.[18] In this case we have no commentary from William, who must surely have been arrested by Ruskin's opening sentence: 'I am, and my father was before me, a violent Tory of the old school;—Walter Scott's school, that is to say, and Homer's.'[19] Two of the most famous 'Englishmen' of their day had Scottish, evangelical, and Tory backgrounds, and shared similar tastes in classical and modern literature. Yet the contrast between Ruskin's pessimism and William's optimism in their maturity was so great that the first visit to Hawarden had begun nervously.[20] William caught up with *Præterita* again on 1 October 1886, six weeks after the resignation of his third ministry. He finished the first volume on the 16th, the day on which he regretfully burned the letters of two 'cases of great interest', Mrs Dale, *née* Summerhayes, and Mrs Davidson, *née* Cowper.[21] Anxious lest these old letters 'might in parts have suggested doubt & uneasiness,' after his death, he now also had a possible model for his future 'Autobiographica' in Ruskin's 'outlines of scenes and thoughts'.

Fiction also provided rich seams of pseudo-biography and pseudo-autobiography, as in the beloved novels of Scott. (When beginning Cross's life of his wife, George Eliot, in 1885, he told Acton that he was 'wrath' with him and his daughter Mary for 'lifting her above Walter Scott'.[22]) His reading of Stevenson's *The Strange Case of Dr. Jekyll and Mr. Hyde*, in February 1886, while grappling with Irish home rule legislation, passes without commentary.[23] (It also goes unremarked by Travis L. Crosby, author of *The Two Mr. Gladstones*.) Six years earlier, however, William did comment on Dickens's favourite offspring, *The Personal History of David Copperfield*, which he read with 'increasing admiration'. He finished the novel on a particularly busy day. Early in the morning of Saturday 4 September 1880 he arrived at Gravesend from Yarmouth, reached London at 10.30, chaired a cabinet meeting, and attended the Commons: 'Made rather a long speech on the Eastern question, in great heat; & was much fatigued. Twelve to dinner. Retired early. Read D. Copperfield: to the end. A most noteworthy book—It alters my estimate of Dickens.'[24] The departure of 'The Emigrants' for Australia, witnessed by David at Gravesend in chapter 57, would have been of more than immediate topical interest to William, as the group included two rescue cases: Martha the prostitute and Little Emily, the fallen woman from Yarmouth.

A year later, having just finished George Eliot's *Scenes from Clerical Life*, William was captivated by a historical novel set in the seventeenth century, *John Inglesant: A Romance* (1881). Its author was Joseph Henry Shorthouse of Edgbaston, a wealthy individual who worked in the family chemical business and wrote in the evenings. Over a period of ten years he produced the novel that unexpectedly became a publishing sensation, ironically through an intervention by Mary Ward, who took a privately printed copy to Alexander Macmillan. John Inglesant comes from a line of 'Papists at heart' who had conformed to the Church of England during and after the English Reformation. He is tutored by a Jesuit, who grooms him as a pro-Catholic Anglican, so that he can serve as a mediator between Canterbury and Rome in the years leading up to the Civil War. As a supporter of King Charles, Inglesant narrowly escapes execution before travelling to Italy in search of his brother's murderer. Having found and forgiven the assassin, Inglesant—'England's saint', who is mistaken for St George— stands trial for Molinism, being both a Benedictine novice and 'an accredited agent of the Queen Mother of England', Henrietta Maria. The novel ends with the hero offering his reflections upon Catholicism and Anglicanism, based on an unusually wide experience of both traditions.

William started on this remarkable work on 14 July 1881, while piloting the Irish Land bill through the Commons, and finished it a month later. He wrote to the poet Sir Francis Doyle, on 22 October 1881, 'I wonder whether you have read John Inglesant, & what you think of it? It is certainly no common book.'[25] He was photographed holding a copy, and, on 3 May 1882, welcomed the author and his wife to a reception at Downing Street attended by the Prince of Wales. Mrs Shorthouse recorded William's response as they entered the room. 'I never saw a more delighted expression upon a face,' she wrote, 'than that which beamed upon his as he bowed and greeted my husband.'[26] Next day there were 'Nine to breakfast, including Mr Shorthouse'.[27] Mary Gladstone recorded that 'the poor author has an appalling impediment in his speech, really almost like a sort of convulsion.'[28]

Several explanations for William's beaming face present themselves, including the sheer charm of the narrative, and especially Shorthouse's treatment of Nicholas Ferrar's Anglican community at Little Gidding. Primarily, however, he would have seen aspects of his own spiritual journey in that of Inglesant, ranging from trivial matters such as the hero's admiration for St Peter's, Rome, to significant parallels with his own unpublished story, such as the tension that lies at the heart of the novel: like William, Inglesant 'desired to live a life of holiness, but the only life that seemed possible to him was one of business and intrigue.'[29] Inglesant, like William, believes that 'We must suffer for the sin of others as for our own; and in this suffering we find a healing and purifying power and element.'[30] When alone with the lovely Lauretta, and 'heated with wine', 'the temptation came upon him with a force which he had neither power nor desire to resist'; but a rustling breeze 'was like a whisper from heaven that reminded him of his better self'.[31] As Inglesant travelled through Italy he encountered people 'of the peasant class, and heard the story of their lives'.[32]

Like William's famous perorations, however, it is the closing chapter of the novel that lingers in the memory. Inglesant is asked whether he prefers 'the Romish system' or that of 'the English Church'. 'This is the supreme quarrel of all,' he replies. 'This is not a dispute between sects and kingdoms; it is a conflict within a man's own nature—nay, between the noblest parts of man's nature arrayed against each other. On the one side obedience and faith, on the other, freedom and the reason. What can come of such a conflict as this but throes and agony?'[33] Like William, Inglesant argues that 'Upon the altars of the Church the divine presence hovers as surely, to those who believe it, as it does upon the splendid altars of Rome.' And his belief that Christ 'won the world by placing Himself in harmony with that law of gradual development which the Divine Wisdom had planned' was also William's in the 1880s, as he aligned himself with Anglican liberal catholicism.

Catholics old and new

During the 1880s William reviewed his Tractarian past and investigated the ideas of a younger generation of high churchmen. He also explored the borderlands between Anglican liberal catholicism and liberal Roman Catholicism. His attitude towards Vaticanism and ultramontanism had been shaped partly by Ignaz von Döllinger, at whose feet he had sat for many years. Pio Nono's Syllabus of Errors of 1864, anathema to William, was aimed partly at Döllinger, whose rejection of papal infallibility led to his excommunication in 1871. The Old Catholics on the continent, who also rejected infallibility, were strongly influenced by Döllinger, but failed to recruit him to their denomination. An outstanding historian, he was remarkably well informed on British current affairs, both political and ecclesiastical. He followed William's prime ministerial career closely and corresponded with him on questions such as church establishment and unbelief. In September 1879 he was photographed with members of the Gladstone family (William, Catherine, Mary, and Herbert) and Lord Acton's wife and children, at Acton's home at Tegernsee.[34] Acton had lived in Döllinger's house in Munich in his student days, and now, as that friendship waned, formed a bond with Mary Gladstone, who fell in love with him during the stay.[35] Their correspondence includes detailed discussions on the political and ecclesiastical challenges that confronted 'Mr. Gladstone' (Acton), or 'the P. M.' (Mary). Many years later, Mary wrote of her father's friendship with Acton, 'It was of little moment to which branch of the Holy Catholic Church—the Anglo-Catholic or the Roman Catholic—the two men belonged. Both were Catholic in the deepest and widest sense of the term, both were conscious and proud of their membership in the Apostolic and Universal Church . . . Both were staunch believers in religious liberty, and both were possessed of a deep longing for the reunion of Christendom.'[36]

While sharing these grand principles and aspirations with a sophisticated cosmopolitan like Acton, William retained a deep desire for members of his own family to remain staunchly high Anglican. Principle and practice collided on 16 January 1880, when his sister Helen died in Cologne, a month after his first Midlothian campaign. He had been mortified when she converted to Rome in 1842. Now he rushed to her deathbed, anxious to discern the current state of her faith. The evening before she died was 'for the most part distressing from her piteous cravings' (for laudanum), he wrote in the diary, adding, 'She has been led into a great error: I cannot say whether it may not have been a great sin: yet I can dismiss her fearlessly to the great account, mine is a sadder & a darker tale.'[37] On the 17th he made funeral arrangements and worked obsessively on her effects, including about 1,200 books, looking for evidence. As he explained to Catherine in a letter, they first had to certify the death:

I believe she would have asked to be buried in the Church of her youth & her home—but I cannot prove it. Today a Mr Henkel, who had been in friendly intercourse with her, went to arrange about certifying the death and wished to enter her religion as Old Catholic. Apropos to this he told us that she said to him in so many words 'I am Old Catholic.' But the officials do not permit it and the Old Catholics of Cologne when they die are entered simply as Catholics like the Romans. They would take 'Anglican' but this we are not entitled to say. We must settle before Monday. Catholic is a good name, none better; but the advantage of Old Catholic would have been that it would at once have prevented any ultramontane intrusion or objection.[38]

Her religion was registered as 'katholischer'.[39]

On the 18th, a Sunday, William attended a 'quiet soothing service' of his own communion and 'wrote to C. G. (fully)', sharing the results of his bibliographical research and referring to the weekly high Anglican newspaper, *The Guardian*, and Keble's poems for children and *Christian Year*:

I have made a most curious & interesting examination of her books of devotion, and have also learned much from her Library. She took in no one [*sic*] of the English R. C. Journals, but took in the Guardian. The Psalms in the English Prayerbook Version are *worn out*. Latterly she took to a copy of large print, using these and the Gospels of N. T. every day, & never having them off her bed. The *Lyra Innocentium* is very much worn. She got a large Christian Year, & read it incessantly. It was always on her bed, & if it was mislaid (says Watkins) for half a day she was most unhappy about it. Hardly any new *R. C.* books of devotion have come in since 1870; about 4 or 5: and these are not in the least used. She seems to have used a R. C. Church Calendar for the last time *in 1871*. Is not all this most extraordinary, and a perfect substantial proof that she finally lived & died in unity with us? I have much time to write a long account to Dr Döllinger.[40]

Diligence and a close attention to detail, learned at Eton and Oxford, were undiminished, as William sifted through the time-worn devotional books of a departed sister.

By Sunday 25th he was at Fasque, attending services in the episcopalian chapel, 'so full of dear memories', the coffin resting in the hall. Helen was buried with the Anglican rite two days later: 'Mr B[elcher] . . . had not the sympathetic spirit of Mr Harris: nor was the commendatory blessing given. However we ought to be most thankful that as if in answer to our prayer our dear sister has been freely restored to the unity of the Spirit and the bond of peace.—I miss sorely the funeral communion.'[41] On his return to Hawarden he seems to have requested communion on Friday 30th, 'in the place of Funeral Communion'. His duties were not over, however, as an 'account' of Helen's life and death was needed, along the lines of those discussed in Chapter 3. His 'Memorandum on the religious profession of my sister Helen Jane Gladstone', dated 8 February 1880, begins defensively. Having explained that the decision to bury her at Fasque was shared with his brother Thomas, he wrote, 'Let me begin by stating that, for my share in the matter, I have felt myself under the most sacred obligation to proceed judicially, and to exclude from my mind, to the best of my ability, everything in the nature of sectarian or ecclesiastical prepossession. I have done what I think an upright Roman Catholic brother would have been bound to do; namely, in the absence of a direct statement of her wishes, to examine the evidence bearing upon the point, and to act upon it if sufficient.'[42] Before reviewing four sources as evidence, and giving an account of recent days in Cologne, he weakened his claim to judicial neutrality still further by referring to the fact that the most powerful of the female converts to Rome over the previous forty years had, as far as he knew, 'reverted or shown a disposition to revert to the communion of the Church of England'. A month later, having returned from electioneering in Midlothian, he was troubled by rumours in London. His letter to Acton of 6/7 March 1880 is marked 'Most private'. 'I am given to understand', he wrote, 'that in Roman circles here I am accused (it should be my brother and I) of disregarding her wishes in not having her buried with the rites of the Anglo-Roman Church.'[43] An exchange of letters ensued, as William continued to wrestle with his conscience on a matter that he intellectualized: 'the question about my sister', he wrote on 14 March, 'is one of deep interest'. Borderlands are dangerous territory.

Turning to matters related to his beloved Church of England, William particularly enjoyed memoirs that took him back to earlier periods of his spiritual life. When Lord Rosebery joined the party for luncheon at Dollis Hill, on Sunday 12 June 1882, he brought Thomas Mozley's recently published *Recollections of the Oxford Movement* (1882), which included anecdotes relating to William and his friend Samuel Wilberforce, among others. Mary noted that the book 'enchanted and enthralled Papa'.[44] Four years earlier he had shared his own reflections on the movement during a visit to Keble College, Oxford.

The foundation of Keble in 1870 was in certain respects similar to that of King's College, London, being overtly Anglican and welcoming students of moderate means. Unlike King's, however, Keble was a high church institution, and was regarded as being conservative, for all Butterfield's use of modern materials in its design: the streaky bacon was *contra mundum*.[45] Founded in memory of John Keble, the college was intended to carry the torch for the Oxford Movement into the last quarter of the nineteenth century and beyond. The first warden was Edward Stuart Talbot, who married Lavinia Lyttelton, Mary Gladstone's favourite cousin, in 1870. Lavinia recorded in her diary, 'Uncle W. in great form willing to see and be seen,' when William made a flying visit to the college in November 1872, the month in which the college acquired the Oxford Movement's most famous icon, *The Light of the World*, by William Holman Hunt. (Ruth Clayton Windscheffel has shown how Hunt's familiar image of Christ was to feature in an imaginary stained-glass window behind the figure of William reading the lesson, in an illustration entitled 'The Aged Reader' and dated 1898.[46])

William and Hunt's painting were in the same room on 25 April 1878, when the former prime minister joined in prayers at the opening of the college library by the Bishop of Oxford, John Mackarness, who was standing near the east end 'near to Mr. Holman Hunt's now unveiled picture'.[47] Mary Gladstone recorded in her diary that she 'joined the procession marching round the quadrangle singing psalms' that morning, 'a most impressive sight with its scores of past and present Kebleites, and then the choristers in their scarlet gowns, and the very brightest sun and sky above. The library was opened with a short form of service, and then after some dawdling all went to luncheon in the beautiful big hall ... Papa long and good but a little dry for him.'[48]

At the luncheon, William was 'greeted with loud, long, and enthusiastic cheering, and waving of hats and caps', as he rose to propose the health of the college in a speech which ranged over the history of the Oxford Movement and offered some pointed advice to the college, where his son Herbert had recently become a lecturer in history:

> There would be no greater calamity, in my opinion, than that we should see founded in Oxford any new college which was marked out by fanciful peculiarities or any new college which could be open, in any sense of the word, to the charge of bearing a sectarian character . . . Oxford, I believe, is as much as at any period of English history in no weak sense the heart and centre of the religious life of the country. It has also been the scene of the most painful—I might say without exaggeration the most agonising—convulsion of that religious life within the last half century. There are great names connected with the religious movement of our time. There is the great name commemorated for ever, as we hope, in this work. (Cheers.)—There, too, is the name of Dr. Pusey—(cheers)—who I believe commands in full the respect—perhaps even the veneration—of many who differ, perhaps, from some of his particular opinions. But there is a name which, as an academical name, is greater than either of those—I mean the name of Dr. Newman. (Cheers.) When the history of Oxford during that time comes to be written, the historian will have to record the extraordinary, the unexampled career of that distinguished man in the University. We know how his influence was sustained by his extraordinary purity of character and the holiness of his life. (Cheers.) We know also the catastrophe—I cannot call it less—which followed. (Cheers.) . . . It is said in a beautiful expression by a brilliant writer still living [Goldwin Smith] that the effect of that secession, and what was justly called, perhaps, the failure of the movement connected with it, threw all the brightest and noblest intellects of the University as wrecks upon every shore. If that be true—and I as a pathetic observer, fully believe it was—the time had come when it was well to make a new protest recalling Oxford to its first principles.[49]

William speaks as one who witnessed the events he describes and who was dismayed by Newman's conversion. Yet he has moved on in his understanding of the role of the church in religious education, as becomes clear later in the speech, when he says 'There has been appropriately noticed the notable local conjunction of Keble College with the Museum [of Natural History] on the other side of the way. It has been well said that they appropriately represent the sacred and the secular at Oxford . . . It is an illustration of the harmony which ought to prevail, and I trust ever will, between the branches of education within this great University.' As Windscheffel points out, Gladstone was 'publicly allying himself with liberal, not conservative religious opinion.'[50] Increasingly he sympathized with the younger generation of Henry Scott Holland, Edward Talbot, and Charles Gore.

Scott Holland was born in 1847, the same year as his friend and supporter Mary Gladstone, who called him 'the Flying Dutchman', 'in some sense associated with wings', and liked to play tennis with him.[51] William came to share his daughter's high opinion of him through social contact: he walked with him at Hawarden in December 1880, entertained him at a London breakfast in July 1882, and read his memorial sermon on Pusey at Cannes in February 1883.[52] Preferment ensued the following year. While mixing with Acton, Liddon, Holland, and Jowett in Oxford, in February 1884, Mary recorded the morning on which Holland 'got the P. M.'s letter asking him to be St. Paul's Canon, but by no sign did he show, or I, that anything had happened.'[53] Mary's cousin by marriage, Edward Talbot, born in 1844, had been a Hawarden habitué in his youth and later reciprocated by entertaining the Gladstones at Keble College. When William walked with him at Hawarden, in 1884, he described him as 'a model of dispassionate uprightness'.[54] Four months later, he took two walks at Hawarden with Charles Gore, born in 1853 and now the librarian of Pusey House, Oxford, and shared his opinion of him with Acton: 'Mr. Gore, head of the Pusey Institute, a man of very high promise, has already a society of twenty Tutors formed for Theological study under or with him. I really doubt (but this may be extravagant) whether there is any single place in Christendom which might—if any single place could be so honoured—be more truly termed its heart, than Oxford.'[55]

As so often in the nineteenth century, however, Oxford was embroiled in religious controversy in the later 1880s and early 1890s. When he stayed at All Souls, of which he was an honorary fellow, in January 1890, William canvassed opinion on biblical criticism, the current subject of dispute.[56] A controversial 'series of studies in the religion of the incarnation' had appeared a few months earlier under the title *Lux Mundi* (1889), edited by Gore. Contributors included Gore, Holland, Talbot, and other members of the 'Holy Party', half of whom were associated with Keble College. In his preface, dated from Pusey House, Gore wrote: 'We are sure that Jesus Christ is still and will continue to be the "Light of the World".'[57] Here was a subject close to William's heart, as well as central to his theology. He read 'Gore's Masterly paper' on 'The Holy Spirit and Inspiration' in *Lux Mundi* on his first day at All Souls.[58] He also read Liddon's sermon denouncing Gore and found a position halfway between the two, as reflected in his book *The Impregnable Rock of Holy Scripture* (1890), one section of which is entitled 'On the recent corroborations of Scripture from the regions of history and natural science'. Although the arguments put forward by several authors in *Lux Mundi* for theology to accommodate scientific developments, including theories of evolution, were in line with William's Keble speech of 1878, he retained a conservative position on the specific question of biblical criticism.

When he stayed at Keble in November 1888, the year before *Lux Mundi*, he had a particular project of his own that he wanted to discuss. Having lost his voice after addressing 18,000 people at Bingley Hall, Birmingham, on the 7th, he arrived at the college 'soon after six' on Saturday 10th, and at nine o'clock, still a little hoarse, he talked to 'Mr. Gore' for two hours 'on meditated Hawarden foundation & other matters'.[59] Gore thought it was a joke that William could focus upon 'a scheme he has got for the furtherance of theological study amongst the clergy, as if he had no other thought in the world.'[60] The intensity, however, with which William followed up this conversation was typical of him. Politics could wait. Next day, he attended three services in Oxford and read Gore's new book on *The Ministry of the Christian Church*. On the Monday, still with a slight sore throat, he dined in hall at Keble and had a 'full conversation' with his host, Talbot, and Gore 'on Meditated foundation. Made Mem[orandum] of heads'. So the first detailed document regarding the future St Deiniol's Library was drafted in a specifically liberal catholic context, and in response to discussions with two leading figures of their generation at Oxford. Under '*Purpose*, Higher', William wrote 'Divine learning and worship' and 'Gradual formation of a body'; and under 'Secondary & possible', 'Aid to the local Church', 'Home for retired clergy', and so on.[61]

Next day he was off to London, where he was soon caught up in discussions with parliamentary colleagues on Ireland.

Two years before this Keble visit, he had shared his vision of some kind of foundation, based upon a large collection of his books, with members of the family, and particularly his son Stephen, Rector of Hawarden.[62] His children would have to support such a heritage project after his death, and he had to ensure that his gift to the Church of England was in safe hands. Having built a fireproof 'octagon', adjacent to the Temple of Peace, he began the 'very formidable business' of arranging his papers as a duty to his children, 'whom it wd sorely perplex', in August 1888.[63] The books, however, were to be housed on a separate site in the village, which he surveyed with Stephen that summer, taking professional advice, and later dragging guests along to share the vision. By August 1889, plans for the temporary library building were at an advanced stage: 'My ground floor is to be Theological & planned for 25000 volumes.'[64] Large sections of his collection on literature, history, philosophy, and other subjects broadened the agenda of 'divine learning', William's term for a serious engagement with the God-given wisdom of the ages, epitomized in his own eclectic reading. Over the Christmas period, and the celebration of his eightieth birthday, he was shelving books in the 'Tin Tabernacle', as it was affectionately known, aided by the village joiner and his daughter Helen, having taken his turn pushing the famous wheelbarrow, laden with volumes, up from the Castle. As he solemnly recorded on his birthday, his 'physical conservation' was 'noteworthy'. He could never 'get at the true measure' of his sinfulness, however, until he was 'permitted to pass into the condition of a simply private person'.[65] Meanwhile, according to Mary, seven people worked round a mountain of presents for an hour that day, 'without making very much perceptible difference. Flowers, blankets, gingerbreads, pocketbooks, sausages, crumpets, pictures, books, lamps, vases, rings, cushions, etc., etc.'[66]

Employed for His purposes

William's lifelong belief in divine providence, discussed in earlier chapters, deepened in the 1880s, a decade in which his political or public life—'the best part of my life'—became more taxing as he got older. In late March 1884 it was his duty as prime minister to propose an 'Address of Condolence' on the death of the haemophiliac Prince Leopold, Duke of Albany, at the age of thirty. His immediate response to the sad news from Windsor—'He would have made his mark'—provided the theme for his address: 'When, in extremely early life, it is the will of Providence to cut the thread of that life before the bud has in any degree opened into flower, deep regret is felt; but, at the same time, no one can measure the loss experienced. But in the case of the Duke of Albany . . . both the gifts which it had pleased Providence to bestow upon him and the cultivation which had been incessantly applied to them gave the richest and most certain promise.'[67] The two references to providence convey a sense of divine guidance being at work in every human life.

Whereas such references remained standard features of public discourse at times of national mourning, William's private reflections on the role of providence in external events were those of an older generation. In February 1881 he received news of a skirmish at Majuba Hill which left ninety-six English troops dead. 'Sad Sad news from South Africa', he recorded: 'is it the Hand of judgment?'[68] When facing electoral defeat, in July 1886, he felt somewhat perturbed by the results, 'but One ever sitteth above'.[69] Two days later it became clear that the defeat was a 'smash'. 'I accept the will of God for my poor country or the English part of it,' he wrote, adding, 'To me personally it is a great relief; including in this cessation of my painful relations with the Queen, who will have a like feeling.'

Whereas royal deaths, colonial skirmishes, and general elections were passing events which invited interpretation, the catholic and apostolic church was for William an institution founded and sustained by Christ himself, to be reaffirmed in each generation, rather than reinterpreted. During Lent in 1881 he had 'much conversation' with one of his high church protégés, the Revd Malcolm MacColl, a Scottish priest and publicist who had been trained at Trinity College, Glenalmond. They discussed an unsuccessful attempt to reprint Palmer's *Treatise on the Church of Christ* (1838).[70] A few days later William wrote to MacColl, 'What I want to have, on the basis of Palmer's work, is a setting forth, according to the methods which theological science provides, of the Civitas Dei, the City set on a hill, the pillar and ground of truth, the Catholic and Apostolic Church . . . not as against

Nonconformists, nor even principally as against the Jesuit aggressive Church of Rome, but as a positive dispensation, a form divinely given to the religious idea, which challenges with authority, but agreeably to reason, the assent of the rational and right-minded man, in competition with all the other claimants on that assent.' In the midst of many competing systems of belief and unbelief in the modern world, he looked for a 'textbook' on 'the case of the English Church, under the shadow of which our lot is providentially cast'. The following year he referred to Newman's Roman Catholic classic in a private memorandum: 'I too have my "Grammar of Assent." The frame & constitution of things wherein we live teach me to believe in an Author of unbound intelligence who works towards justice truth and mercy' (Micah 6.8). 'I am not surprised', he added, that for 'the conservation of the record, & for organising and guiding the tradition there should have been founded in the world by Christ our Lord a Society for perpetual though not perfect life, which we term the Church.'[71]

How, then, was William's understanding of the workings of providence in the world at large related to his sense of divine guidance in his own life? The most obvious connection between the external and the internal occurs when William is the agent in a major political event, as in his second Midlothian campaign, which finished on 2 April 1880: 'so ends the second series of the speeches in which I have hammered with all my little might at the fabric of the present Tory power.'[72] But a larger force was at work during the election. The next day at Dalmeny was quiet, but his correspondence and 'incoming news' made it busy: 'It seemed as if the arm of the Lord had bared itself for work He has made His own.' When he travelled home all night on the 6th, by train, he 'had time to ruminate on the great hand of God so evidently displayed'. Hawarden awaited him, with a chance to reread *Guy Mannering* and to begin cabinet-making, before a 'reluctant goodbye' on the 19th and a journey to London which he vaguely felt to be 'a plunge, out of an atmosphere of peace into an element of disturbance. May He who has of late so wonderfully guided, guide me still in the critical days about to come.' Chiasmus (has guided/guide me still) dramatizes the transition from the past conflict (the election) to the future challenge (government).

On 20 May he went down to the House with his son Herbert, newly elected as MP for Leeds, and was greeted by a 'great & fervent crowd in Palace Yard: & much feeling in the House'.[73] In the diary, the business of the day is described briskly—'Spoke 1 hour on the Address'—whereas considerable space is given to spiritual reflection, with an echo of Newman's hymn, 'Lead, kindly Light':

> It almost overpowered me as I thought by what deep & hidden agencies I have been brought back into the midst of the vortex of political action and contention. It has not been in my power during these last six months to make notes as I could have wished of my own thoughts & observations from time to time: of the new access of strength which in some important respects has been administered to me in my old age: and of the remarkable manner in which Holy Scripture has been inwardly applied to me for admonition & for comfort. Looking calmly over this course of experience I do believe that the Almighty has *employed me for His purposes in a manner larger or more special than before*, and has strengthened me & *led me on accordingly*, though I must not forget the admirable saying of Hooker that evil ministers of good things are like torches, a light to others, waste & destruction to themselves.[74] In all things, at all times, by all instruments & persons, may His will be done. (My emphases.)

These reflections were written at the beginning of his second administration. On his seventy-sixth birthday, 29 December 1885, he looked back at the year in which it had come to an end. 'What is my true standing before God?' he asked. 'How much has He shown me! yet this I have not learned.' He would only see clearly after extricating himself from 'the life of contention' in politics; but, he adds, 'I know truly that I am not worthy of this liberty with which Christ makes free His elect. In His own good time something I trust will for me too be mercifully devised.'[75] Not yet, however. A month later the Tory government was defeated and on 3 February 1886 William formed his third administration. On 8 April he introduced the Government of Ireland (home rule) bill in a spell-binding speech of three and a half hours. As so often on big occasions, he was supported by words from the Psalms: 'The message came to me this morning: "Hold thou up my goings in thy paths: that my footsteps slip not"' (Psalms 17.5).[76] When the bill was rejected on its second reading in June, he went to the country, and found during long speeches in Midlothian that his voice 'held out in a marvellous manner. "I went in bitterness, in the heat of my spirit: but the hand of the Lord was strong upon me"' (Ezekiel 3.14).[77] He was defeated in July. A minor ailment in October made bed rest necessary, affording William 'great opportunities of review. Especially as to politics and my politics are now summed up in the word Ireland, for probing inwardly the intention, to see whether all is truly given over to the Divine will.'[78] Only by retiring to his closet can he discern whether God's will is at work in his long and highly personal campaign for Ireland.

Earlier in William's political career, the demands of long hours in the Commons, long journeys, and long speeches out of doors had taken their toll: the onset of head colds, chest infections, or diarrhoea often sent him to bed. The pattern was repeated in old age, but he was amazed to find 'new access of strength' as he battled on, in his view a gift from God. On 12 February 1884 Northcote moved a vote of censure on his Sudan policy, presenting him with one of the greatest challenges of his career. He wrote in the diary, 'Speech of 1 h. 50 m, history & controversy. Thank God it is off. This has been rather a sore time combining difficulties in Council constantly renewed with effort for & in the House. But God sent to me His words: "when thou passest through the waters, I will be with thee; through the rivers, they shall now overthrow [*recte* overflow] thee" [Isaiah 43.2]. So I have been in His sight: praise be to His great Name.'[79] Mary, who was in the gallery, wrote: 'I never before saw the House absolutely crammed between 8 and 9: there was a wonderful play and variety of emotion, indignation, scorn, earnestness and a certain amount of banter even, but for force and feeling I never heard it surpassed; he held the House in his hands and did with them what he would.'[80]

It was specifically when speaking that William felt a strong sense of divine support. Having addressed the House for almost two hours, for example, in February 1882, he wrote, 'A sustaining power seemed to come down upon me'; and in November 1888, when he addressed that vast crowd at Bingley Hall, he noted, 'I was at once conscious of a great strain upon the chest: yet strength & voice were given me for a speech of 1¾ hours.'[81] There was, however, more than a vague sense of support in his continued belief in what is called universal providence, of the kind taught by Calvin, and which we saw in his accounts of accidents, earlier in life. According to this, 'God is in direct control of every event, including every human thought and action.'[82] Two days after speaking at Bingley Hall he wrote, 'I woke without a voice: and in pouring rain, after the *four* days of fair weather while we wanted them. How He maketh all things in measure & in number [Wisdom 11.20]. I think there have been since 1879 not less than fifty of these fair days: and not *one* has failed us. And I am asked to believe there is no Providence, *or* He is not "knowable".'[83] Victorian England's most famous political orator also believed that words were put into his mouth, as Jesus promised his followers when they came to trial. When preparing his speech on Ireland and foreign and colonial questions at the Lord Mayor's banquet, in November 1880, he wrote, 'Ruminated much on what I should say: felt myself more than ever a poor creature. "But I will give you a mouth and wisdom"' (Luke 21.15).[84]

From time to time in the 1880s William wistfully looked forward to retirement and discussed the possibility with family and friends, most of whom responded negatively to the idea. Early in 1883, when still at Hawarden during the recess, he brought the Almighty into the argument. On 5 January the Psalm of the day for Morning Prayer in the Book of Common Prayer seemed to offer a lifeline. He wrote in the diary, 'Ch 8½ a.m. Sleep say 5–5½ hours . . . In the Psalms this day, as so often in the straiter passages of my life, God's love supplied me with a touching telling word. "Mine eyes are ever looking unto the Lord: for he shall pluck my feet out of the net." [Psalms 25.14] Can it be that He is backing, & thus taking, my side in the controversy over my early retirement?'[85] The answer proved to be negative, as it did in the 1890s, when he was to form his fourth and final administration.

Notes

1. Letter dated 8 April 1888, in William S. Peterson, 'Gladstone's Review of *Robert Elsmere*: Some Unpublished Correspondence', *Review of English Studies*, 21, 84 (1970), 442–61 (451). In his friendly review of the novel, William objected that 'A great creed, with the testimony of eighteen centuries at its back, cannot find an articulate word to say in its defence' (445).
2. Psalm 42 features in William's 'Collection of Psalms', kept since Oxford days: BL, 44, 833, f. 27r.
3. *Diaries*, vol. XI, p. 88. 31 December 1883.

4. *Diaries*, vol. XII, p. 60.
5. *The Prime Ministers' Papers: W. E. Gladstone, Autobiographica and autobiographical Memoranda*, ed. John Brooke and Mary Sorensen, 4 vols. (London: HMSO, 1971–81), vol. I, p. 3.
6. *Diaries*, vol. XI, pp. 219, 251. James Harris was a Tory foreign secretary before his elevation to the Lords.
7. See *Diaries*, vol. XI, pp. 222–27; BL, 44,768. f. 125.
8. GL, WEG/I 56/MOZ and GladCat.
9. *Diaries*, vol. X, p. 152.
10. *Diaries*, vol. VII, p. c
11. GL, WEG/I 56/WIL/ASH. On the annotations see Michael Wheeler, 'Gladstone Reads His Contemporaries', in *The Edinburgh History of Reading: Modern Readers*, ed. Mary Hammond (Edinburgh: Edinburgh University Press, 2020), pp. 83–103 (pp. 95–99).
12. *Diaries*, vol. IX, p. 434, 6 August 1879; BL 44,460. f. 305.
13. *Diaries*, vol. IX, p. 440, 3 September 1879.
14. *Diaries*, vol. XI, p. 537.
15. *Diaries*, vol. XII, p. 15. 27 February 1887.
16. BL, 44,733 f.13; *Diaries*, vol. XII, p. 19. 19 March 1887.
17. *Mary Gladstone (Mrs. Drew), Her Diaries and Letters*, ed. Lucy Masterman (London: Methuen, 1930), p. 65.
18. *Diaries*, vol. XI, p. 360.
19. *The Works of John Ruskin*, Library edition, ed. Edward Tyas Cook and Alexander Wedderburn (London and New York: Allen/Longmans, Green, 1903–12), vol. 35, p. 13.
20. See Michael Wheeler, 'Gladstone and Ruskin', in *Gladstone*, ed. Peter Jagger (London and Rio Grande: Hambledon, 1998), pp. 177–95 (p. 187).
21. *Diaries*, vol. XI, pp. 617–20.
22. Letter to Acton, 11 February 1885, *Diaries*, vol. XI, p. 295.
23. *Diaries*, vol. XI, pp. 495–97.
24. *Diaries*, vol. IX, pp. 573, 575.
25. *Diaries*, vol. X, p. 151.
26. *Life, Letters, and Literary Remains of J. H. Shorthouse*, ed. Sarah Scott Shorthouse, 2 vols. (London and New York: Macmillan, 1905), vol. I, p. 113.
27. *Diaries*, vol. X, p. 251.
28. *Mary Gladstone Diaries*, p. 248.
29. Joseph Henry Shorthouse, *John Inglesant: A Romance* (London: Macmillan, 1911), p. 197.
30. *John Inglesant*, p. 259.
31. *John Inglesant*, pp. 335–36.
32. *John Inglesant*, p. 402.
33. *John Inglesant*, p. 441.
34. See *Letters of Lord Acton to Mary, Daughter of the Right Hon. W. E. Gladstone*, ed. Herbert Paul (London: Allen, 1904), facing p. 1.

35. See Roland Hill, *Lord Acton* (New Haven and London: Yale University Press, 2000), p. 309.
36. Mary Drew, *Acton, Gladstone and Others* (London: Nisbet, 1924), pp. 1–2.
37. *Diaries*, vol. IX, p. 477.
38. GL, GLA/GGA/2/10/1/25/112.
39. Historisches Archiv mit Rheinischem Bildarchiv, Köln (Nr. 184/1880 Standesamt Köln).
40. GL, GLA/GGA/2/10/1/25/113. Papal infallibility was promulgated in 1870.
41. *Diaries*, vol. IX, p. 480.
42. *Prime Ministers' Papers*, vol. IV, p. 38.
43. *Prime Ministers' Papers*, vol. IV, p. 45.
44. *Mary Gladstone Diaries*, p. 253.
45. See William Whyte, *Oxford Jackson: Architecture, Education, Status, and Style, 1835–1924* (Oxford: Oxford University Press, 2006), p. 112, cited in Ruth Clayton Windscheffel, *Reading Gladstone* (Basingstoke and New York: Palgrave Macmillan/St Martin's Press, 2008), p. 160.
46. See Windscheffel, *Reading Gladstone*, p. 187.
47. Supplement to *The Guardian*, no. 1,691, double number, 1 May 1878, p. 614; 'Keble College, Oxford', *Illustrated London News*, 72, 2027 (4 May 1878), 16–17.
48. *Mary Gladstone Diaries*, p. 137.
49. *The Guardian*, p. 615.
50. Windscheffel, *Reading Gladstone*, p. 162.
51. Drew, *Acton, Gladstone and Others*, p. 57.
52. *Diaries*, vol. IX, p. 648; *Mary Gladstone Diaries*, p. 255; *Diaries*, vol. X, p. 402.
53. *Mary Gladstone Diaries*, p. 302.
54. *Diaries*, vol. XI, p. 216. 30 September 1884.
55. *Diaries*, vol. XI, pp. 274, 283.
56. See David W. Bebbington, *The Mind of Gladstone: Religion, Homer, and Politics* (Oxford: Oxford University Press, 2004), p. 243.
57. *Lux Mundi: A Series of Studies in the Religion of the Incarnation*, 8th edn (London: Murray, 1890), p. vii.
58. *Diaries*, vol. XII, p. 268. 31 January 1890.
59. *Diaries*, vol. XII, p. 160. See also Windscheffel, *Reading Gladstone*, pp. 174–75.
60. G. L. Prestige, *The Life of Charles Gore, A Great Englishman* (London and Toronto: Heinemann, 1935), p. 79.
61. *Diaries*, vol. XII, p. 161.
62. See, for example, *Diaries*, vol. XI, p. 589. 12 July 1886.
63. *Diaries*, vol. XII, p. 139. 10 August 1888.
64. *Diaries*, vol. XII, p. 226. 21 August 1889.
65. *Diaries*, vol. XII, p. 258. 29 December 1889.
66. *Mary Gladstone Diaries*, p. 411.
67. *Diaries*, vol. XI, p. 129. 28 March 1884; *Hansard*, vol. 286, cols. 1176–77.
68. *Diaries*, vol. X, p. 25. 28 February 1881.

69. *Diaries*, vol. XI, p. 583. 6 July 1886.
70. *Diaries*, vol. X, p. 37. 20 March 1881.
71. *Diaries*, vol. X, pp. 312–13. 14 August 1882.
72. *Diaries*, vol. IX, p. 497.
73. *Diaries*, vol. IX, p. 526.
74. See Richard Hooker, *Of the Laws of Ecclesiastical Polity*, Bk V, Ch. lxii, para. 10.
75. *Diaries*, vol. XI, p. 466.
76. *Diaries*, vol. XI, p. 526. Book of Common Prayer, Morning Prayer, day 3.
77. *Diaries*, vol. XI, p. 576. 28 June 1886.
78. *Diaries*, vol. XI, p. 619. 12 October 1886.
79. *Diaries*, vol. XI, p. 112.
80. *Mary Gladstone Diaries*, p. 301.
81. *Diaries*, vol. X, p. 212. 20 February 1882; vol. XII, p. 150. 7 November 1888.
82. M. J. Langford, 'Providence', in *A New Dictionary of Christian Theology*, ed. Alan Richardson and John Bowden (London: SCM, 1983), pp. 478–79 (p. 478).
83. *Diaries*, vol. XII, p. 160. 9 November 1888.
84. *Diaries*, vol. IX, p. 610. 9 November 1880.
85. *Diaries*, vol. X, p. 392.

8
Lead, Kindly Light

Lead, Kindly Light, amid the encircling gloom,
Lead Thou me on!
The night is dark, and I am far from home—
Lead Thou me on!

John Henry Newman, *The Pillar of the Cloud*[1]

William had described himself as old since 1880 and had sometimes wanted to retire during his second and third administrations. That wish intensified as he moved into the patriarchal phase of his Grand Old Manhood. On 29 December 1891 he wrote in the diary, 'I struck 82. In my *trunk* there seems still to be much life. I have the inconveniences of old age: but not such as to stop my work. It is a singular lot: I am not permitted the rest I long for: Amen. But I am called to walk as Abraham walked, not knowing whither he went. What an honour. Yet I long, long, long, to be out of contention: I hope it is not sin'.[2] Having established an unrivalled reputation as an energetic parliamentarian, gifted with remarkable stamina, he dealt with the inconvenience of old age by pacing himself rather more effectively. He now took to his bed at the first sign of a cold, for example. 'Threat of cold—early bed', he recorded on Tuesday 11 November 1890. Having stayed in bed until the evening of Wednesday, he could congratulate himself on the Thursday: 'Cold thrown off—by *early* care'.[3] He increasingly relied upon Catherine and the children for support, and he accepted invitations from two wealthy Liberal politicians to rest and recuperate in their grand houses, or to stay in a house or hotel on the Mediterranean at their expense.[4] On a good day, Mary could describe her parents as 'frisky as 3-year-olds';[5] but William knew that his poor hearing and sight affected his performance as a politician. On 15 July 1892 he quoted Newman's famous hymn in a diary entry: 'Frankly: from the condition (*now*) of my senses, I am no longer fit for public life: yet bidden to walk in it. "Lead Thou me on" '.[6] Later that month, his chancellor of the exchequer, Sir William Harcourt, was shocked by his deterioration, describing him as 'confused and feeble'.[7]

During William's fourth and final premiership (August 1892–March 1894), he succeeded in getting the second Government of Ireland (home rule) bill through the Commons, only to see it rejected by the Lords. When staying with Lord Aberdeen at Dollis Hill, in May 1894, he wrote to his son Stephen, misquoting another Newman hymn: 'Never did I see more plainly the Divine handwriting. Here had I been scheming for twenty years to get out of public life without dishonour, and never could make any approach to it. Then comes in the providence of God, and arranges to set me free by means of this cataract! from which in its turn I have good hope of being set free in a short time . . . Praise to the Highest in the height, and in the depth be praise!'[8]

Along with old age came the inevitable losses. He was the only member of his circle at Eton to see 1890. Between 1891 and 1893 several friends and confidants died, including Lords Granville, Tennyson, and Northbourne (Walter Charles James). He also lost his devoted doctor, Sir Andrew Clark, and Zadok Outram, the valet who had 'fitted into the nooks & crannies' of his life for many years.[9] Alcoholism had led to Outram's demotion (he was taken out of livery) and eventually his mysterious disappearance on 1 December 1893. According to Lionel Tollemache, on the following morning 'Mr. Gladstone thought that he saw him waiting at the breakfast-table, and asked the butler whether he was not there. Mr. Gladstone had no reason to think that this occurred at the moment of the servant's death; but he said it was the only occasion on which he remembered himself to have been the victim of an ocular delusion'.[10] By the 3rd, William was alarmed by Outram's absence, writing in the diary, 'Ever since I began to feel I was growing old I have been his daily care & he has served me with daily intelligence & daily affection'.[11] Outram's drowning in the Thames was a 'great sorrow', and the remains were taken back to Hawarden for burial.

William's greatest loss, however, was that of his eldest son, Willy, who died on Saturday 4 July 1891, following the removal of a brain tumour. Mary woke her father at Hawarden early that morning, but only told him the worst when they were 'within half an hour of London. He was terribly shocked and broken down'.[12] Next day he recorded that 'the services spoke to us at so many points . . . Among ourselves we spoke much of the beloved, not lost, only hidden for a time . . . Praised be God for all His goodness. The God of the widow and the fatherless'.[13] Back at Hawarden, he recorded on the 7th, 'Harry and Herbert brought the precious remains from Chester after midnight', and on the 8th, 'Our son in the prime of middle life was followed to the grave, with its wide and inspiring outlook, between twelve and one, by his mother in her 80th, and his unworthy Father in his 82^d year. We had all attended a Celebration in the Orphanage at nine. The devoted widow went to the service & the grave. It was more than she could bear'. He wrote the inevitable 'account', a copy of which survives in Mary's hand,[14] and discussed the question of succession with the family. Mary's summary of the 9th reads, 'Parents very, very much broken. He wrote a little memoir on the day of the funeral. He read *Pilgrim's Progress* through on the day of death'. He had also reread his childhood favourite the year before, on Easter Day, noting 'a clear cut objectivity reminding one of Dante'.[15]

This chapter examines the last phase of William's spiritual life, when he avoided writing a spiritual autobiography, but took a close interest in the biographies of former friends and colleagues. He also reflected upon death and the future life, particularly in his published work on Bishop Butler. His willingness to speak in public on the Armenian massacres when he was physically frail, and thus to spread the news around the world, is still highly appreciated in that country today. Armenian associations with St Deiniol's Church, Hawarden, were carried over into ceremonies associated with his death and his burial in Westminster Abbey, when the hymns chosen for the funeral service represented several strands of Christian tradition. Finally, William's spiritual life is reviewed in a short coda on his memorialization.

Our perpetual spiritual conflict

In 1881 William had hoped that a 'textbook' might be prepared on 'the case of the English Church, under the shadow of which our lot is providentially cast'.[16] Twelve years later, Charles Gore went some way towards fulfilling that hope. 'I have been reading with great delight

Mr. Gore's "Mission of the Church"', William wrote to Stephen on 20 March 1893, adding, 'I do not know when I have seen so much matter in so small a book and in general so admirably stated. If you have it not I should like to give it you'.[17] The book is based upon four lectures delivered by Gore at a St Asaph diocesan conference the previous summer, when he argued along lines that are often similar to William's on 'church principles'. For example, this passage could have come from William's own pen: 'As we move down the road of history we find the Church in different parts of the world assuming different characteristics. In the West, where the Roman genius prevails, the special characteristic is that of order and discipline. In Alexandria Christianity is regarded primarily as the truth, which is to attract, to satisfy, to educate, the intellect and life of man. But this variety in the local characteristics of churches only throws into higher relief the common underlying creed and conception of the visible Church'.[18] Similarly, Gore's lecture on 'Unity within the Church of England' focuses upon the apostolic succession and the sacraments, and in his final lecture, on 'The Mission of the Church in Society', he argues that the divorce act is against the law of Christ and pays particular attention to the ministry to the poor and to women.

His third lecture, on 'The Relation of the Church to independent and hostile Opinion', addresses what William had described as 'the real battle against unbelief', discussed in Chapter 6. Like William, he relates the journey of the individual soul to that of the church. 'We ought to study more, perhaps, than we do the message of the Apocalypse', he suggests. 'It is the book of the New Testament which conveys one particular lesson—the lesson that the Bride of Christ is for ever passing through those same phases of fortune that Christ in His human life passed through . . . The Apocalypse lays down the main conditions and principles of our perpetual spiritual conflict . . . We are to be like Christ . . . Through the grave and gate of death the Church passes to her triumph'.[19] In October 1859 William had argued that the key to our salvation lies in Christ's physical suffering, and that 'in what He suffered, in His experience, lay the discipline which made that Body fit and ready for its function, as the mould and model of the human race'.[20]

While celebrating Gore's fresh interpretation of high church principles, William frequently looked back to the crisis of 1845 in Oxford, the subject of his speech at Keble College in April 1878, when he presented Newman's conversion as a tragedy. This was Richard Church's central theme in his history of the Oxford Movement, a book that William began on Good Friday 1891, described as 'admirable' over Easter and as a 'great book' when he finished it on Sunday 5 April.[21] Church, Dean of St Paul's since 1871 on William's recommendation, had been one of the survivors in the shipwreck of 1845. His last appearance at St Paul's had been to officiate at the funeral of Canon Liddon in September 1890. Church and Liddon had been living proof that the church could pass through the 'grave and gate of death'.

When William finally began work on his fragmentary 'Autobiographica', in July 1892, there were no Augustinian descriptions of his own 'perpetual spiritual conflict'. Rather, he focused upon passages from childhood and his time at Eton, turning to his friendship with Arthur Hallam in November 1893. In *Præterita* (1885–89) Ruskin avoided subjects that might have angered or distressed him, and thus threaten his fragile mental stability. William's avoidance of difficult subjects, such as his mid-life crisis of 1859–60, or his subsequent relationship with Laura Thistlethwayte, was for other reasons. His diary and his letters to Laura had served as a confessional at the time. He still felt that he lacked 'a true self knowledge'.[22] There was an obvious need for secrecy. So there seems to have been no plan for a true spiritual autobiography. His fragments of retrospection on his mature adult life focus upon politics and religion, but in the latter case on the workings of the mind rather than of the heart and soul.

On 10 December 1893, the second Sunday of Advent, he was the guest of George Armitstead at Lion Mansions, a Brighton hotel, for a long weekend. 'Chapel Royal mg. Afternoon prayers at home: a congregation of 7', he recorded in the diary. 'Wrote Eucharistic Devotions out: great part'.[23] These prayers and meditations, some of them in Latin, were for private use at various points in the eucharist, such as after returning from the altar. Writing and copying material of this kind, for practical spiritual application associated with the eucharist, was the habit of a lifetime, alongside the reading of dozens of books on the sacrament over six decades.[24]

He spent the next weekend in London. Catherine travelled to Hawarden on Saturday 16 December ('What a spirit! By the same train, the remains of Z. Outram'), and on the third Sunday of Advent William attended the Chapel Royal, morning and afternoon, and 'Wrote Autob. MS. and Euch. Devotions'.[25] The Autobiographica moved slowly forwards chronologically, with an account of his thinking on auricular confession in the 1840s.[26] Recalling that, in 1841 or 1842, his '*mind* had attained a certain fixity of state in a new development' (my emphasis), he continues, 'I had been gradually carried away from the moorings of an education Evangelical in the party sense to what I believe history would warrant me in calling a Catholic position . . . I do not mean here to touch upon the varied stages of this long journey . . . I am now speaking all through not of spiritual life, a very interior subject, but of convictions and opinions in theology, a much lower and less inward matter: not that I am ignorant how these things are connected, but I am not entitled to assume that in my case the connection was a vital one'. His aims and objectives are markedly different from Newman's in the *Apologia*. Turning to auricular confession, a burning issue in the 1840s, he moves into the present tense to summarize the position that he still maintains: 'The healthy soul ought to be able to discharge its burdens at the foot of the great throne without the assistance of an intermediate person'.

Next day he recorded 'a troubled night physically, in brain only', adding, 'This is certainly the weakness of old age unfitting me for Parliamentary effort'.[27] Three months later, on 3 March 1894, he resigned the premiership and soon succumbed to 'a stiff bronchial cough' that required Brighton air for four weeks.[28] Work on Bishop Butler had resumed immediately, however, and he was soon ready to take up his translations of Horace and his Autobiographica. In a document marked '*Autobiog. Mch. 94. Secret*', he gave thanks for his newfound freedom before launching into commentary on recent events, and particularly his disagreement with members of his cabinet over the navy estimates, which he characterizes as 'accursed militarism'. Politics, he writes,

> are like a labyrinth, from the inner intricacies of which it is even more difficult to find the way of escape, than it was to find the way into them . . . It is the state of my sight which has supplied me with effectual aid in exchanging my imperious public obligations for what seems to be a free place on [']the breezy common of

humanity' . . . This operation of retirement . . . must I think be considered to be among the chief *momenta* of my life. And like those other chief *momenta* which have been numerous they have been set in motion by no agency of mine, and have all along borne upon them the marks of Providential ordination . . . The withdrawal of the demands, excitements and appliances of responsible office may leave behind at the moment the sense of a blank. But . . . it is not from inside but from outside the political circle that man if at all is to be redeemed. This is a new and great subject, not now to be opened with any good effect.'[29]

Further reflection is deferred, never to be taken up again in writing, although the 'chief *momenta*', shaped by providence, that we have considered in this book, form the very spine of his spiritual life. Modern liberal theologians have 'reduced the notion of special divine action to our subjective response to ordinary natural events'.[30] William is not one of their number. Yet his 'breezy common' quotation is from a famous passage in Harriet Martineau's radical *Autobiography* (1877), which he had described as 'a strange but instructive book'.[31] Ironically, it was precisely by letting go her Christian faith that she had achieved her own freedom. 'At length', she wrote, 'I recognised the monstrous superstition in its true character of a great fact in the history of the race, and found myself, with the last link of my chain snapped,—a free rover on the broad, bright breezy common of the universe'.[32]

Four months after the Brighton sojourn, an operation on William's cataract led to an interruption in the daily diary. On 25 July 1894 he wrote, 'For the first time in my life there has been awarded to me by the Providence of God a period of compulsory leisure, reaching at the present date to four and a half months. Such a period drives the mind in upon itself, and invites, almost constrains, to recollection, and the rendering at least internally an account of life'.[33] Here was 'a good opportunity for breaking off the commonly dry daily Journal, or ledger as it might almost be called, in which for seventy years I have recorded the chief details of my outward life'. He disparages the secret diaries that in fact reveal so much about his inner life, and he continues to defer the challenge of writing a spiritual autobiography. In February 1897, for example, he added a scholarly note to his Autobiographica of December 1893 on confession, announcing that his own ideas on absolution 'are more or less indicated in a paper on the Atonement of 1894', and that 'What is strictly personal to myself I shall probably reserve for a more confidential chapter'.[34]

In reality he could only render 'an account of life' internally. Most of the fragments of Autobiographica written in 1896–97 registered the hurt caused by Queen Victoria on his final resignation as prime minister, when she failed to acknowledge William's outstanding service to the nation. In the first of these fragments, he tentatively suggests that 'We may *sometimes*, even if it be *rarely*, obtain a *morsel* of self knowledge through the medium of a dream' (my emphases).[35] The previous night he had dreamed that he was at Windsor and was summoned to breakfast alone with the monarch at ten o'clock, an unprecedented invitation. 'But the dream had lost its tail. The hour never came. And the sole force and effect of the incident is to show that the subject of my personal relation to the Queen, and all the unsatisfactory ending of my over half a century of service, had more hold upon me, down at the root, than I was aware'. These words were written on 2 January 1896, during one of his holidays in Cannes as a guest of Lord Rendel. In the diary entry of the same day, covering events of the past week, he wrote, 'While it is on my mind, I place on record here awaiting some more formal method, my strong desire that after my decease my family shall be most careful to keep in the background all information respecting the personal relations of the Queen and myself during these later years, down to 1894 when they died a kind of natural death'. A rare foray into the unconscious, 'down at the root', sits alongside a characteristic piece of practical business relating to his legacy.

While carefully limiting the scope of his Autobiographica in the 1890s, he kept up his voracious reading of the lives of others, and particularly of contemporaries who had 'gone before'. He read Wemyss Reid's two-volume life of Lord Houghton (Richard Monckton Milnes) 'for many hours' in November 1890 and published a review of it.[36] (Among many references to William in the book is a shrewd comment made by a guest at a private dinner, that 'if Lord Beaconsfield was a good judge of men Mr. Gladstone was a still better judge of mankind'.[37]) Two months later he was immersed in Anne Mozley's newly published collection of Newman's letters as an Anglican, marking his copy frequently and adding a long index of his own, including a page reference to 'WEG'.[38] His review of Samuel Smiles's life and correspondence of John Murray, published in May 1891, ends with the boast of an elderly literary gentleman: 'I am the only man now living, who has had Mr. Murray, second of his race, for his publisher'.[39] During a Sunday in bed, on 14 June 1891, he 'read largely' Randall Davidson's life of Archbishop Tait: 'no slight exercise', he recorded, 'tho' the book is most attractive'.[40] And so it went on, with 'Mrs Carlyle's Life' in July 1891, presented by the author, Mrs A. E. Ireland; the life of the 4th Earl of Aberdeen by his son, in which he inserted many marginal notes, in February 1893; and Liddon's life of Pusey, in January 1894.[41]

On 17 December 1894, shortly before his eighty-fifth birthday, this inveterate chronicler and writer of lists recorded that, while enjoying 'the relief from the small grind of the Daily Journal', he thought 'it may be well still to note certain dates: and also books read. For a main difficulty with me now is to know *where* I have read this and that: and a list will be a help'.[42] He begins with three biographies of 1894, 'strange in succession, still more in their mixture'. His copy of Mary Church's *Life and Letters* of her father, Dean Church, is full of marginal marks and contains one of his additional indexes. Here there is much that aligns with William's own views and experience. In a letter of 1880, for example, Church referred indirectly to the formation of the fiercely anti-Ritualist Church Association in 1865, when writing on the danger of 'rooting out true Church doctrines and liberty by a policy of persecution which has been going on for the last fifteen years'. William underlines 'fifteen years', and mutters in the margin, 'nearer 50'.[43] Next in this strange succession came the *Life and Work* of Charles Bradlaugh by his daughter, Hypatia Bonner. The interminable controversy over Bradlaugh's refusal to take the parliamentary oath had clogged up parliamentary business during William's second ministry. Bonner complained that authors constantly referred to the atheist Bradlaugh as one who denied God, to which William responds sardonically in the margin, 'no wonder?'[44] Third in the list, and the most prolifically annotated and indexed, was Maria Bishop's memoir of the Roman Catholic novelist Pauline Craven, whose fiction depicts the glamorous world of continental salons.[45] In 1875 she published an article responding to William's views on Vaticanism: 'disappointing' in his view.[46] Having dined with the Cravens at the British Embassy in Paris in 1883, he had written to thank her for her article on the

Salvation Army and the Church of England, explaining that he was 'a traditionist' (*sic*).[47]

William's annotations indicate a particular interest in these biographers' 'accounts' of final illnesses and deaths. He also maintained his lifelong engagement with the question of a future state, reading works on the subject by a wide range of theologians and philosophers. For example, his reading list of December 1894 included a recent book with the encouraging title *The Bottomless Pit: a discursive Treatise on eternal Torment*, by William Ross.[48] During a stay at Biarritz, in January 1893, he had told a local Anglican chaplain that 'the popular teaching on Eschatology was most superficial', with the notable exception of *Catholic Eschatology and Universalism* (1876) by the Roman Catholic convert Henry Oxenham.[49] He often turned to earlier sources. Sunday reading in 1890 included *A Philosophical Discourse concerning the Natural Immortality of the Soul*, 2 vols. (1708) by the Platonist John Norris, Rector of Bemerton; and on Sunday 20 September 1891 he read Robert Day's *Free Thoughts in Defence of a Future State* (1700).[50] He was sufficiently well read to suggest, in his essay 'On the Ancient Beliefs in a Future State' (October 1891), that the doctrine of immortality in the Old Testament outlined by the distinguished Hebraist and biblical scholar Thomas Cheyne required 'an important modification'.[51] He ends the article, however, by stating that, 'when the Redeemer, standing in Judea, brings life and immortality fully into light, He propounds a doctrine already not without venerable witness in the conscience and tradition of mankind'.[52]

Oxenham had Matthew Arnold in mind when acknowledging that the doctrine of future retribution, based upon 'the exceeding sinfulness of sin', was 'peculiarly repugnant to the spirit of the age'. 'The conviction of sin', he argued, 'whether original or actual, is abhorrent alike to the pride and sensuality ... of the dominant "*Zeitgeist*"'.[53] William agreed. He was concerned that the relegation of hell to 'the far-off corners of the Christian mind' represented a highly selective reading of the scriptures.[54] He made this point in his *Studies subsidiary to the Works of Bishop Butler* (1896), the product of decades of study and reflection. His commentary on Butler, one of his four 'doctors', often reads like a personal *summa*, so close are the positions of teacher and taught. Early in his introduction, for example, when commenting on Butler's treatment of the 'great governing agency' of the 'higher world', and on his 'strong statements of the ruin of the world through sin', he is reiterating principles that have dominated his own spiritual reflections throughout his life.[55] Elsewhere he offers personal observations that are inspired by Butler, as when he writes, 'In labour there is effort, growth, development, advance; in the absence of labour there is remission, poverty, stagnation'.[56] Similarly, he writes on the future life in the light of Butler, but with his own emphasis: 'The Christian dead . . . are in a progressive state', and the 'perversely wicked . . . disappear into pain and sorrow; the veil drops upon them in that condition'.[57] And when he comments on a rare example of speculation in Butler, relating to death as 'an enlargement of existence', he confesses to feeling 'like one resting on the wings of a great and strong bird, when it takes an excursion in mid-air, and is felt to mount as easily as it will descend'.[58] In old age, after decades of 'perpetual spiritual conflict', he reflects on death and the future life with Butler alongside.

That eminent parishioner of Hawarden

Theology engaged William's mind most often in the Temple of Peace. His heart and soul, however, found the most profound spiritual refreshment in church. Two or three Sunday services were normal, wherever he found himself, and preferably included a celebration of the eucharist. On weekdays at Hawarden, Mattins at St Deiniol's Church, led by his son Stephen or one of the curates, was a fixture in his routine. Once he became a political celebrity, the image of him reading the lesson there became a familiar aspect of his public persona.[59] When illness struck in the early 1890s, and his doctors forbade him from churchgoing, he registered deep regret in the diary.[60] An inconvenience of old age also played its part, as he recorded in October 1894: 'I am unable to continue attendance at the daily morning service, not [on] account of eyesight but because the condition of the bowel department does not allow me to rise before ten at the earliest. And so a Hawarden practice of over 50 years is interrupted'.[61] Evening Prayer became a substitute.

Two months later, on 29 December 1984, a representative of the Armenian community in Paris marked William's eighty-fifth birthday by presenting a chalice to St Deiniol's Church, in recognition of 'the great life, work, and sympathy of that eminent parishioner of

Hawarden, who had not only assisted the Neapolitan prisoners in their escape over 40 years ago, but whose voice and pen were used in sympathy with the Armenian people'.[62] On this occasion, the Arch-Priest of the Armenian congregation in London informed the rector that his father's sympathies with the Armenian church and nation were 'in harmony with the principles' on which his life had been based. The Anglo-Armenian Association had held a meeting in London on 17 December, to protest against the massacre of the Christians of Armenia by the Ottoman Turks. As William had declined their invitation to address the meeting, through ill health, they now came to him, in the hope of enlisting his further support. In the vestry he thanked the deputation for their choice of a chalice, 'an emblem of Christian love which performs so important a function in the great Sacrament of Christian love, by which Sacrament believers in our Lord and Saviour are permitted to attain to such near communion with God. I think it requires no more words from me in order to make clear why we are here'. He then said, 'the outrages and the scenes and abominations of 1876 in Bulgaria have been repeated in 1894 in Armenia'. Lunch at the Castle followed.

The eminent parishioner of Hawarden and his family received a further delegation on Easter Sunday, 1895. A leader in *The Times* commented on the fact that a number of Armenian refugees were present, and that William's address to them was 'very sympathetic, while containing pointed references to his age and to his retirement from public affairs'.[63] By early August, however, he had decided to speak publicly on the matter, knowing that his words would be both influential and widely reported. In some ways it was like old times, although in this final campaign he had to ask for an assembly room at Chester's town hall to be used, as he could not 'stand the strain of speaking in a larger room'.[64] Hundreds were turned away. William's family and supporters joined him on the platform, along with Arch-Priest Baronian, 'attired in his official robes and wearing the cross and purple biretta'. The Duke of Westminster, presiding, asked the audience whether England realized that ten thousand men, women, and children had been massacred in appalling circumstances. William then declared that nothing but 'a strong sense of duty' could have induced a man of his age, and 'not without other difficulties', to speak on this question. He examined the evidence of 'plunder, murder, rape, and murder. ("Shame")', and cited overwhelming evidence for the massacres, while carefully distinguishing between Turkish misrule and the precepts of their religion. A *Times* leader commented that he spoke for more than an hour, with much of his old fervour and 'oratorical brilliancy'.[65] Linley Sambourne's approving cartoon in *Punch* shows the Duke thanking a sprightly and dapper William as they leave the hall.[66]

William's second great speech on Armenia was more demanding for him, being delivered to an audience of around 6,000 at Hengler's Circus in Liverpool. On 24 September 1896, he and an impressive number of family members travelled there by special train, to be welcomed by Lord Derby, the Lord Mayor of the city and chairman of the meeting.[67] Again, he detailed the atrocities and distinguished between Islam and bad government. Of the victims he said, 'I confidently affirm, that if instead of being Christians, they were themselves Mahomedans, Hindus, Buddhists, Confucians—call them what you like—they would have precisely the same claims upon our support, and the motives which brought us here today would be incumbent upon us with the same force and with the same sacredness that we recognize at the present moment'. In contrast to most parliamentarians of the day, for whom the national interest was of primary importance, he offered a global vision. 'The ground on which we stand here', he declared, 'is not British or European, but it is human. Nothing narrower than humanity could pretend for a moment justly to represent it. (Cheers.)' And he ended by referring to 'the most terrible and most monstrous series of proceedings that has ever been recorded in the dismal and the deplorable history of human crime. (Loud and prolonged cheering.)'

A leader in *The Times* anticipated that the circumstances in which the speech was delivered would contribute to its impact. 'The spectacle', the writer suggests, 'of the veteran statesman quitting for a moment his well-earned repose, in order to plead the cause of the oppressed is well calculated to move the sympathy and the admiration of the nation'.[68] The speech would be 'read with eagerness from one end of England to the other'; it would be 'carefully studied by all the Cabinets of Europe'; and it would 'penetrate, we may trust, the recesses of the Palace in Constantinople itself'. All 'sober politicians' would, however, part with him on 'practical remedies', including coercion. *Punch* was strongly approving, however, with Tenniel portraying William as an elderly knight in full armour and with sword drawn, making 'A Strong Appeal' to Britannia for action.[69] When Lord Rosebery resigned from the leadership of the Liberal Party, twelve days later, he cited William's speech as the 'last straw on his back'.[70]

On 20 October 1896, William listed seven matters 'entailing anxiety in various degrees' which had occurred recently. These included the crisis of the leadership, the Armenian question, and 'the sudden death of Archbishop Benson while he was our guest at Hawarden'.[71] On 11 October, Edward Benson had died of heart failure at the Castle, having collapsed during the general confession and absolution at Mattins in St Deiniol's Church, when seated next to Catherine.[72] At the funeral service there, his coffin was covered with a white silk pall that had been donated to William by the Armenians, on which the words 'Requiescat in Pace' and 'In Memory of Archbishop Benson, Hawarden, October 1896' were embroidered. The association between Armenia and St Deiniol's Church was strengthened further on Catherine's eighty-fifth birthday, 6 January 1897, when another Armenian deputation arrived at Hawarden Castle, and presented her with a portrait of the Catholicos of All Armenians. The party then moved to the church, where the Martyrs of Armenia window was blessed by Alfred Edwards, Bishop of St Asaph. Edward Frampton's window depicts St Bartholomew, said to have taken Christianity to Armenia and been martyred there in the first century, and St Gregory, the monk responsible for the country's becoming the first nation on earth to officially embrace Christianity in 301 AD. The pleasure afforded to that eminent parishioner of Hawarden, no longer a daily diarist, can only be imagined. During a subsequent stay in Cannes, he wrote a pamphlet entitled *The Eastern Crisis: A Letter to the Duke of Westminster, K. G.*, in which he suggested that 'the great and terrible tragedy of Armenia' was now 'out of sight if not out of mind'.[73]

While holding Armenia in mind throughout 1896, he had also focused upon the question of the future life, the subject of a lengthy paper on Bishop Butler that was printed in parts over six months in the *North American Review* that year. On 3 February he wrote to his son Stephen from Biarritz, summarizing the contents. 'My impressions about "Eternal Hope" are much like yours', he wrote: 'What I find in Scripture is, a flood of light upon the blessed future of the righteous, but much reserve, *beyond* a certain line or precinct, on that of the wicked'.[74]

The concluding words of his paper draw upon a lifetime's Butlerian reflection on universal laws and on reserve in the scriptures: 'The specific and limited statements supplied to us are, after all, only expressions in particular form of immovable and universal laws—on the one hand, of the irrevocable union between suffering and sin; on the other hand, of the perfection of the Most High—both of them believed in full, but only in part disclosed, and having elsewhere, it may be, their plenary manifestation, in that day of the restitution of all things for which a groaning and travailing Creation yearns'.[75]

Although his health declined in 1897, William noted in the final fragment of Autobiographica, dated 18 November, that old age had not prevented him from working on Homer until the previous August. He continued, 'With respect to the other world, my only special call to it was that of my age. The attitude therefore in which I endeavoured to fix myself was as follows. I desired to consider myself as a soldier on parade, in a line of men drawn up, ready to march, and waiting for the word of command. Only it was not to be "march" but "die" and I sought to be in preparation for prompt obedience ... firmly convinced that whatever He ordains for us is best for us and for all'.[76] His faith in divine providence was about to be put to the ultimate test.

Over the subsequent three months, while staying in Cannes as Rendel's guest, he suffered considerable pain. He then spent a month in Bournemouth. Facial cancer was diagnosed, and the public was informed of his terminal illness. 'His pain seemed to increase a little day by day', Mary recorded, 'and he had very wretched nights'. She wrote to her cousin, Lavinia Talbot, 'In his worst bouts you may hear him in a voice of extraordinary fervour, "Praise to the Holiest in the height," and all that verse, so that no one can say he is not an angel in the way he accepts the suffering, but I never saw anybody mind it as he does, and I can't say what my thankfulness is that it has not come till his 88th year, for he has the sort of organisation that is knocked all to pieces by it'.[77] 'Praise to the Holiest in the height, / And in the depth be praise: / In all His words most wonderful; / Most sure in all His ways!'[78]

On 22 March 1898 he returned to Hawarden to die. By mid-May the village was watching and waiting, along with much of the Anglophone world, frequently updated by a squadron of newspaper reporters.[79] Over a thousand letters of sympathy have survived, many of them full of praise for William's 'distinctively Christian contribution to public life'. Religious minorities 'recalled his sympathy for their cause'.[80] The end came on Ascension Day, Thursday 19 May: 'Just after 5 a.m. . . . with his wife, eight other members of the family and three doctors round the bed, Gladstone was pronounced dead. However much anticipated, this was an event reported throughout the world. The pressmen were waiting in the smoking room immediately underneath Gladstone's bedroom and they knew that he was dead when the stentorian voice of Stephen Gladstone intoning the prayers for the dying and the dead echoed around the corridors of Hawarden Castle'.[81]

Two days later, a full-page drawing on the cover of the *Illustrated London News* showed a light shining from the sickroom window at the Castle, as onlookers watched in the darkness. On an inside page, reporters are shown reading telegrams in the hall. Also illustrated is the body lying in the Temple of Peace, to which estate workers and others who lived in the village were invited.[82] Wearing his doctoral robes from Oxford University, he lay on the white silk pall from Armenia that had been used for the archbishop. A scarlet embroidered cloth, also a gift from Armenia, covered the feet. After lying in state in St Deiniol's Church, the simple coffin, made in the village, was displayed to the 300,000 people who paid their respects in Westminster Hall. *The Times* reported that the only colour to be seen was in 'the white silk pall, with subdued gold and blue embroideries . . . which hung at the foot of the bier, displaying to the people as they advanced up the passages the words "Requiescat in Pace"'.[83]

William was given a state funeral, the first since Wellington's in 1852. Appropriately, there were no military uniforms to be seen, apart from those worn by the guard of honour, formed by cadets from his beloved Eton. Those who could not attend the Abbey were offered further drawings in the *Illustrated London News*. Its cover for 4 June showed Catherine and some of her grandchildren next to the open grave, an intimate and highly unusual scene.[84] But for Catherine, as for William, the grave held no fears, rather a wide and inspiring outlook. The order of service for the Burial of the Dead included William's favourite hymn, 'Rock of Ages', by Augustus Montague Toplady, a Calvinist opponent of John Wesley; Newman's 'Praise to the Holiest'; and 'O God, our help in ages past', by Isaac Watts, a Congregational minister and theologian.[85] As in life, so in death, universal Christian truths were affirmed across the spectrum of traditions. He was buried beneath the aisle of the north transept. Canon Holland commented, 'He lies there in the thick of the throng . . . All the great ones who lie there are become the property of the people'.[86]

Requiescat in pace

Close to the grave stands Thomas Brock's marble statue of William in his doctoral robes, erected in 1904. Edwardian visitors to the National Liberal Club, London, encountered a statue or bust of the GOM at every turn. Monuments appeared in town centres across the country. Penmaenmawr, his favourite bathing resort, erected a bust by public subscription in 1899, in memory of 'Gladstone, Statesman, Orator, Scholar'. (It was stolen in 1977, but replaced, again by public subscription, by a local sculptor in 1991.) In St Deiniol's Church lie the marble figures of William and Catherine, side by side and shielded on the 'boat of life' by an angel. This extraordinary work of 1906 by Sir William Richmond is too large for its allotted space, forcing the visitor to squeeze around it, in order to admire the literary and religious figures depicted on the tomb chest. The sculptural heritage is as awkward as it is reverential. How to capture this remarkable polymath?

A further effort was made by John Hughes, whose bronze Gladstone Monument, commissioned in 1910 by the National Gladstone Memorial Committee, was destined for Phoenix Park, Dublin. It features four allegorical figures: Erin, Classical Learning, Finance, and Eloquence. When the city council rejected the gift, however, following Irish independence, it was relocated in front of St Deiniol's Library, Hawarden, in 1925. Catherine's last public act had been to lay the foundation stone of John Douglas's handsome library building in September 1899, erected by 'a grateful nation' and opened in 1902. Two years later the family contributed £8,000 towards the cost of an integrated residence, to incorporate a fireproof muniments room to secure the Glynne/Gladstone manuscripts. William's gift to the Church of England, 'for the advancement of divine learning', was now a national memorial. The Wardenship, however, was to be held by an ordained priest of the Church of England, as it is to this day in the rebranded Gladstone's Library, with its quarter of a million books (including 5,000 annotated by William) and 70,000 family letters; its courses, research programmes, writers in residence, and public lectures; and its twenty-six beds. Here, if anywhere, William's heritage is both honoured and interrogated, as in the library's support of research into the family's involvement in slavery.

The difficulty of grappling with William as a human being rather than a hero on a pedestal is captured by Michael (M. R. D.) Foot in his introduction to volume I of the *Diaries* (1968). 'Anyone', he writes, 'who has ever looked into Lady Frederick Cavendish's diary will appreciate at once the distinction between the wholly human and delightful Uncle William of her pages and the thirty-two-bites-to-a-mouthful Titan of Morley'.[87] And then there is the question of the rescue work, for which, strangely, William is best known in our own prurient age. As Foot goes on to explain, Henry and Herbert were exasperated by Peter Wright's false accusation of 1925 that their father had pursued and possessed 'every sort of woman'. Following a court case, vindicating 'the high moral character of the late Mr. W. E. Gladstone', the brothers thought it prudent to hand the manuscript diaries and the Thistlethwayte papers to the Archbishop of Canterbury in 1928, to be housed as his property, and that of his successors, at Lambeth Palace Library. As we have seen in earlier chapters, it is largely through the minutely inscribed agonizing of the diary, and the stabs at self-analysis in the letters to Laura, that we encounter a multifaceted and conflicted personality.

William's story turns upon a series of collisions between the real and the ideal: between the political fixer and the lone crusader on the side of the oppressed; between the reformer who embraced modernity and the conservative upholder of tradition in church and state; between the Soho adulterer in the heart and the distinguished parishioner of Hawarden. As he confessed to Laura Thistlethwayte, he was a strange mixture of art and nature. In this richest of lives devoted to reading, writing, and speaking on the widest range of subjects, the 'chief *momenta*' that he recorded in his diaries and memoranda were religious rather than political: confirmation at Eton, mourning for Canning, grasping the nature of the church in Rome, seeing a way forwards in Norwich Cathedral, Holy Matrimony, losing Jessy, reinventing himself as a writer and scholar, finding freedom in retirement. All were regarded as providential acts of grace, for which he was profoundly grateful. None was regarded as a fitting reward for effort, because a highly sensitive conscience constantly reminded him of the all-seeing eye. The memorials to this great statesman are the products of a nation that regarded itself as the greatest in the world. In fact, William is most truly the quintessential Victorian in the very complexity of his spiritual life.

Notes

1. John Henry Newman, *Verses on various Occasions*, 2nd edn (London: Burns, Oates, 1869), p. 148.
2. *Diaries*, vol. XII, p. 428.
3. *Diaries*, vol. XII, pp. 334–35.
4. Stuart Rendel MP was created Baron Rendel of Hatchlands in Byfleet when William resigned in 1894, and George Armitstead MP turned down an offer of a peerage in 1893.
5. *Mary Gladstone (Mrs. Drew), Her Diaries and Letters*, ed. Lucy Masterman (London: Methuen, 1930), p. 418, 1 March 1892.
6. *Diaries*, vol. XIII, p. 43.
7. Roy Jenkins, *Gladstone* (London: Macmillan, 1995), p. 585.
8. *Correspondence on Church and Religion of William Ewart Gladstone*, ed. D. C. Lathbury, 2 vols. (London: Murray, 1910), vol. II, p. 334.
9. *Diaries*, vol. XIII, p. 343. Letter to Catherine, 23 December 1893.
10. *Gladstone's Boswell: Late Victorian Conversations by Lionel A. Tollemache and other Documents*, ed. Asa Briggs (Brighton and New York: Harvester/St. Martin's, 1984), p. 161.
11. *Diaries*, vol. XIII, p. 331.
12. *Mary Gladstone Diaries*, p. 416.
13. *Diaries*, vol. XII, p. 393.
14. BL, 46,269. f. 144.
15. *Diaries* vol. XII, p. 284. 6 April 1890.
16. *Diaries*, vol. X, p. 37. 20 March 1881.
17. *Diaries*, vol. XIII, p. 216. William asked Murray to send him twenty copies for distribution.
18. Charles Gore, *The Mission of the Church: Four Lectures Delivered in June, 1892, in the Cathedral Church of St. Asaph* (London: Murray, 1899), pp. 19–20.
19. Gore, *Mission of the Church*, pp. 88–91.
20. BL, 44,781.f.124r.
21. Richard W. Church, *The Oxford Movement: Twelve Years, 1833–1845* (London and New York: Macmillan, 1891); *Diaries*, vol. XII, pp. 376–77.
22. *Diaries*, vol. XIII, p. 172. 29 December 1892.
23. *Diaries*, vol. XIII, p. 335; *Correspondence on Church*, 421–27.

24. See, for example, *Diaries*, vol. II, p. 98; vol. III, pp. 430, 432.
25. *Diaries*, vol. XIII, pp. 340–41.
26. See *The Prime Ministers' Papers: W. E. Gladstone, Autobiographica and autobiographical Memoranda*, ed. John Brooke and Mary Sorensen, 4 vols. (London: HMSO, 1971-81), vol. I, pp. 158–61.
27. *Diaries*, vol. XIII, p. 341.
28. *Diaries*, vol. XIII, pp. 390–98.
29. *Diaries*, vol. XIII, p. 402 (19 March 1894); *Prime Ministers' Papers*, vol. I, pp. 121–22.
30. Robert John Russell and Kirk Wegter-McNelly, 'Science', in *The Blackwell Companion to Modern Theology*, ed. Gareth Jones (Oxford: Blackwell, 2004), pp. 512–56 (p. 520).
31. *Diaries*, vol. IX, 209. 7 April 1877. She had declined William's offer of a civil-list pension in 1873 (ODNB).
32. Harriet Martineau, *Autobiography*, 2nd edn, 3 vols. (London: Smith, Elder, 1877), vol. I, p. 116.
33. *Diaries*, vol. XIII, p. 415; Add MS 44,790, f. 142.
34. *Prime Ministers' Papers*, vol. I, p. 161.
35. See *Diaries*, vol. XIII, p. 424 (2 January 1896); *Prime Ministers' Papers*, vol. I, p. 168.
36. *Diaries*, vol. XII, p. 334.
37. Thomas Wemyss Reid, *The Life, Letters, and Friendships of Richard Monckton Milnes, first Lord Houghton*, 3rd edn, 2 vols. (London: Cassell, 1891), vol. II, p. 462.
38. *Diaries*, vol. XII, pp. 359–61. 18–24 January 1891. The book contains fifteen references to William, who included 'WEG' among his own additional index entries: GL, WEG/I 56.6/MOZ and GladCat.
39. 'Memoir of John Murray', *Murray's Magazine*, 9 (January–June 1891), 577–87 (587). See *Diaries*, vol. XII, p. 379.
40. *Diaries*, vol. XII, p. 389.
41. *Diaries*, vol. XII, pp. 396–98; vol. XIII, pp. 204–6 (GL, WEG/M 34.9/GOR and GladCat); vol. XIII, pp. 352–66.
42. *Diaries*, vol. XIII, p. 421.
43. *Life and Letters of Dean Church*, ed. Mary Church (London and New York: Macmillan, 1894), p. 282. GL, WEG/I 56.7/CHU and GladCat.
44. Hypatia Bradlaugh Bonner, *Charles Bradlaugh: A Record of his Life and Work*, 2 vols. (London: Unwin, 1894), vol. I, p. 87. GL, WEG/E 39/BON and GladCat.
45. Maria Catherine Bishop, *A Memoir of Mrs. Augustus Craven (Pauline de la Ferronnays)*, 2 vols. (London: Bentley, 1894). GL, WEG/I 49 CRA/B15 and GladCat.
46. See Bishop, *Memoir*, vol. I, p. 357; *Diaries*, vol. IX, p. 30. 19 April 1875.
47. *Diaries*, vol. X, p. 412. 3 March 1883.
48. *Diaries*, vol. XIII, p. 421.

49. Briggs, *Gladstone's Boswell*, p. 95.
50. *Diaries*, vol. XII, p. 306 (6 July 1890); vol. XII, p. 408 (20 September 1891).
51. 'On the ancient Beliefs in a future State', *Nineteenth Century*, 30 (July–December 1891), 658–76 (658).
52. 'On the Ancient Beliefs', 676.
53. Henry Nutcombe Oxenham, *Catholic Eschatology and Universalism: An Essay on the Doctrine of Future Retribution*, 2nd edn (London: Allen, 1878), p. xxxvii.
54. *Studies Subsidiary to the Works of Bishop Butler* (Oxford: Clarendon, 1896), p. 206.
55. *Studies*, p. 3.
56. *Studies*, p. 10.
57. *Studies*, pp. 253, 259.
58. *Studies*, p. 249.
59. See, for example, Asa Briggs, 'Victorian Images of Gladstone', in *Gladstone*, ed. Peter J. Jagger (London and Rio Grande, 1998), pp. 33–49 (p. 39).
60. *Diaries*, vol. XII, p. 390 (21 June 1891); vol. XIII, p. 259 (2 July 1893); vol. XIII, p. 396 (7 March 1894).
61. *Diaries*, vol. XIII, p. 421. 1 October 1894.
62. 'Mr. Gladstone: The Armenian Question', *The Times*, 31 December 1894, p. 6.
63. *The Times* 16 April 1895, p. 7.
64. 'Mr. Gladstone on the Armenian Question', *The Times*, 7 August 1895, p. 4.
65. *The Times*, 7 August 1895, p. 7.
66. *Punch*, 109 (July–December 1895), 62.
67. 'Mr. Gladstone on the Armenian Question', *The Times*, 25 September 1896, p. 5.
68. *The Times*, 25 September, 1896, p. 7.
69. 'A Strong Appeal!', *Punch*, 111 (July–December 1896), 151 (26 September 1896).
70. See Jenkins, *Gladstone*, p. 628.
71. *Diary*, vol. XIII, p. 427.
72. *Mary Gladstone Diaries*, p. 433.
73. *The Eastern Crisis: A Letter to the Duke of Westminster, K. G.* (London: Murray, 1897), p. 10.
74. Lathbury, *Correspondence*, vol. II, pp. 123–24.
75. 'Man's Condition in the Future Life', *The North American Review*, 162 (June 1896), 740–56 (756).
76. *Prime Ministers Papers*, vol. I, p. 175. 18 November 1897.
77. *Mary Gladstone Diaries*, p. 444.
78. Newman, *Verses*, p. 348.
79. Detailed accounts are given in H. C. G Matthew, 'Gladstone's Death and Funeral', *Journal of Liberal Democrat History*, 20 (Autumn 1998), 38–42, and John Wolffe, *Great Deaths: Grieving, Religion, and Nationhood in Victorian and Edwardian Britain* (Oxford: Oxford University Press/British Academy, 2000), pp. 169–91.

80. Wolffe, *Great Deaths*, pp. 172, 177.
81. Matthew, 'Gladstone's Death', p. 39.
82. *Illustrated London News*, 112, 3084 (28 May 1898), 1, 4, 13.
83. 'The Death of Mr. Gladstone: the Lying in State', *The Times*, 27 May 1898, p. 4.
84. *Illustrated London News*, 112, 3085 (4 June 1898), 1.
85. GL, GG/1727, The Funeral Box.
86. Mary Drew, *Acton, Gladstone and Others* (London: Nisbet, 1924), p. 84.
87. *Diaries*, I, p. xxxii.

Selected Bibliography

Primary Sources

Unpublished materials
Gladstone Papers, British Library, London.
Glynne-Gladstone Manuscripts, Gladstone's Library, Hawarden.
Gladstone's Diary and other Manuscripts, Lambeth Palace Library, London.

Published Works by W. E. Gladstone
Address delivered at the Distribution of Prizes in the Liverpool College, Decr 21, 1872, London: Murray, 1873.
Address and Speeches delivered at Manchester on the 23rd and 24th of April, 1862, London: Murray, 1862.
Bulgarian Horrors and the Question of the East, London: Murray, 1876.
A Chapter of Autobiography, London: Murray, 1868.
Church Principles considered in their Results, London: Murray, 1840.
The Eastern Crisis: a Letter to the Duke of Westminster, K. G., London: Murray, 1897.
'Ecce Homo', London: Strahan, 1868.
England's Mission, p.p., 1878.
Gleanings of Past Years, 1843–78, 7 vols., London: Murray, 1879.
Homer, London: Macmillan, 1878.
The Impregnable Rock of Holy Scripture, revised and enlarged from 'Good Words', London: Isbister, 1890.
Juventus Mundi: the Gods and Men of the Heroic Age, London: Macmillan, 1869.
Landmarks of Homeric Study, London: Macmillan, 1890.
Later Gleanings, London: Murray, 1897.
A Manual of Prayers from the Liturgy, arranged for Family Use, London: Murray, 1845.
The Odes of Horace translated into English, London: Murray, 1894.
The Psalter, with a Concordance and other auxiliary Matter, London and New York: Murray/Scribner's, 1895.
Remarks on the Royal Supremacy, as it is defined by Reason, History, and the Constitution: a Letter to the Lord Bishop of London, London: Murray, 1850.
Rome and the newest Fashions in Religion, London: Murray, 1875.
Speeches on great Questions of the Day, London: Hotten, 1870.
The State in its Relations with the Church, 4th ed., 2 vols., London: Murray, 1841.
Studies on Homer and the Homeric Age, 3 vols., Oxford: Oxford University Press, 1858.
Studies subsidiary to the Works of Bishop Butler, Oxford: Clarendon, 1896.

Substance of a Speech for the Second Reading of the Maynooth College Bill, in the House of Commons, on Friday, April 11, 1845, London: Murray, 1845.

Two Letters to the Earl of Aberdeen, on the State Prosecutions of the Neapolitan Government, London: Murray, 1851.

The Vatican Decrees in their Bearing on Civil Allegiance: a political Expostulation, London: Murray, 1874.

ed., *The Works of Joseph Butler, D. C. L.*, 2 vols., Oxford: Clarendon, 1896.

(For a full list, including journal articles, see *Diaries*, vol. XIV, pp. 797–803.)

Subsequently Published Writings by W. E. Gladstone

Correspondence on Church and Religion of William Ewart Gladstone, ed. D. C. Lathbury, 2 vols. London: Murray, 1910.

The Correspondence of Henry Edward Manning and William Ewart Gladstone: the complete Correspondence, 1833–1891, ed. Peter C. Erb, 4 vols., Oxford: Oxford University Press, 2013.

The Gladstone Diaries, ed. M. R. D. Foot and H. C. G. Matthew, 14 vols., Oxford: Clarendon, 1968–94.

Gladstone to his Wife, ed. A. Tilney Bassett, London: Methuen, 1936.

Midlothian Speeches 1879, intro. M. R. D. Foot, Leicester and New York: Leicester University Press/Humanities Press, 1971.

The Political Correspondence of Mr. Gladstone and Lord Granville, 1876–1886, ed. Agatha Ramm, 2 vols., Oxford: Clarendon, 1962.

The Prime Ministers' Papers: W. E. Gladstone, Autobiographica and Autobiographical Memoranda, ed. John Brooke and Mary Sorensen, 4 vols., London: HMSO, 1971–81.

Other Published Works

Acton, John Emerich Edward Dalberg, *Letters of Lord Acton to Mary, Daughter of the Right Hon. W. E. Gladstone*, ed. Herbert Paul, London: Allen, 1904.

Argyll, 8th Duke of, *George Douglas, Eighth Duke of Argyll, K. G., K. T. (1823–1900): Autobiography and Memoirs*, ed. Ina, Dowager Duchess of Argyll, 2 vols., London: Murray, 1906.

Ashwell, Arthur Rawson and Reginald Wilberforce, *Life of the Right Reverend Samuel Wilberforce, D. D., Lord Bishop of Oxford and afterwards of Winchester, with Selections from his Diaries and Correspondence*, 3 vols., London: Murray, 1880.

Bonner, Hypatia Bradlaugh, *Charles Bradlaugh: A Record of his Life and Work*, London: Unwin, 1894.

Carter, Thomas Thelluson, *The First Five Years of the House of Mercy, Clewer*, London: Masters, 1855.

Church, Richard W., *The Oxford Movement: twelve Years, 1833–1845*, London and New York: Macmillan, 1891.

Davidson, Randall Thomas and William Benham, *Life of Archibald Campbell Tait, Archbishop of Canterbury*, 2 vols., London and New York: Macmillan, 1891.

Drew, Mary, *Mary Gladstone (Mrs. Drew); Her Diaries and Letters*, ed. Lucy Masterman, London: Methuen, 1930.

Gaskell, James Milnes, *Records of an Eton Schoolboy*, ed. Charles Milnes Gaskell, p.p., 1883.

Gore, Charles, ed., *Lux Mundi: A Series of Studies in the Religion of the Incarnation*, 8th edn, London: Murray, 1890.

Gore, Charles, *The Mission of the Church: Four Lectures Delivered in June, 1892, in the Cathedral Church of St. Asaph*, New York: Scribner's, 1893.

Greville, Charles C. F., *The Greville Memoirs: A Journal of the Reigns of King George IV and King William IV*, ed. Henry Reeve, 4th edn, 3 vols., London: Longmans, Green, 1875.

Greville, Charles C. F., *The Greville Memoirs (Second Part): A Journal of the Reign of Queen Victoria from 1837 to 1852*, 3 vols., London: Longmans, Green, 1885.

Guedalla, Philip, *Gladstone and Palmerston, Being the Correspondence of Lord Palmerston with Mr. Gladstone, 1851–1865*, London: Gollanz, 1928.

Guedalla, Philip, *The Queen and Mr. Gladstone*, 2 vols., London: Hodder, Stoughton, 1933.

Hallam, Arthur Henry, *The Letters of Arthur Henry Hallam*, ed. Jack Kolb, Columbus, OH: Ohio State University Press, 1981.

Heygate, William Edward, *Care of the Soul; Or, Sermons upon Some Points of Christian Prudence*, London: Rivington, 1851.

Heygate, William Edward, *The Good Shepherd; Or, Meditations for the Clergy upon the Example and Teaching of Christ*, 3rd rev. edn, London: Rivingtons, 1884.

Hodder, Edwin, *The Life and Work of the Seventh Earl of Shaftesbury, K. G.*, 3 vols., London: Cassell, 1886.

Keble, John, *The Christian Year: Thoughts in Verse for the Sundays and Holydays throughout the Year*, London: Bickers, 1875.

Keble, John, *On Eucharistical Adoration*, Oxford and London: Parker, 1857.

Keble, John, *Lyra Innocentium: Thoughts in Verse on Christian Children, their Ways, and their Privileges*, 13th edn, Oxford and London: Parker, 1870.

Keble, John, *Sermons, Academical and Occasional*, Oxford and London: Parker/Rivington, 1847.

Kempis, Thomas à, *The Imitation of Christ, in Three Books*, trans. John Payne, introductory essay by Thomas Chalmers, 7th edn, Glasgow: Collins, 1830.

Kempis, Thomas à, *The Imitation of Christ*, trans. Leo Sherley-Price, Harmondsworth: Penguin, 1952.

Kingsley, Charles, *Charles Kingsley: His Letters and Memories of his Life*, ed. Frances Kingsley, London and New York: Macmillan, 1895.

Liddon, Henry Parry, *Life of Edward Bouverie Pusey*, 4 vols., London: Longmans, Green, 1893–97.

Maurice, Frederick, ed., *The Life of Frederick Denison Maurice, Chiefly Told in His Own Letters*, 2 vols., Macmillan, 1884.

Mozley, Thomas, *Reminiscences, Chiefly of Oriel College and the Oxford Movement*, 2 vols., London: Longmans, Green, 1882.

Newman, John Henry, *Apologia Pro Vita Sua: Being a History of his Religious Opinions*, ed. Martin J. Svaglic, Oxford: Clarendon, 1967.

Newman, John Henry, *Letters and Correspondence of John Henry Newman during his Life in the English Church, with a Brief Autobiography*, ed. Anne Mozley, 2 vols., London and New York: Longmans, Green, 1891.

Newman, John Henry, *The Letters and Diaries of John Henry Newman*, ed. C. S. Dessain et al., 31 vols., London and Oxford: Oxford University Press, 1961–77.

Ornsby, Robert, *Memoirs of James Robert Hope-Scott of Abbotsford, D. C. L., Q. C., late Fellow of Merton College, Oxford, with Selections from his Correspondence*, 2 vols., London: Murray, 1884.

Oxenham, Henry Hutcombe, *Catholic Eschatology and Universalism: An Essay on the Doctrine of future Retribution*, 2nd edn, London: Pickering, 1878.

Purcell, Edmund Sheridan, *Life of Cardinal Manning, Archbishop of Westminster*, 2 vols., London: Macmillan, 1896.

Pusey, Edward Bouverie, *The Doctrine of the Real Presence as Contained in the Fathers . . . preached A. D. 1853, before the University of Oxford*, Oxford and London: Parker / Rivington, 1855.

Reid, Thomas Wemyss, *The Life, Letters, and Friendships of Richard Monckton Milnes, First Lord Houghton*, 3rd edn, 2 vols., London: Cassell, 1891.

Reid, Thomas Wemyss, ed., *The Life of William Ewart Gladstone*, London: Cassell, 1899.

Ruskin, John, *The Works of John Ruskin*, Library edition, ed. Edward Tyas Cook and Alexander Wedderburn, London and New York: Allen/Longmans, Green, 1903–12.

Russell, George W. E., *Mr. Gladstone's Religious Development*, London: Rivingtons, 1899.

Seeley, J. R., *Ecce Homo: A Survey of the Life and Work of Jesus Christ*, London and New York: Macmillan, 1900.

Shorthouse, Joseph Henry, *John Inglesant: A Romance*, London: Macmillan, 1911.

Stephen, Leslie, *The Life of Sir James Fitzjames Stephen, Bart., K. C. S. I., a Judge of the High Court of Justice*, 2nd edn, London: Smith, Elder, 1895.

Tennyson, Alfred, *The Poems of Alfred Tennyson*, ed. Christopher Ricks, London and New York: Longman/Norton, 1969.

Thirlwall, Connop, *Letters, Literary and Theological, of Connop Thirlwall, Late Lord Bishop of St. David's*, ed. J. J. Stewart Perowne and Louis Stokes, London: Bentley, 1881.

Thirlwall, Connop, *Remains, Literary and Theological, of Connop Thirlwall, Late Lord Bishop of St. David's*, ed. J. J. Stewart Perowne, 3 vols., London: Daldy, Isbister, 1877–78.

Tollemache, Lionel A., *Gladstone's Boswell: Late Victorian Conversations by Lionel A. Tollemache and other Documents*, ed. Asa Briggs, Brighton and New York: Harvester/St. Martin's, 1984.

Victoria, Queen, *The Letters of Queen Victoria: A Selection of Her Majesty's Correspondence between the Years 1837 and 1861*, ed. Arthur Christopher Benson and Viscount Esher, 3 vols., London: Murray, 1908.

Wilberforce, Samuel, ed., *Eucharistica: Meditations and Prayers on the most Holy Eucharist from old English Divines*, London: Burns, n.d.

Secondary Sources

Aitken, Ros, *The Prime Minister's Son: Stephen Gladstone, Rector of Hawarden*, Chester: Chester University Press, 2012.

Aldous, Richard, *The Lion and the Unicorn: Gladstone vs Disraeli*, London: Pimlico, 2007.

Askwith, Betty, *The Lyttletons: A Family Chronicle of the Nineteenth Century*, London: Chatto, Windus, 1975.

Bassett, Arthur Tilney, *Gladstone to his Wife*, London: Methuen, 1936.

Bassett, Arthur Tilney, *Gladstone's Speeches: Descriptive Index and Bibliography*, London: Methuen, 1916.

Battestin, Martin C., *The Providence of Wit: Aspects of Form in Augustan Literature and the Arts*, 1974; rpt. Charlottesville: University Press of Virginia, 1989.

Battiscombe, Georgina, *Mrs. Gladstone: The Portrait of a Marriage*, London: Constable, 1956.

Bebbington, David, 'Gladstone's "Church Principles considered in their Results": A Layman's Church Principles considered in their Result', *Nineteenth Century Prose*, 50, 1/2 (2023), pp. 281–300.

Bebbington, David, 'Gladstone's Preaching and Gladstone's Reading', *Nineteenth Century Prose* 39, 2 (2012), 113–36.

Bebbington, David, *The Mind of Gladstone: Religion, Homer, and Politics*, Oxford: Oxford University Press, 2004.

Bebbington, David, 'The Spiritual Home of W. E. Gladstone: Anne Gladstone's Bible', in *Religion and the Household*, ed. John Doran, Charlotte Methuen, and Alexandra Walsham, Woodbridge: Boydell, 2014, pp. 343–53.

Bebbington, David, *William Ewart Gladstone: Faith and Politics in Victorian Britain*, Grand Rapids, MI, and Cambridge: Eerdmans, 1993.

Bebbington, David and Roger E. Swift, eds., *Gladstone Centenary Essays*, Liverpool: Liverpool University Press, 2000.

Beer, John, *Providence and Love: Studies in Wordsworth, Channing, Myers, George Eliot, and Ruskin*, Oxford: Clarendon, 1998.

Bradley, Ian, *Abide with Me: The World of Victorian Hymns*, London: SCM, 1997.

Brady, Ciaran, *James Anthony Froude: An Intellectual Biography of a Victorian Prophet*, Oxford: Oxford University Press, 2013.

Brown, Alan Willard, *The Metaphysical Society: Victorian Minds in Crisis, 1869–1880*, 1947; rpt. New York: Octagon, 1973.

Brown, David, *Palmerston: A Biography*, New Haven and London: Yale University Press, 2010.

Butler, Perry, *Gladstone, Church, State and Tractarianism: A Study of His Religious Ideas and Attitudes, 1809–1859*, Oxford and New York: Clarendon / Oxford University Press, 1982.

Cannadine, David, *The Decline and Fall of the British Aristocracy*, New Haven: Yale University Press, 1990.

Chadwick, Owen, *The Victorian Church*, Ecclesiastical History of England, ed. J. C. Dickinson, vols. VII–VIII, London: Black, 1966–70.

Chamberlain, Muriel E., *Lord Aberdeen: A Political Biography*, London and New York: Longman, 1983.

Chapman, Raymond, *J. H. Shorthouse: Anglo-Catholic Novelist*, London: Anglo-Catholic History Society, 2009.

Checkland, Sydney George, *The Gladstones: A Family Biography, 1764–1851*. Cambridge: Cambridge University Press, 1971.

Colley, Linda, *Britons: Forging the Nation, 1707–1837*, New Haven and London: Yale University Press, 1992

Collini, Stefan, *Public Moralists: Political Thought and Intellectual Life in Britain, 1850–1930*, Oxford: Clarendon Press, 1991.

Crosby, Travis L., *The Two Mr. Gladstones: A Study in Psychology and History*, New Haven and London: Yale University Press, 1997.

Drew, Mary, *Acton, Gladstone and Others*, London: Nisbet, 1924.

Drew, Mary, *Catherine Gladstone*, London: Nisbet, 1919.

Fitzmaurice, Edmond, *The Life of Granville George Leveson Gower, second Earl Granville, K. G., 1815–1891*, 2 vols., Longmans, Green, 1905.

Galloway, Peter, *A Passionate Humility: Frederick Oakeley and the Oxford Movement* Leominster: Gracewing, 1999.

Ghosh, Peter and Lawrence Goldman, eds., *Politics and Culture in Victorian Britain: Essays in Memory of Colin Matthew*, Oxford: Oxford University Press, 2006.

Gladstone, William, *Gladstone: A Bicentenary Portrait*, Wilby: Russell, 2009.

Hawkins, Angus, *The Forgotten Prime Minister: The 14th Earl of Derby*, Oxford: Oxford University Press, 2007.

Hawkins, Angus, *Victorian Political Culture: 'Habits of Heart and Mind'*, Oxford: Oxford University Press, 2015.

Herring, George, *The Oxford Movement in Practice: The Tractarian Parochial World from the 1830s to the 1870s*, Oxford: Oxford University Press, 2016.

Hill, Roland, *Lord Acton*, New Haven and London: Yale University Press, 2000.

Hilton, Boyd, *The Age of Atonement: The Influence of Evangelicalism on Social and Economic Thought, 1795–1865*, Oxford: Oxford University Press, 1988.

Hinchliff, Peter, *Frederick Temple, Archbishop of Canterbury: A Life*, Oxford: Clarendon, 1998.

Hinchliff, Peter, *John William Colenso, Bishop of Natal*, London: Nelson, 1964.

Jagger, Peter J., *Gladstone: The Making of a Christian Politician: The Personal Religious Life and Development of William Ewart Gladstone, 1809–32*, Allison Park, PA: Pickwick, 1991.

Jagger, Peter J., ed., *Gladstone*, London and Rio Grande: Hambledon, 1998.

Jenkins, Roy, *Gladstone*, London and Basingstoke: Macmillan, 1995.

Jenkyns, Richard, *The Victorians and Ancient Greece*, Oxford: Blackwell, 1980.

Johnston, John Octavius, *Life and Letters of Henry Parry Liddon*, London: Longmans, Green, 1904.

Ker, Ian, *John Henry Newman: A Biography*, Oxford and New York: Oxford University Press, 1990.

Larsen, Timothy, *John Stuart Mill: A Secular Life*, Spiritual Lives, Oxford: Oxford University Press, 2018.

Larsen, Timothy, *A People of one Book: The Bible and the Victorians*, Oxford: Oxford University Press, 2011.

Ledger-Lomas, Michael, *Queen Victoria: This Horny Crown*, Spiritual Lives, Oxford: Oxford University Press, 2021.

Livingstone, Natalie, *The Mistresses of Cliveden*, London: Hutchinson, 2015.

Lubenow, William C., *The Cambridge Apostles, 1820–1914: Liberalism, Imagination, and Friendship in British Intellectual and Professional Life*, Cambridge: Cambridge University Press, 1998.

Lubenow, William C., *Liberal Intellectuals and Public Culture in Modern Britain, 1815–1914: Making Words Flesh*, Woodbridge and Rochester, NY: Boydell, 2010.

McKelvy, William Ralston, *The English Cult of Literature: Devoted Readers, 1774–1880*, Charlottesville, VA, and London: University of Virginia Press, 2007.

Magnus, Philip, *Gladstone: A Biography*, London: Murray, 1954.

Marlow, Joyce, *Mr and Mrs Gladstone: An Intimate Biography*, London: Weidenfeld, Nicolson, 1977.

Marshall, Catherine, Bernard Lightman, and Richard England, eds., *The Papers of the Metaphysical Society, 1869–1880*, 3 vols., Oxford: Oxford University Press, 2015.

Mason, Michael, *The Making of Victorian Sexuality*, Oxford and New York: Oxford University Press, 1994.

Matthew, H. C. G., *Gladstone, 1809–1898*, Oxford: Clarendon, 1997.

Matthew, H. C. G., 'Gladstone's Death and Funeral', *Journal of Liberal Democrat History*, 20 (Autumn 1998), 38–42.

Matthew, H. C. G., 'Gladstone, Evangelicalism, and "The Engagement"', in *Revival and Religion since 1700: Essays for John Walsh*, ed. Jane Garnett and Colin Matthew, London and Rio Grande: Hambledon, 1993, pp. 111–26.

Matthew, H. C. G., 'Gladstone, Rhetoric and Politics', in *Gladstone*, ed. Peter J. Jagger, London and Rio Grande: The Hambledon Press, 1998, pp. 213–34.

Meisel, Joseph S., *Public Speech and the Culture of Public Life in the Age of Gladstone*, New York: Columbia University Press, 2001.

Monypenny, William Flavelle and George Earle Buckle, *The Life of Benjamin Disraeli, Earl of Beaconsfield*, rev. edn., 2 vols., London: Murray, 1929.

Morley, John, *The Life of William Ewart Gladstone*, 3 vols., London and New York: Macmillan, 1903.

Nead, Lynda, *Victorian Babylon: People, Streets and Images in Nineteenth-Century London*, New Haven and London: Yale University Press, 2000.

Newsome, David, *The Convert Cardinals: John Henry Newman and Henry Edward Manning*, London: Murray, 1993

Newsome, David, *The Parting of Friends: A Study of the Wilberforces and Henry Manning*, London: Murray, 1966.

Nockles, Peter Benedict, *The Oxford Movement in Context: Anglican High Churchmanship, 1760–1857*, Cambridge: Cambridge University Press, 1994.

Orton, Diana, *Made of Gold: A Biography of Angela Burdett Coutts*, London: Hamilton, 1980.

Parry, J. P., *Democracy and Religion: Gladstone and the Liberal Party, 1867–1875*, Cambridge: Cambridge University Press, 1986.

Peterson, William S., 'Gladstone's Review of *Robert Elsmere*: Some Unpublished Correspondence', *Review of English Studies*, 21, 84 (1970), 442–61.

Pointon, Marcia, *William Dyce, 1806–1864: A Critical Biography*, Oxford: Clarendon, 1979.

Prestige, G. L., *The Life of Charles Gore, a Great Englishman*, London and Toronto: Heinemann, 1935.

Pritchard, T. W., *The Glynnes of Hawarden*, p.p., 2017.

Quinault, Roland, Roger E. Swift, and Ruth Clayton Windscheffel, eds., *William Gladstone: New Studies and Perspectives*, Farnham: Ashgate, 2012.

Richards, Jeffrey, *Sir Henry Irving: A Victorian Actor and his World*, London and New York: Hambledon and London, 2005.

Shannon, Richard, *Gladstone: I, 1809–1865*, London: Methuen, 1982.

Shannon, Richard, *Gladstone and the Bulgarian Agitation 1876*, London: Nelson, 1963.

Shannon, Richard, *Gladstone, God and Politics*, London: Hambledon Continuum, 2007.

Shannon, Richard, *Gladstone: Heroic Minister, 1865–1989*, London: Lane/Penguin, 1999.

Shorthouse, Joseph Henry, *Life, Letters, and Literary Remains of J. H. Shorthouse*, ed. Sarah Scott Shorthouse, 2 vols., London and New York: Macmillan, 1905.

Talbot, Edward Stuart, *Memories of Early Life*, London: Mowbray; Milwaukee, WI: Morehouse, 1924.

Vance, Norman, *The Sinews of the Spirit: The Ideal of Christian Manliness in Victorian Literature and Religious Thought*, Cambridge: Cambridge University Press, 1985.

Vidler, Alec R., *The Orb and the Cross: A Normative Study in the Relations of Church and State with Reference to Gladstone's Early Writings*, London: SPCK, 1945.

Vincent, John R., *The Formation of the Liberal Party, 1857–1868*, London: Constable, 1966.

Waller, Philip, *Writers, Readers, and Reputations: Literary Life in Britain, 1870–1918*, Oxford: Oxford University Press, 2006.

Weliver, Phyllis, *Mary Gladstone and the Victorian Salon: Music, Literature, Liberalism*, Cambridge: Cambridge University Press, 2017.

West, Jenny, 'Gladstone and Laura Thistlethwayte, 1865–75', *Historical Research*, 80, 209 (August 2007), 368–92.

Wheeler, Michael, 'Gladstone Reads his Contemporaries', in *The Edinburgh History of Reading: Modern Readers*, ed. Mary Hammond, Edinburgh: Edinburgh University Press, 2020, pp. 83–103.

Wheeler, Michael, 'Gladstone and Ruskin', in *Gladstone*, ed. Peter J. Jagger, London and Rio Grande: The Hambledon Press, 1998, pp. 177–95.

Wheeler, Michael, *Heaven, Hell, and the Victorians*, Cambridge: Cambridge University Press, 1994.

Wheeler, Michael, *The Old Enemies: Catholic and Protestant in Nineteenth-Century English Culture*, Cambridge: Cambridge University Press, 2006.

Wheeler, Michael, *Ruskin's God*, Cambridge: Cambridge University Press, 1999.

Wheeler, Michael, *St John and the Victorians*, Cambridge: Cambridge University Press, 2012.

Wheeler, Michael, *The Year that Shaped the Victorian Age: Lives, Loves and Letters of 1845*, Cambridge: Cambridge University Press, 2022.

Windscheffel, Ruth Clayton, *Reading Gladstone*, Basingstoke: Palgrave Macmillan; New York: St Martin's Press, 2008.

Witheridge, John, *Excellent Dr Stanley: The Life of Dean Stanley of Westminster*, London: Russell, 2013.

Wolffe, John, *Great Deaths: Grieving, Religion, and Nationhood in Victorian and Edwardian Britain*, Oxford: Oxford University Press/British Academy, 2000.

Zeepvat, Charlotte, *Prince Leopold: The Untold Story of Queen Victoria's Youngest Son*, Stroud: Sutton, 1998.

Index

For the benefit of digital users, indexed terms that span two pages (e.g., 52–53) may, on occasion, appear on only one of those pages.

Aberdeen, 4th Earl of (George Hamilton-Gordon) 71, 80–81, 86, 87, 88–89, 90–92, 110–11, 180–81
Aberdeen, 1st Marquess of (John Campbell Hamilton-Gordon) 174
  Dollis Hill 159–60, 174
Abraham 173–74
Acland, Henry Wentworth 14, 45
Acland, Thomas Dyke 14–15, 35, 37, 45
Acton, 1st Baron (John Emerich Edward Dalberg Acton) 116, 134–35, 151, 154, 156–57, 159, 162
Afghanistan, hill villages of 143
Albert, Prince (Prince Consort) 98, 106
Alexander, Cecil Frances 106
  'All things bright' 106
Alexandria 175–76
America 151
  Civil War 105–6, 108
Anglicanism *see* Church of England
Anne, Sister (Miss Thorn) 103
Anstice, Joseph 14–15, 21–22, 35, 58
Arabian Nights 5–6, 127
Argyll, 1st Duke of (UK peerage, George Douglas Campbell) 98, 104
Aristotle 31–32, 72
Armenia
  church 183–85
  massacres 175, 183–86
Arminianism 17–18
Armistead, 1st Baron (George Armistead) 177
Arnold, Matthew 182–83
Ashwell, Arthur Rawson 152
  (ed.) *Life of Samuel Wilberforce* 152

Atonement 55–56, 179–80
Augustine, St 34, 35, 177
  Confessions 34
Austen, Jane 3–4
  Mansfield Park 3–4
Autobiography 5–6, 20, 124, 127–29, 130–31, 151–54, 175, 177, 178–79

Bampton Lectures 17–18
Baptism 11, 13–14, 29, 35, 43, 59–60
  baptismal regeneration 13–14, 17–18, 43, 62, 78–79
Barnes, Thomas 109
Baronian, Arch-Priest 184–85
Bartholomew, St 186
Bathurst, 5th Earl (William Lennox Bathurst) 132–33
  Oakley Park 132–33
Bauer, Karoline 151–52
  Nachgelassene Memoiren 151–52
Bazely, Henry Casson Barnes 153
Beaconsfield, Earl of (Benjamin Disraeli) 84, 86, 87–88, 101–2, 124, 142–43, 149–50, 180–81
Bemerton 182
Benson, Edward White 186, 188–89
Bible 2–4, 7–8, 11, 12, 13, 15–18, 29, 31–32, 34, 39, 43–44, 51–52, 54–55, 56–57, 58, 90, 115–16, 117, 134, 162–63, 167, 182–83, 186–87
  books of
    I Corinthians 17, 114–15
    Ecclesiastes 20
    Ephesians 44–45

Bible (*cont.*)
  Exodus 108
  Ezekiel 167–68
  Genesis 9, 42–43, 65–66, 91–92
  Isaiah 168
  Jeremiah 117
  Job 16
  John 44–45, 51
  I John 1, 34
  Luke 20, 33–34, 43, 66–67,
    91, 168–69
  Matthew 12, 23, 27–28, 56–57,
    60–61, 71, 75, 76–77, 110–11,
    114–15, 117–18
  Micah 165–66
  I Peter 67–68
  II Peter 102
  Philippians 11, 91
  Proverbs 84
  Psalms 11, 21, 39–40, 65–66,
    73, 77–78, 87–88, 89–90, 117,
    141–42, 143–44, 149, 158, 160,
    167–68, 169
  Revelation (Apocalypse) 60–61, 176
  Romans 17, 56–57, 62
  Samuel 3
  I Timothy 42–43, 97, 123–24
  commentaries on 8, 12, 56–57
  New Testament 8, 13, 176
  Old Testament 5–6, 182
Biography 51, 113, 151–54, 181–82
Birmingham
  Bingley Hall 163–64, 168–69
Bishop, Maria 181–82
  Life of Craven 181–82
Blair, Hugh 8, 11
Blomfield, Charles James 75–76, 78–79
Bolton 108–9
  Farnworth 109
Bonner, Hypatia Bradlaugh 181–82
  Life of Charles Bradlaugh 181–82
Book of Common Prayer 3–4, 7–8,
  15–16, 27, 29, 30, 33–34, 39–40,
  44–45, 65–66, 72–73, 141–42,
  149, 169

Baptism 29
Burial of Dead 29, 53–54, 188–89
Churching of Women 43
Collects 7–8, 30
Confirmation 11–12, 29, 40–41, 90,
  114, 190–91
Evening Prayer (Evensong) 7–8, 30,
  74, 183
Holy Communion 12, 40–41, 42–43,
  44–45, 67, 74–75, 76–78, 90, 113
  (*see also* eucharist)
Holy Matrimony 27, 29, 44–45, 190–91
Litany 7–8
Morning Prayer (Mattins) 3–4, 54–55,
  87–88, 169, 183
Ordination 8, 11, 13, 21–23,
  29, 39–40
Psalms 7–8, 141–42, 158, 169
Bournemouth 187
Boveridge 129–30
Bradlaugh, Charles 181–82
Brampford Speke 59–60
Bramwell, William 55–56
  Life & Death of Ann Cutler 55–56
Brighton 177
  Lion Mansions 63–64, 177, 178, 179
Brock, Sir Thomas 189
Buchanan, George 8
  Psalmorum Davidicorum 8
Buddhism 185
Bulgarian atrocities 138–39, 140–41, 183
Bull, John 139–40
Bulteel, Henry Bellenden 9–16
Bunyan, John 5–6
  Pilgrim's Progress 5–6, 174–75
Burdett-Coutts, Angela 75–76
Burke, Edmund 37
Butler, Joseph 17–18, 72, 149, 175, 178,
  182–83, 186–87
  Analogy of Religion 17–18, 105
Butterfield, William 45, 160
  Keble College 160

Calvinism 2–3, 4, 6, 17–18, 30, 168–
  69, 188–89

Cambridge University 6, 9–10, 13, 14–15, 35
  Trinity College 9, 14–15
Canning, George 4–5, 31, 52, 55, 190–91
Canterbury, Archbishop of 8, 115–16, 129, 133, 155, 185–86, 188–89, 190
Carlyle, Thomas 23, 151–52
  'Signs of Times' 23
Carnegie, Andrew 151
Castle Howard 141
Catholic Emancipation Act 9–10, 15
Cavendish, Lady Frederick, née Lyttelton (Lucy) 190
Chalmers, Thomas 2–3, 8, 21
Charles I, King 155
Chester 85, 126–27, 174–75, 183–84
  diocese of 16, 18–19
  town hall 183–84
Cheyne, Thomas Kelly 182
China 91–92
Christadelphians 141–42
Christendom 113, 126, 156–57, 162
Christian Socialism 106
Church, the 1–2, 6–7, 11, 17–18, 27, 29–30, 32–33, 40–41, 44–45, 126, 133–34, 165–66, 175–77
Church, Mary 181–82
  Life of Richard Church 181–82
Church, Richard William 176–77
  Oxford Movement 176–77
Church Association 181–82
Church of England 3–4, 8, 12, 13–14, 17–18, 19, 28–29, 30, 35, 39–40, 59–60, 77–80, 81–82, 83, 91, 100–1, 112–13, 115, 117, 123–24, 133–34, 135, 136–38, 150, 155, 156, 158, 159, 160, 161–62, 164, 175–76, 181–82, 189–90
  broad church 113, 115
  catholic 10, 13–14, 44–45, 123–24, 134, 156
  divine society 17–18
  'high and dry' 15

  latitudinarianism in 27–28, 134–35
  liberal 113, 115
  liberal catholic 116, 150, 156–57, 163–64
  low church 134
  ritualism 134–37
  sisterhoods 77–78
  'third order' of 39–40
Cicero 13
Civil War, English 155
Clapham Sect 2–3
Clark, Sir Andrew 174
Clifton, Emma 79–80
Colenso, John William 115
Coleridge, Samuel Taylor 21, 37, 75–76
  'Ancient Mariner' 75–76
Collins, Elizabeth 82–83, 84, 87–88, 89–90
Commons, House of 15, 64, 76–78, 81–82, 83, 84, 86–88, 91–92, 97, 108, 116, 124, 136–37, 138–39, 141–42, 143, 150, 154, 168, 174
Comte, Auguste 133–34
  Catechism of Positive Religion 133–34
Confucianism 185
Congregationalism 188–89
Conservative Party 15, 32, 80–81, 84, 86, 138–39
  see also Tory Party
Constitution, British 8–9, 10, 11, 15
Contemporary Review, The 135–37
Conversion 5–6, 17–18, 55–56, 71, 81–82, 112–13, 116–17, 161–62, 176–77
Convocation 34, 85
Court, the 106, 142–43
Coverdale, Miles 7–8, 65–66, 141–42
Cowper, E. 103, 153–54
Cranmer, Thomas 7–8
  see also Book of Common Prayer
Craven, Mrs Augustus (Pauline de La Ferronnays) 181–82
Crimean War 71, 90
Croker, John Wilson 151–52
  Croker Papers 151–52

Cross, John Walter 154
    George Eliot's Life 154
Cuddesdon 13–14, 21–22

Daily News, The 134–35, 138–39
Dante (Alighieri) 72, 99, 174–75
    Divina Commedia 99
Davidson, Randall Thomas 180–81
    Life of Tait 180–81
Day, Robert 182
    Future State 182
Dearmer, Percy 106
Death 12, 20, 21–22, 36–37, 51–68, 174–75, 187
Derby, 14th Earl of (Edward George Geoffrey Smith-Stanley) 80–81, 84
Derby, 17th Earl of (Edward George Villiers Stanley) 185
Devil 54, 123–24, 132–33
Devotional books 12, 21–22, 84, 158
Dickens, Charles Huffam 75–76, 154
    David Copperfield 154
Disraeli, Benjamin *see* Beaconsfield, Earl of
Dissenters *see* Nonconformists
Dodsworth, William 37
Döllinger, Ignaz von 111, 116, 134–35, 156–57, 158
Douglas, John 189–90
Douglas, Lady Frances (Harriet) 38
Doyle, Francis 10, 11, 14–15, 35, 37
Drew, Mary, née Gladstone 42, 59–60, 138–39, 149–50, 154, 155, 156–57, 159–60, 162, 164, 168, 173–75, 187
Dyce, William 99
    Lady with Coronet of Jasmine 99

Eastern Question 91–92, 123–24, 135–36, 137, 138, 139–40, 143–44, 154
Edinburgh Review, The 137–38
Edwards, Alfred George 186
Eliot, George (Marian Evans) 154, 155
    Scenes from Clerical Life 155

Ellesmere, Dowager Lady (Mary Louisa Egerton) 110–11
    Worsley Hall 110–11
Engagement, the 39–41, 45, 72, 75–76
English Hymnal, The 106
Episcopalianism 2–3, 37, 40–41, 159
Erastianism 17
Erskine, 1st Baron (Thomas Erskine) 17
    Brazen Serpent 17
Essays and Reviews 115–16
Eton College 1–2, 6–15, 19, 31, 35, 38, 40–41, 52, 110–11, 158, 174, 177, 188–89, 190–91
    Eton Miscellany 8–10, 52
    Eton Society 8–10
Eucharist 12, 40–41, 58, 63–64, 159, 177, 183
Euclid 13
Evangelicalism 2–5, 6, 8, 10, 11, 12, 13–14, 15–16, 18–19, 20, 28, 32, 44–45, 53–54, 55–56, 58, 113, 130–31, 153–54, 177–78
Exeter, diocese of 59–60

Fabliaux et Contes 73, 98–99
Farquhar, Caroline 38, 54–55, 56–57
Farquhar, Lady Sybella Martha 54–55
Farr, William Wyndham 9–10, 14–15, 20, 72–73
Fasque 3–5, 33–34, 35, 40–41, 54–55, 59–61, 63–68, 72, 79–80, 81–82, 159
Fathers of church 13–14, 17–18
Ferrar, Nicholas 155–56
Flintshire 27, 85, 87–88
Formularies 17–18
Forster, William Edward 133
Frampton, Edward Reginald 186
France 137–38, 152
    Biarritz 182, 186–87
    Cannes 162, 180, 186, 187
    Cobden-Chevalier Treaty 152
    Henrietta-Maria of 155
    Paris 182–84
        British Embassy 183–84

Index

Franco-Prussian War 137–38
Freeman, Henry 55–56
  Life of Ann Freeman 55–56
Frith, William 149–50
  Private View 1881 149–50
Froude, James Anthony 151–52
  Thomas Carlyle 151–52

Gaskell, Elizabeth Cleghorn 75–76
  Mary Barton 75–76
Gaskell, James Milnes 10, 14–15, 35, 58
George IV, King 21–22
Gerbet, Olympe-Philippe 40–41
Germany 40, 137–38
  Bad Ems 40
  Baden 72, 73
  Cologne 157–58, 159
  Munich 72, 116, 156–57
  Tegernsee 156–57
Gladstone, Agnes (daughter) *see* Wickham, Agnes
Gladstone, Anne (mother) 2, 3, 5–7, 8, 27–28, 32–33, 38, 42, 43–44, 51, 53–59, 66–67
Gladstone, Anne (sister) 2, 3, 11, 16, 38, 42, 53–54, 56–57
Gladstone, Catherine, née Glynne (wife) 27, 40–45, 60, 61, 63–64, 66, 72–73, 74–75, 76–78, 80–81, 82, 85, 86–90, 98, 100, 101–2, 103–4, 105–6, 109, 111, 127, 130, 132–33, 143, 156–57, 173–74, 177–78, 186, 188–90
Gladstone, Catherine Jessy (daughter) 51, 59–64, 65–66, 67, 72–73, 80, 190–91
Gladstone, Helen (daughter) 3, 59, 164
Gladstone, Helen (sister) 4–5, 13–14, 39–40, 53, 54, 56–57, 63, 67, 72, 157–59
Gladstone, Herbert (son) 59, 101–2, 156–57, 160–61, 166–67, 174–75, 190
Gladstone, John Neilson (brother) 3, 6, 11, 28, 54, 56–57

Gladstone, Sir John (father) 2, 3–5, 6–7, 21–22, 30–33, 37, 52, 54–55, 60–62, 64–67, 83
Gladstone, Mary (daughter) *see* Drew, Mary
Gladstone, Robertson (brother) 3, 6, 56–57, 109–10
Gladstone, Stephen (son) 59, 114, 164, 174, 175–76, 183, 186–88
Gladstone, Thomas (brother) 3, 6–7, 14, 19, 32, 53, 54, 57, 67, 79–80, 159
Gladstone, William Ewart
  adultery in the heart 71, 75, 78–79, 82, 100, 130, 140–41, 190
  baptism 2
  beaten up 19–20
  bereavements 51–68, 174–75
  bible reading *see* Bible
  birthdays 1–2, 18–19, 35–36, 43–44, 77–78, 80, 87, 89–90, 91, 102–3, 118, 130, 164, 167–68, 181–82, 183–84
  childhood 1–14
  on Christian experience 36–37, 105–6
  confirmation 11–12, 29, 40–41, 190–91
  conversations 8–9, 13–14, 34–35, 36–37, 58, 59–60, 72, 76, 79–81, 101–2, 129–30, 134, 135–36, 151, 163–64, 165–66
  and conversion 5–6
  deathbeds, accounts of 51–68
  depression 39–40
  diary 1–2, 7–8, 18–19, 36–37, 38, 42, 53, 54–55, 56–57, 60, 61–62, 63, 65, 71, 72, 74–75, 80–81, 82, 84, 101–2, 117, 141, 166–67, 177, 179–80, 190
  on discipline 33–34, 36–37, 42, 76, 81–82, 97, 100–1, 102, 103, 104–8, 114–15, 153, 175–76
  on 'divine learning' 43, 108, 150, 163–64, 189–90
  education 6–23, 133, 177–78
  eucharistic devotions, collections of 40–41, 177

Gladstone, William Ewart (*cont.*)
  as father 42–44, 59–60, 72–73, 80, 85, 87, 91, 100, 102, 103, 114, 149–50, 156–57, 164, 173–74
  heaven, hope of 16, 38–39, 51–52, 53–54, 60–61, 66, 124–25, 186–87, 188–89
  high churchmanship 30, 37, 45, 58, 59–60, 77–78, 84, 99, 113–14, 134, 156–57, 160, 165–66, 176–77
  letter writing 9–10, 11, 59–60, 63–64, 82, 101–2, 123–24, 127, 129, 152, 174
  marriage 38–39, 40–41, 44–45, 72–73, 76–77, 78–80, 82, 98–99, 103–4, 130, 132–33, 189
  masturbation 1–2, 18–19, 72, 98–99
  memoranda 1–2, 17–18, 36–37, 39–40, 59, 66–67, 73, 74–75, 135, 153, 159, 165–66, 190–91
  memorials to 189–91
  on obedience 17, 33–34, 100–1, 106, 156, 187
  and ordination 8, 11, 13, 21–23, 29, 39–40
  parliamentary oath 27, 181–82
  and pornography 72, 98–99
  prayer 7–8, 11, 13, 20, 33–34, 40–41, 43–44, 77–78, 159, 160, 177
  and prostitutes 13–14, 59–60, 71–72, 75–78, 80–81, 82, 89–90, 91, 98, 101–2, 103–4, 127, 140–41, 190
  providence, belief in *see* Providence
  psalms, collections of 21, 39, 65–66, 73
  reading 1–2, 8, 12, 17–19, 21–22, 30, 34, 35, 40, 73, 75, 78–79, 84, 85, 99, 116–17, 123–24, 132, 151, 153, 154, 164, 175–76, 177, 180–81, 182, 190–91
  as scholar 1–2, 6–23, 73, 135–36, 179–80, 180, 189 (*see also* Butler, Joseph; Homer)
  scourge, use of 59–60, 72, 74–75, 76–77, 81–82, 100
  sermons of 40–41, 43–45, 87–88, 97, 100–1, 103, 114–16
  sin, conviction of 1–2, 5–6, 17, 18–19, 21–22, 39–41, 60–61, 72, 73, 74–75, 76–77, 80–81, 82, 84, 87, 90–91, 100–1, 108, 112–13, 143–44, 149, 155–56, 173–74, 182–83, 186–87
  slavery and 4, 31–32, 139–40, 189–90
  Sunday observance 8, 9, 16–17, 28–29, 31, 34, 36–37, 44–45, 72, 74–75, 99, 115–16, 129–30, 133–34, 142–43, 158, 159, 177–78, 182, 183
  on unbelief 123–24, 133–34, 135, 137, 143–44, 156–57, 165–66, 176
  women, idealization of 38, 54, 99, 134–35, 190–91
  work ethic 13, 33–34, 35–36, 71, 78–79, 80, 84, 85, 89–91, 136–37, 138, 173–74
  major writings:
    'Autobiographica' 151, 153–54, 177–78, 179–80, 180, 187
    Bulgarian Horrors and the Question of the East 123, 138–39
    Chapter of Autobiography 124
    Church Principles considered in their Results 41–42, 112–13, 175–76
    Gleanings of Past Years 108
    The Impregnable Rock of Holy Scripture 162–63
    Remarks on the Royal Supremacy 78–79
    The State in its Relations with the Church 27, 35, 37, 39–40, 81–82
    Studies in Homer and the Homeric Age 90–92, 111–12
    Studies subsidiary to the Works of Bishop Butler 182–83
    (ed.) *The Works of Joseph Butler* 17–18, 72, 105

Gladstone, William Henry (son) 42–44, 59, 61–62, 63, 65, 80, 85, 90, 114, 174–75
Gladstones, Thomas (grandfather) 4
Glynne, Henry 40, 80
Glynne, Lady Mary 40
Glynne, Lavinia 71, 80, 83
Glynne, Sir Stephen 40, 85, 105–6
Gordon, Charles George 151–52, 168
Gore, Charles 161–64, 175–76
  (ed.) *Lux Mundi* 162–63
  Ministry of Christian Church 163–64
  Mission of Church 175–76
Gorham, George Cornelius 59–60, 61–62, 64, 77–79, 83, 112–13
Graham, Sir James 37, 91–92, 110–11
Granville, 2nd Earl (Granville George Leveson-Gower) 116, 138–39, 174
Gravesend 154
Greece 111–12
  independence of 139–40
  Ionian Islands 91–92
    Corfu 91–92
    Platutera 91–92
Greek 6, 8, 13, 115
  see also Homer
Greenwich 124, 141
Greg, William Rathbone 79–80
Gregory, St 186
Gregory XVI, Pope 28–29
Grey, 2nd Earl (Charles Grey) 15
Guardian, The 158

Hagley Hall 74–75
Hallam, Arthur Henry 9, 14–15, 17, 35, 177
Hallam, Henry 35
Hamilton, Walter Kerr 10, 21–22, 34, 37
Harcourt, Sir William 173–74
Harrison, Benjamin 14–15, 34
Hartington, Marquess of (Spencer Compton Cavendish) 129, 138–39

Hastings, H. 100–1
Hawarden 187–88
  Castle 27, 40, 59–60, 71, 74, 83, 85, 87, 90, 91–92, 126, 136, 153–54, 162, 174–75, 183–84, 186, 187–88
  orphanage 174–75
  'Temple of Peace' 89–90, 164, 183, 188
  Rectory 40, 163–64
  St Deiniol's Church 40, 85, 117, 126, 175, 183–84, 185–86, 189
  St Deiniol's Library (now Gladstone's Library) 150, 163–64, 186, 188, 189–90
Hawthorne, Nathaniel 82
  Scarlet Letter 82
Hawtrey, Edward Craven 6–7
Heaven 12, 34, 51–52, 57, 67–68, 90, 112–13, 155–56
Hebrew 13–14, 111–12, 182
Hell 12, 75, 182–83
Heygate, William Edward 84, 91
  Care of Soul 84
  Good Shepherd 84
Hicks, Edward Lee 153
  Henry Bazely 152
Hinduism 185
Hodder, Edwin 153
  Life of Shaftesbury 153
Holland, Henry Scott 161–63, 188–89
Holy Spirit 11, 84, 159, 162–63
Homer 90–92, 111–12
Hooker, Richard 17–18, 37, 167
  Ecclesiastical Polity 17–18, 37
Hope, James 10, 14–15, 30, 37, 72, 79–80
Hope, William 10
Houghton, 1st Baron (Richard Monckton Milnes) 180–81
Hughes, John 189–90
Hunt, William Holman 160
  Light of World 160
Huskisson, William 4–5

Huxley, Thomas Henry 136

Illustrated London News 188–89
Incarnation 40–41, 44–45, 97, 100–1, 108, 114–16, 126, 134, 149–50
Ireland 37, 72, 116, 123–24, 125–26, 130–31, 151–52, 153, 154, 155, 167–68, 174, 189–90
   Belfast 125
   Church of 124
   Dublin 125, 189–90
      Phoenix Park 189–90
   Protestant ascendency 124
Irving, Edward 23
   'Signs of Times' 23
Irving, Sir Henry 149–50
Islam 139–40, 185
Italian 38–39, 73, 82
Italy 30, 35–36, 40, 60, 76–77, 137, 155–56
   Calabria 40
   Como, Lake 76–77, 185
   Messina 40–41
   Naples 40, 80–81
   Rome 40
      Colosseum 40
      St Peter's 155–56
      St Peter's Square 28–29
      Sistine Chapel 28–29
   Sicily 40

Jebb, Henry Gladwyn 100–1
   Out of Depths 100–1
Jennings, Henry James 151–52
   Lord Tennyson 151–52
Jerram, Charles 55–56
   Tribute of parental Affection 55–56
Jesus Christ 1–2, 11, 12, 17, 19, 20, 33–34, 40–41, 42–43, 44–45, 51, 62, 64, 75, 76–77, 90, 97, 107–8, 112–13, 114–15, 117–18, 123–24, 126, 135, 149–50, 156, 160, 162–63, 165–66, 167–69, 175–76
Jowett, Benjamin 115, 162

Judgment 12, 20, 42–43, 114–15, 137–38, 165
   last judgment 12, 124–25

Keble, John 13–14, 16–17, 44–45, 158, 160
   Assize Sermon 34
   Christian Year 158
   Lyra Innocentium 158
Kempis, Thomas à 21, 40–41, 63, 64, 91, 114–15
   Imitation of Christ 21, 40–41, 63, 64, 114–15
Kingsley, Charles 116–17
Kinnaird, Arthur Fitzgerald 37, 40, 126–27, 129–30
Knowles, James 135–36

Lancashire 88–89, 108, 113–14
   South Lancashire MP 97
   Wigan 124
   see also Bolton; Liverpool; Manchester
Langtry, Lillie 149–50
Latin 21, 34, 177
Lawrence, David Herbert 18–19
   Fantasia of Unconscious 18–19, 75
   'Pornography and Obscenity' 18–19
Leamington 4–5, 16, 21–22
Leeds 166–67
Leopold, Prince (Duke of Albany) 164–65
Liberal Party 71, 92, 97, 98, 113–14, 135, 138–39, 151, 173–74, 185–86
Liddon, Henry Parry 162, 176–77
Lightfoot, P. 80–81, 82
Lincoln, Earl of *see* Newcastle, 5th Duke of
Lincoln, Lady Charlotte 60, 76–77, 98–99
Little Gidding 155–56
Liverpool 2–5, 52, 54, 109–10, 133–34
   College 133–34
   Free Library 109–10

Index

Hengler's Circus 185
Museum 109–10
St Andrew's 54
St George's Hall 109–10
London 10, 13–14, 35, 40, 59–60, 85–86, 91, 138–39, 141, 149–50, 151–52, 159, 166, 183–84
   Argyll Rooms 79–80
   Bedfordbury 74–75, 80–81
   Berkeley Square 40
   British Museum 134–35
   Buckingham Palace 80–81
   Carlton Gardens 38
   Carlton House Terrace 40, 99, 103, 111, 135–36
   Chapel Royal 100, 177–78
   Church of Scotland church 153
   diocese of 78–79
   Downing Street 87–88, 100, 104, 153–54, 155
   Farm Street 80–81
   Fulham 40–41
   Gower Street 133
   Grillion's 151
   Grosvenor Hotel 136
   Grosvenor Square 125
   Harley Street 138–39
   Haymarket Theatre 138–39
   Hyde Park 125, 138–39
   Kensington Gardens 42
   King's College 133, 160
   Lambeth Palace Library 190
   Lord Mayor of 168–69
   Lyceum Theatre 149–50
   Margaret Street 45
     Margaret Chapel (later All Saints) 39–40, 45, 72, 114
   National Liberal Club 189
   Oxford and Cambridge Club 100
   Piccadilly 33–34
     Albany 33–34
     St James's 33–34, 42–43, 100
   St James's Hall 141
   St Martin-in-the-Fields 44–45
   St Paul's Cathedral 162, 176–77
   Soho 60, 75–76, 190–91
     House of St Barnabas 75–76
     St Anne's 60
   University College 133
   Westminster 15, 39–40, 109–10
     Abbey 32–33, 39–40, 52, 175
     Bridge 141
     Hall 188
   Willis's Rooms 98, 133, 138–39
Longley, Charles Thomas 115–16
Lyttelton, 4th Baron (George William Lyttelton) 40–41, 64, 77–78
Lyttelton, Lady Mary, née Glynne 160
Lyttelton, Lavinia *see* Talbot, Lavinia

Macaulay, Thomas Babington 40
MacColl, Malcolm 165–66
Mackarness, John Fielder 160
Macmillan, Alexander 155
Malmesbury, 3rd Earl of (James Howard Harris) 151–52
Memoirs of an Ex-Minister 151–52
Manchester 75–76, 88–89, 105–8
   Assize Courts 109–10
   Cathedral 108
   Exchange 88–89, 109–10
   Free Trade Hall 105–6, 109–10
   Town Hall 88–89, 108, 109–10
Manning, Henry Edward 40, 43, 58, 59, 72, 77–79, 80, 81–82, 116, 129
Mant, Richard 8, 11, 17–18
Martin, Abbé Jean-Pierre-Paulin 137
Martineau, Harriet 179
Autobiography 179
Mary, Blessed Virgin 43
Maynooth grant 27, 72
Metaphysical Society 136, 138–40
Methodists 17–18, 125
Midlothian campaigns 138, 143–44, 157, 159, 166, 167–68
Mill, John Stuart 109
Monasticism 21, 91–92
Monsell, Harriet O'Brien 103–4

Index

Monsell, John Samuel Bewley 123–24
   'Fight the good fight' 123–24
More, Hannah 2–3
Morley, John 51, 90–91, 113, 152, 190
   Life of Cobden 152
   Life of Gladstone 51, 90–91, 113, 190
Mozley, Anne 180–81
   (ed.) *Letters of Newman* 180–81
Mozley, John Bowline 151–52
   Letters 151–52
Mozley, Thomas 159–60
   Recollections of Oxford Movement 159–60
Müller, Friedrich Max 151–52
   Biographical Essays 151–52
Murray, Grenville 141–42
Murray III, John 135–36

Natal, diocese of 115
Neale, John Mason 77–78
Newark 30–32, 35–36
Newcastle, 4th Duke of (Henry Pelham-Clinton) 30
Newcastle, 5th Duke of (Henry Pelham Fiennes Pelham-Clinton) 10, 125–26
   Clumber 110–11
Newman, John Henry 10, 13–14, 16–17, 34, 35, 72, 116–17, 136, 137–38, 161, 173, 174, 176–78, 180–81, 188–89
   Apologia pro Vita sua 116–17, 177–78
   Arians 35
   Grammar of Assent 165–66
   'Lead kindly light' 166–67, 173–74
   Pillar of Cloud 173
   'Praise to the Holiest' 174, 187, 188–89
Newton, John 153
   'Amazing Grace' 153
Nineteenth Century, The 135–36, 142–43
Nonconformists 17–18, 113–14, 135, 153, 165–66
Norris, John 182
   Natural Immortality 182
North American Review 186–87
Northbourne, 1st Baron (Walter Charles) 174
Northcote, Sir Stafford 168

Norwich 38–39, 190–91
   Cathedral 38–39, 190–91
   Julian of 60

Oak Farm 71, 74–75, 85
Oakeley, Frederick 45
Onania 18–19
Outram, Zadok 174, 177–78
Oxenham, Henry Nutcombe 182–83
   Catholic Eschatology 182
Oxford 13–14, 153
   diocese of 114, 160
   Essay Society (WEG) 14–15
   Martyrs' Memorial 153
   Movement *see* Tractarians
   Pusey House 162–63
   St Ebbe's 16–17
   St Mary's 16–17
   Union 31–32, 104–5
   University 1–2, 14–23, 71, 114, 188
      All Souls College 114, 162–63
      Christ Church 1–2, 14–23
      Keble College 149, 159–64, 176–77
      Merton College 34
      MP for 59–60, 74, 85, 97, 110–11, 114, 117
      Museum of Natural History 161–62
      Oriel College 10
      Pusey House 162
      St Mary Hall 16
      Worcester College 34

Paley, William 13
   Evidences of Christianity 13
Palmer, Roundell 45
Palmer, William Patrick 30, 34, 37, 40, 165–66
   Origines Liturgicæ 30
   Treatise of Church of Christ 30, 37, 40, 165–66
Palmerston, 3rd Viscount (Henry John Temple) 71, 90–92, 97, 98, 104, 108, 111–12, 152
Panizzi, Sir Anthony 134–35
Pastoralia 13, 115–16

Paul, St 56–57
Peel, Sir Robert 14, 15, 27, 35–37, 79–80, 83, 87–89
  Peelites 77–78, 83, 84, 90–91
Pelham, George 12
Phillpotts, Henry 59–60
Pickering, Edward Hayes 10, 11
Pitt, William, the younger 52
Pius IX, Pope 116, 156–57
  Syllabus of Errors 116, 156–57
Platonism 182
Plymouth Brethren 16
Pope, Alexander 105
  Essay on Man 105
Pornography 18–19, 72, 98–99
Powys, Horatio 13
Praed, William 37
Predestination 9, 17
Presbyterianism 2, 33–34
Privy Council 59–60, 78–79
Protestantism 15, 17–18, 28, 124, 126
Providence 32, 35, 38–39, 40–41, 88–89, 97, 104–6, 107, 109–10, 111–12, 113, 117, 123–24, 127, 135–36, 137–38, 142–43, 150, 164–65, 166, 168–69, 174, 178–80, 187, 190–91
Pugin, Augustus Welby Northmore 137
Punch 99, 101–2, 124, 184–86
Puritanism 20
Pusey, Edward Bouverie 13–14, 34, 35, 37, 40–41, 44–45, 77–78, 161, 162, 180–81
Pusey, Philip 37
Putnam's Sons, G.P. (publisher) 151

Quarterly Review, The 91–92, 100–1, 135–36

Ramsay, Edward Bannerman 33–34, 38
Rawson, William 6, 27–28, 54
Reform Act (1832) 15, 22–23, 28, 104–5
Reform Bill (1866) 97
Reformation 17–18, 155
Reid, Stuart J. 151–52
  Sydney Smith 151–52

Reid, Sir Thomas Wemyss 180–81
  Life of Houghton 180–81
Rendel, 1st Baron (Stuart Rendel) 180
Richmond, Sir William Blake 189
Roberts, Robert 141–42
Rogers, Frederic 10, 14–15, 34, 45
Roman Catholic Church 28–30, 37, 72, 81–82, 116–17, 134–35, 137, 156–57, 159, 165–66, 181–82
  Benedictines 165–66
  Jesuits 155, 165–66
  Liberal 116, 134–35, 156–57
  Molinism 155
  Old Catholics 156–57, 158
  transubstantiation 40–41
  Ultramontanism 116
  Vaticanism 116, 181–82
  see also Catholic Emancipation Act
Rosebery, 5th Earl of (Archibald Philip Primrose) 159–60, 185–86
Ross, William Stewart 182
  Bottomless Pit 182
Royal Academy of Arts 99, 149–50
Royalists 15
Ruskin, John 14, 51, 153–54, 177
  Praeterita 153–54, 177
Russell, George W.E. 33–34
Russell, John, first Earl 8–9, 97, 98
Russia *see* Eastern Question

Salisbury, diocese of 21–22, 34
Salvation 11, 34, 40–41, 62, 100–1, 108, 176
Salvation Army 181–82
Sambourne, Edward Linley 184–85
Sandringham 133–34
Saunders, Augustus Page 13, 21–22
Scotland 2–4, 37, 54–55, 67–68, 89–90, 138, 153–54, 165–66
  Aberdeen 99
  Balmoral 104–5, 111
  Dalkeith 143
    Corn Exchange 143
    Forester's Hall 143
  Dingwall 2–3, 125

Scotland (*cont.*)
  Edinburgh 4, 33–34, 35–36, 38, 65, 143
    Dalmeny House 166
    St John's 33–34
    University 111–12
      Rectorship of 111–12
  Glenalmond (Trinity
    College) 37, 165–66
Scotsman, The 141–42
Scott, Sir Walter 153–54, 166
  Guy Mannering 166
Seaforth 4–5, 6, 8, 13, 17–18, 21–22,
    52, 54, 85
Seeley, Sir John Robert 98–99, 117–18
  Ecce Homo 98–99, 117–18
Selwyn, George Augustus 10, 37
Sermon on the Mount 12, 27–28, 71, 75,
    76–77, 110–11
Sermons 2, 8, 9, 11, 12, 13–14, 16–17,
    27–28, 34, 40–41, 43–45, 60–61,
    84, 87–88, 97, 100–1, 103, 109–
    10, 114–16, 129–30, 162–63
Seymer, Henry Kerr 14–15
Shaftesbury, 7th Earl (Anthony Ashley-
    Cooper) 129–30, 153
  Life 153
  St Giles 129–30
Shelley, Lady Frances 40–41
Shorthouse, John Henry 155–56
  John Inglesant 155–56
Simeon, Charles 6, 8
Slavery 4, 31–32, 139–40, 189–90
Smiles, Samuel 108, 180–81
  Memoir of Murray 180–81
Socrates 152
Sodor and Man, diocese of 13
South Africa 115, 165
  Majuba Hill 165
Spain 137
Spiritual autobiography 20, 130–31, 175,
    177, 179–80
Stafford 86–87
Stephen, James Fitzjames 139–40
Stevenson, Robert Louis 154
  Jekyll and Hyde 154

Strauss, David 133–34
  Der alte under der neue Glaube 133–34
Sudan 168
  Khartoum 151–52
Summerhayes, Marion 99, 101–2, 123,
    140–41, 152, 153–54
Sumner, John Bird 8, 16, 18–19
  Sermons on Principal Festivals 16
  Treatise on Records of Creation 18–19
Sutherland, Duchess of, Harriet 89–90,
    98, 124–25, 129
  Cliveden House 98, 100, 104, 116–17
  Stafford House 98
Switzerland
  Geneva 30
  Lausanne 76–77

Tait, Archibald Campbell 133, 136–
    37, 180–81
Talbot, Edward Stuart 85, 160, 161–64
Talbot, Lavinia, née Lyttelton 160, 187
Taylor, Jeremy 21
  Holy Living 21
Tenniel, Sir John 124, 180
Tennyson, Alfred Lord 9, 92, 97, 98–
    101, 111–12, 129–30, 132–33,
    136, 138–39, 140–41, 151–52,
    153, 174
  Idylls of King 92, 97, 98–101, 132,
    140–41, 153
  In Memoriam 9
Terry, Ellen 149–50
Thirlwall, Connop 115–16, 117–18
Thirty-Nine Articles 15–16, 29–30
Thistlethwaite, Frederick 123–24
Thistlethwaite, Laura 104, 123–24, 125–
    26, 132–33, 140–41, 143–44,
    151, 177, 190–91
Times, The 76, 86–87, 105–6, 139–40,
    141–42, 185–86, 188
Tollemache, Sir Lionel Arthur 174
Tomline, Sir George Pretyman 8, 11
  Elements of Christian Theology 8, 11
Toplady, Augustus Montague 188–89
  'Rock of ages' 188–89

Index

Tory Party 3, 9, 15, 32, 38, 52, 110–11, 153–54, 166, 167–68
  see also Conservative Party)
Tractarians 13–14, 34, 35, 77–78, 111–12, 159–60, 161, 176–77
  Tracts for Times 35
Trevelyan, Sir Charles 139–40
Trinity 9
Tupper, Martin Farquhar 32
Turkey *see* Eastern Question
Turner, John Matthias 13

Utilitarianism 133

Victoria, Queen 10, 27, 39–40, 80–81, 98–99, 104–6, 134, 165, 180

Wakefield, diocese of 10
Wales 90–91
  Flintshire 27, 85, 87–88
  Penmaenmawr 100, 189
  Prince of 126–27, 155
  St Asaph, diocese of 175–76, 185–86
  St David's, diocese of 115
  see also Hawarden
Walpole, Lord, 4th Earl of Orford (Horatio William Walpole) 60, 76–77
Walters, Catherine ('Skittles') 129
Ward, Mary 149, 155
  Robert Elsmere 149
Waterhouse, Alfred 109–10
Watts, Isaac 188–89
  'Oh God, our help' 188–89
Wellesley, Arthur *see* Wellington

Wellesley, Gerald Valerian 10
Wellington, 1st Duke of (Arthur Wellesley) 10, 15, 188–89
Wesley, Charles 55–56, 188–89
  Death of Mrs Richardson 55–56
Wesley, John 17–18, 188–89
West Indies 4–5, 31, 32–33
Westminster, 1st Duke of (Hugh Grosvenor) 184–85, 186
Westminster Review, The 143
Whig Party 9, 10, 15, 35–36, 40, 81–82, 98
Whitefield, George 17–18
Wickham, Agnes, née Gladstone 59, 80
Wilberforce, Robert Isaac 37, 60
Wilberforce, Samuel 40–41, 60, 75–76, 88–89, 114, 115, 152, 159–60
  Eucharistica 40–41
  Life of 152
Wilberforce, William 2–3, 31, 32–33, 75–76
William IV, King 15, 35–36
Winchester 21
  diocese of 85
Windsor 10, 77–78, 164–65
  Castle 98, 116–17, 123–24, 164–65, 180
  Clewer House of Mercy 77–78, 79–80, 103–4
Wordsworth, William 141
  'Westminster Bridge' 141
Wright, Peter 190

Yarmouth 154

Titles in the *Spiritual Lives* series:

George Eliot
Whole Soul
Ilana M. Blumberg

Ebenezer Howard
Inventor of the Garden City
Frances Knight

Walter Lippmann
American Skeptic, American Pastor
Mark Thomas Edwards

Mark Twain
Preacher, Prophet, and Social Philosopher
Gary Scott Smith

Benjamin Franklin
Cultural Protestant
D. G. Hart

Arthur Sullivan
A Life of Divine Emollient
Ian Bradley

Queen Victoria
This Thorny Crown
Michael Ledger-Lomas

Theodore Roosevelt
Preaching from the Bully Pulpit
Benjamin J. Wetzel

Margaret Mead
A Twentieth-Century Faith
Elesha J. Coffman

W. T. Stead
Nonconformist and Newspaper Prophet
Stewart J. Brown

Leonard Woolf
Bloomsbury Socialist
Fred Leventhal and Peter Stansky

John Stuart Mill
A Secular Life
Timothy Larsen

Christina Rossetti
Poetry, Ecology, Faith
Emma Mason

Woodrow Wilson
Ruling Elder, Spiritual President
Barry Hankins